SPECIFICATION CASE STUDIES

Prentice-Hall International
Series in Computer Science

C. A. R. Hoare, Series Editor

BACKHOUSE, R.C., *Program Construction and Verification*
BACKHOUSE, R.C., *Syntax of Programming Languages, Theory and Practice*
de BAKKER, J.W., *Mathematical Theory of Program Correctness*
BJÖRNER, D., and JONES, C.B., *Formal Specification and Software Development*
BORNAT, R., *Programming from First Principles*
CLARK, K.L., and McCABE, F.G., *micro-PROLOG: Programming in Logic*
DROMEY, R.G., *How to Solve it by Computer*
DUNCAN, F., *Microprocessor Programming and Software Development*
ELDER, J., *Construction of Data Processing Software*
GOLDSCHLAGER, L., and LISTER, A., *Computer Science: A Modern Introduction*
HAYES, I., (Ed.), *Specification Case Studies*
HEHNER, E.C.R., *The Logic of Programming*
HENDERSON, P., *Functional Programming: Application and Implementation*
HOARE, C.A.R., *Communicating Sequential Processes*
HOARE, C.A.R., and SHEPHERDSON, J.C., (Eds.), *Mathematical Logic and Programming Languages*
INMOS LTD., *Occam Programming Manual*
JACKSON, M.A., *System Development*
JOHNSTON, H., *Learning to Program*
JONES, C.B., Systematic Software Development Using VDM
JONES, G., *Programming in Occam*
JOSEPH, M., PRASAD, V.R., and NATARAJAN, N., *A Multiprocessor Operating System*
LEW, A., *Computer Science: A Mathematical Introduction*
MacCALLUM, I., *Pascal for the Apple*
MacCALLUM, I., *UCSD Pascal for the IBM PC*
MARTIN, J.J., *Data Types and Data Structures*
POMBERGER, G., *Software Engineering and Modula-2*
REYNOLDS, J.C., *The Craft of Programming*
TENNENT, R.D., *Principles of Programming Languages*
WELSH, J., and ELDER, J., *Introduction to Pascal, 2nd Edition*
WELSH, J., ELDER, J., and BUSTARD, D., *Sequential Program Structures*
WELSH, J., and HAY, A., *A Model Implementation of Standard Pascal*
WELSH, J., and McKEAG, M., *Structured System Programming*

SPECIFICATION CASE STUDIES

Edited by
IAN HAYES

With contributions by
**BILL FLINN
ROGER GIMSON
CARROLL MORGAN
IB HOLM SØRENSEN
BERNARD SUFRIN**

Prentice/Hall PHI International

Englewood Cliffs, N.J. London Mexico New Delhi
Rio de Janeiro Singapore Sydney Tokyo Toronto

Library of Congress Cataloging-in-Publication Data

Specification case studies.

(Prentice-Hall International series in computer science)
Includes index.
1. Computer programs—Specifications. I. Hayes, Ian, 1956—   . II. Flinn, Bill.   III. Series.
QA76.6.S667 1987   005.3   86-12348

ISBN 0-13-826579-8

British Library Cataloguing in Publication Data

Specification case studies.

(Prentice-Hall International series in computer science)
1.Electronics digital computers - Programming
I. Hayes, Ian II. Flinn, Bill
005. 1' 2   QA76.6

ISBN 0-13-826579-8
ISBN 0-13-826595-X Pbk

Prentice-Hall Inc., *Englewood Cliffs, New Jersey*
Prentice-Hall International (UK) Ltd, *London*
Prentice-Hall of Australia Pty Ltd, *Sydney*
Prentice-Hall Canada Inc., *Toronto*
Prentice-Hall Hispanoamericana S.A., *Mexico*
Prentice-Hall of India Private Ltd, *New Delhi*
Prentice-Hall of Japan Inc., *Tokyo*
Prentice-Hall of Southeast Asia Pte Ltd, *Singapore*
Editora Prentice-Hall do Brasil Ltda, *Rio de Janeiro*

Printed and bound in Great Britain for
Prentice-Hall International (UK) Ltd,
66 Wood Lane End, Hemel Hempstead, Hertfordshire, HP2 4RG
at the University Press, Cambridge.

1 2 3 4 5 90 89 88 87 86

ISBN 0-13-826579-8
ISBN 0-13-826595-X PBK

Contents

Preface

Over the last six years the Programming Research Group at Oxford University has been the home for a number of projects which have made extensive use of mathematics for the specification of computer systems. The style of specification which is used in this monograph has emerged as a result of experience gained on these projects. Specifications are presented using the notation known as Z, which has evolved somewhat since it was originally introduced to us by Jean-Raymond Abrial.

The Software Engineering Project, which began in 1978, has been the backbone of the specification work. Both Tony Hoare and Bernard Sufrin have been associated with the project since its inception. Project staff have included Jean-Raymond Abrial, Tim Clement, Martin Raskovsky, Ib Holm Sørensen, Stefan Sokolowski, and Phil Wadler.

The Distributed Computing Project began in 1982. Its goal is the specification and construction of a loosely-coupled distributed operating system based on the model of autonomous clients having access to shared services. Roger Gimson and Carroll Morgan have been with the project since it began. The application of mathematical specifications to distributed systems has had beneficial consequences both on the style of specifications and on the design of the systems which have been produced.

The Transaction Processing Project also began in 1982. It was initiated to meet the challenge of applying mathematical specification methods in a commercial environment. From the outset Ib Sørensen has run the project from the Oxford end and Peter Collins and John Nicholls have taken responsibility from the IBM end. Tim Clement was associated with this project during its first year; his successor was Ian Hayes. Rod Burstall, Cliff Jones, and Tony Hoare have acted as consultants. The project has demonstrated the benefits to be gained from applying the methods to existing software.

None of the above work could have been done without the generous external support we received. The Software Engineering Project and the Distributed Computing Project were both supported financially by the Science and Engineering Research Council of Great Britain, and the Transaction Processing Project was supported by IBM. And we have had indirect assistance from the many industrial companies who by attending our specification courses have given us the means and motivation to prepare some of our tutorial material.

But we received more than just financial support from these sources, because of course our work could not have been done in a vacuum. The enthusiasm and constant encouragement of our industrial collaborators and S.E.R.C. administrators helped us to concentrate on real problems and to find practical solutions. So to them we are doubly grateful.

The conviction that real software can be specified, and that ordinary mathematics is the proper tool, has been passed on to all of the authors in turn by Tony Hoare and Jean-Raymond Abrial, and to them we owe the greatest debt.

It remains to thank our very painstaking (and forgiving) referees, and others who have helped us with their comments: Nigel Haigh, Jeff Sanders, and Jim Woodcock. And finally we must thank Martin Raskovsky for his marvellous program which made it possible to edit the document exactly as you see it here.

The authors
February, 1986

Foreword

Reading formal texts is like meeting people. Sometimes, you understand them straightaway like good friends who take to each other immediately. At other times, it is more difficult. You may parse what you read, but find it impossible to work out any meaning. With the latter, you have to be patient, ask questions, explore the surroundings; in other words, it is better for you to be introduced through some common good friends who volunteer to help you prepare for the first meeting.

Large computer programs, to say the least, pertain to the category of formal texts whose meanings are not immediately obvious! For that reason, people have been trying — for some time — to find out what kind of intermediate text would be best suited to play the role of go-between.

This book reports on experiments made at Oxford University within this framework: it shows how one may *communicate ideas and meanings* about existing (or even not-yet-written) computer programs, and this by using only the conventional mathematical notations of ordinary logic and elementary set theory.

The choice of a "standard" mathematical notation offers many advantages: it is easy for a scientifically trained reader to understand; it is rigorous; it denotes rich concepts (e.g., functions and their usual attributes: partiality vs. totality, domain, range, etc.); and it is an open notation, because you may enlarge it at will.

Liberated from the burden of obeying the idiosyncracies of a particular language, the authors of the various papers forming this book were free to experiment with *various styles* depending on the problem at hand (but also on their personal taste). In reading the book, I found it very exciting to discover how each situation was formalised in a way different from that of others (or from what I had in mind). This variety of style is reassuring: it indicates, if at all necessary, that there does not exist any "normal" way of describing things rigorously.

However, despite this variety, all authors seem to have encountered at some point or another a difficulty of the same nature — namely that of structuring the formal text. To this common problem they decided to give a common answer in the form of what is called a *Schema*, together with a corresponding *Schema Calculus*.

Roughly speaking, a Schema is a box within which certain *variables of interest* are together declared, given types, and mutually constrained. The Schema Calculus gives rules by which these boxes can be transformed or combined to produce other boxes. The main advantages of this mechanism are its simplicity and immediate "visibility".

In this book, the main emphasis has been put on using ordinary mathematical notations in order to describe (*specify*) computer programs. Another important outcome of any mathematical approach is that of performing proofs: this will be vital, of course, in the process of *software design* by which specifications are gradually transformed in order to obtain concrete programs. Here is the subject of another book.

J.-R. Abrial

GLOSSARY

Mathematical Notation

1. Definitions and declarations.

Let x, x_k be identifiers and let T, T_k be sets.

LHS $\,\hat{=}\,$ RHS	Definition of LHS as syntactically equivalent to RHS.
$x : T$	Declaration of x as type T.

$x_1 : T_1;\ x_2 : T_2;\ \ldots\ ;\ x_n : T_n$
        List of declarations.

$x_1,\ x_2,\ \ldots\ ,\ x_n : T \ \hat{=}\ x_1 : T;\ x_2 : T;\ \ldots\ ;\ x_n : T.$

$[A, B]$	Introduction of generic sets.

2. Logic.

Let P, Q be predicates and let D be a declaration.

$\mathtt{true}, \mathtt{false}$	Logical constants.
$\neg\, P$	Negation: "not P".
$P \wedge Q$	Conjunction: "P and Q".
$P \vee Q$	Disjunction: "P or Q".
$P \Rightarrow Q$	Implication: "P implies Q" or "if P then Q".
$P \Leftrightarrow Q$	Equivalence: "P is logically equivalent to Q".

$P \rightarrow Q, R$ Conditional: "if P then Q else R";
        $(P \rightarrow Q, R) \Leftrightarrow ((P \Rightarrow Q) \wedge (\neg P \Rightarrow R)).$

$\forall\, x : T \cdot P$ Universal quantification: "for all x of type T, P holds".
$\exists\, x : T \cdot P$ Existential quantification: "there exists an x of type T such that P".

$\exists!\ x : T \cdot P_x$
        Unique existence: "there exists a unique x of type T such that P".
        $\hat{=}\ (\exists\, x : T \cdot P_x \wedge \neg(\exists y : T \mid y \neq x \cdot P_y))$

$\forall\; x_1:T_1;\; x_2:T_2;\; \ldots\; ;\; x_n:T_n\; \bullet\; P$

"For all x_1 of type T_1, x_2 of type $T_2, \ldots$, and x_n of type T_n,   P holds."

$\exists\; x_1:T_1;\; x_2:T_2;\; \ldots\; ;\; x_n:T_n\; \bullet\; P$

Similar to $\forall$.

$\exists!\; x_1:T_1;\; x_2:T_2;\; \ldots\; ;\; x_n:T_n\; \bullet\; P$

Similar to $\forall$.

$\forall\; D\; |\; P\; \bullet\; Q\; \;\triangleq\; (\forall\; D\; \bullet\; P \Rightarrow Q).$
$\exists\; D\; |\; P\; \bullet\; Q\; \;\triangleq\; (\exists\; D\; \bullet\; P \wedge Q).$
$t_1 = t_2$ Equality between terms.
$t_1 \neq t_2$ $\triangleq\; \neg(t_1 = t_2).$

3. Sets.

Let S, T and X be sets; t, t_k terms; P a predicate and D declarations.

$t \in S$ Set membership: "t is an element of S".
$t \notin S$ $\triangleq\; \neg(t \in S).$
$S \subseteq T$ Set inclusion:
                     $\triangleq\; (\forall\; x\; :\; S\; \bullet\; x \in T).$
$S \subset T$ Strict set inclusion:
                     $\triangleq\; S \subseteq T \wedge S \neq T.$
$\{\}$ The empty set.

$\{t_1,\; t_2,\; \ldots\; ,\; t_n\}$

The set containing $t_1, t_2, \ldots$ and t_n.

$\{x:T\; |\; P\}$ The set containing exactly those x of type T for which P holds.

$(t_1,\; t_2,\; \ldots\; ,\; t_n)$

Ordered n-tuple of $t_1, t_2, \ldots$ and t_n.

$T_1 \times T_2 \times \ldots \times T_n$

Cartesian product: the set of all n-tuples such that the k th component is of type T_k.

$\{x_1:T_1; \ x_2:T_2; \ \dots \ ; \ x_n:T_n \ | \ P\}$

> The set of n-tuples $(x_1, \ x_2, \ \dots \ , \ x_n)$ with each x_k of type T_k such that P holds.

$\{D \ | \ P \cdot t\}$	The set of t's such that given the declarations D, P holds.
$\{D \cdot t\}$	$\triangleq \ \{D \ | \ true \cdot t\}$.
P S	Powerset: the set of all subsets of S.
F S	Set of finite subsets of S:
	$\triangleq \ \{T: \ \textbf{P} \ S \ | \ T \ is \ finite\}$.
S $\cap$ T	Set intersection: given S, T: **P** X,
	$\triangleq \{x:X \ | \ x \in S \wedge x \in T\}$.
S $\cup$ T	Set union: given S, T: **P** X,
	$\triangleq \{x:X \ | \ x \in S \vee x \in T\}$.
S – T	Set difference: given S, T: **P** X,
	$\triangleq \{x:X \ | \ x \in S \wedge x \notin T\}$.
$\cap$ SS	Distributed set intersection: given SS: **P** (**P** X),
	$\triangleq \{x:X \ | \ (\forall S:SS \cdot x \in S)\}$.
$\cup$ SS	Distributed set union: given SS: **P** (**P** X),
	$\triangleq \{x:X \ | \ (\exists S:SS \cdot x \in S)\}$.
#S	Size (number of distinct elements) of a finite set.
$|S|$	$\triangleq$ #S .

4. Numbers.

N	The set of natural numbers (non-negative integers).
N^+	The set of strictly positive natural numbers:
	$\triangleq$ N – $\{0\}$.
Z	The set of integers (positive, zero and negative).
m..n	The set of integers between m and n inclusive:
	$\triangleq \{k:Z \ | \ m \leqslant k \wedge k \leqslant n\}$.
min S	Minimum of a set; for S: **F** N $| \ S \neq \{\}$,
	$min \ S \in S \ \wedge \ (\forall x:S \cdot x \geqslant min \ S)$.
max S	Maximum of a set; for S: **F** N $| \ S \neq \{\}$,
	$max \ S \in S \ \wedge \ (\forall x:S \cdot x \leqslant max \ S)$.

5. Relations.

A relation is modelled by a set of ordered pairs hence operators defined for sets
can be used on relations.

Let X, Y, and Z be sets; x: X; y: Y; and R: X $\leftrightarrow$ Y.

$X \leftrightarrow Y$ The set of relations from X to Y:
             $\triangleq$ $\mathbf{P}$ (X $\times$ Y).

$x \, R \, y$ x is related by R to y:
             $\triangleq$ (x, y) $\in$ R.

$x \mapsto y$ $\triangleq$ (x, y)

$\{x_1 \mapsto y_1, \ x_2 \mapsto y_2, \ \ldots \ , \ x_n \mapsto y_n\}$
             The relation $\{(x_1, y_1), \ \ldots \ , (x_n, y_n)\}$
             relating x_1 to y_1, $\ldots$, and x_n to y_n.

dom R   The domain of a relation:
             $\triangleq$ $\{x\!:\!X \mid (\exists y\!:\!Y \bullet x \, R \, y)\}$.

rng R   The range of a relation:
             $\triangleq$ $\{y\!:\!Y \mid (\exists x\!:\!X \bullet x \, R \, y)\}$.

$R_1 \; \mathbf{;} \; R_2$ Forward relational composition: given R_1: X $\leftrightarrow$ Y; R_2: Y $\leftrightarrow$ Z,
             $\triangleq$ $\{x\!:\!X; \ z\!:\!Z \mid (\exists y\!:\!Y \bullet x \, R_1 \, y \wedge y \, R_2 \, z)\}$.

$R_1 \circ R_2$ Relational composition:
             $\triangleq$ $R_2 \; \mathbf{;} \; R_1$.

R^{-1} Inverse of relation R:
             $\triangleq$ $\{y\!:\!Y; \ x\!:\!X \mid x \, R \, y\}$.

id X   Identity function on the set X:
             $\triangleq$ $\{x\!:\!X \bullet x \mapsto x\}$.

R^k The relation R composed with itself k times: given R : X $\leftrightarrow$ X,
             $R^0 \triangleq$ id X, $R^{k+1} \triangleq R^k \circ R$.

R*	Reflexive transitive closure: $\triangleq \cup \{n: \mathbb{N} \cdot R^n\}$.
R$^+$	Non-reflexive transitive closure: $\triangleq \cup \{n: \mathbb{N}^+ \cdot R^n\}$.
R⟮S⟯	Image: given $S : \mathbb{P} X$, $\triangleq \{y: Y \mid (\exists x : S \cdot x \ R \ y)\}$.
S ◁ R	Domain restriction to S: given $S: \mathbb{P} X$, $\triangleq \{x: X; \ y: Y \mid x \in S \wedge x \ R \ y\}$.
S ◀ R	Domain subtraction: given $S: \mathbb{P} X$, $\triangleq (X - S) ◁ R$.
R ▷ T	Range restriction to T: given $T: \mathbb{P} Y$, $\triangleq \{x: X; \ y: Y \mid x \ R \ y \wedge y \in T\}$.
R ▶ T	Range subtraction of T: given $T: \mathbb{P} Y$, $\triangleq R ▷ (Y - T)$.
$R_1 \oplus R_2$	Overriding: given $R_1, R_2 : X \leftrightarrow Y$, $\triangleq (\text{dom } R_2 ◀ R_1) \cup R_2$.

6. Functions.

A function is a relation with the property that for each element in its domain there is a unique element in its range related to it. As functions are relations all the operators defined above for relations also apply to functions.

X $\nrightarrow$ Y	The set of partial functions from X to Y: $\triangleq \{f: X \leftrightarrow Y \mid (\forall x: \text{dom } f \cdot (\exists! y: Y \cdot x \ f \ y))\}$.
X $\rightarrow$ Y	The set of total functions from X to Y: $\triangleq \{f: X \nrightarrow Y \mid \text{dom } f = X\}$.
X $\nrightarrowtail$ Y	The set of one-to-one partial functions from X to Y: $\triangleq \{f: X \nrightarrow Y \mid (\forall y: \text{rng } f \cdot (\exists! x: X \cdot x \ f \ y))\}$.

$X \rightarrowtail Y$ The set of one-to-one total functions from X to Y:
$\quad \hat{=} \{f\colon X \twoheadrightarrow Y \mid dom\ f = X\}.$

$X \nrightarrow Y$ The set of finite partial functions from X to Y.
$\quad \hat{=} \{f\colon X \rightarrow Y \mid f \in \mathbb{F}\ (X \times Y)\}.$

$f\ t$ The function f applied to t.

$(\lambda x\colon X \mid P \cdot t)$
$\quad$ Lambda-abstraction: the function that, given an argument x of type X such that P holds, the result is t.
$\quad \hat{=} \{\ x\colon X \mid P \cdot x \mapsto t\ \}.$

$(\lambda\ x_1\colon T_1;\ \dots\ ;\ x_n\colon T_n \mid P \cdot t)$
$\quad \hat{=} \{x_1\colon T_1;\ \dots\ ;\ x_n\colon T_n \mid P \cdot (x_1,\ \dots\ ,\ x_n) \mapsto t\}.$

7. Orders.

`partial_order X`
$\quad$ The set of partial orders on X.
$$\hat{=} \{\ R\colon X \leftrightarrow X \mid \forall x, y, z\colon X \cdot x\ R\ x\ \wedge$$
$$x\ R\ y \wedge y\ R\ x \Rightarrow x{=}y\ \wedge$$
$$x\ R\ y \wedge y\ R\ z \Rightarrow x\ R\ z$$
$\quad$ }.

`total_order X`
$\quad$ The set of total orders on X.
$$\hat{=} \{\ R\colon \texttt{partial\_order}\ X \mid \forall x, y\colon X \cdot x\ R\ y \vee y\ R\ x\ \}.$$

`monotonic X` $<_X$
$\quad$ The set of functions from X to X that are monotonic with respect to the order $<_X$ on X.
$$\hat{=} \{\ f\ \colon\ X \nrightarrow X \mid (\forall x, y\colon X \cdot x <_X y \Rightarrow f(x) <_X f(y))\}.$$

8. Sequences.

`seq X`   The set of sequences whose elements are drawn from X:
$$\hat{=}\ \{\ A\colon \mathbb{N}^+ \nrightarrow X \mid (\exists n\colon \mathbb{N} \cdot dom\ A = 1..n)\ \}.$$

#A   The length of sequence A.

[ ]   The empty sequence {}.

$[a_1, \ldots, a_n]$

$\qquad \hat{=} \{ 1 \mapsto a_1, \ldots, n \mapsto a_n \}.$

$[a_1, \ldots, a_n] ^\frown [b_1, \ldots, b_m]$

Concatenation: $\hat{=} [a_1, \ldots, a_n, b_1, \ldots, b_m],$

$\qquad [] ^\frown A = A ^\frown [] = A.$

head A   The first element of a non-empty sequence:

$\qquad A \neq [] \implies \text{head } A = A(1).$

last A   The final element of a non-empty sequence:

$\qquad A \neq [] \implies \text{last } A = A(\#A).$

tail A   All but the head of a sequence: $\text{tail}([x] ^\frown A) = A.$

front A   All but the last of a sequence: $\text{front}(A ^\frown [x]) = A.$

rev $[a_1, a_2, \ldots, a_n]$

Reverse:

$\qquad \hat{=} [a_n, \ldots, a_2, a_1],$

$\qquad \text{rev } [] = [].$

$^\frown$/AA   Distributed concatenation: given AA : seq(seq(X)),

$\qquad \hat{=} AA(1) ^\frown \ldots ^\frown AA(\#AA),$

$\qquad ^\frown/[] = [].$

$/AR   Distributed relational composition: given AR : seq (X $\leftrightarrow$ X),

$\qquad \hat{=} AR(1) \; \$ \; \ldots \; \$ \; AR(\#AR),$

$\qquad \$/[] = \text{id } X.$

<u>disjoint</u> AS   Pairwise disjoint: given AS: seq ($\mathbb{P}$ X),

$\qquad \hat{=} (\forall i, j : \text{dom } AS \bullet i \neq j \implies AS(i) \cap AS(j) = \{\}).$

AS <u>partitions</u> S

$\qquad \hat{=} \text{disjoint } AS \land \cup \text{ rng } AS = S.$

A <u>in</u> B   Contiguous subsequence:

$\qquad \hat{=} (\exists C, D: \text{seq } X \bullet C ^\frown A ^\frown D = B).$

squash f
: Convert a finite function, $f: \mathbb{N} \twoheadrightarrow X$, into a sequence by squashing its domain. That is,

squash {} = [], and if f ≠ {} then
squash f = [f(i)] ⌢ squash({i} ◁ f)
where i = min(dom f).

For example, squash {2↦A, 27↦C, 4↦B} = [A, B, C].

S 1 A
: Restrict the sequence A to those items whose index is in the set S:
  ≙ squash(S ◁ A)

A ↾ T
: Restrict the range of the sequence A to the set T:
  ≙ squash(A ▷ T).

9. Bags.

bag X
: The set of bags whose elements are drawn from X:
  ≙ $X \twoheadrightarrow \mathbb{N}^+$
  A bag is represented by a function that maps each element in the bag onto its frequency of occurrence in the bag.

[]
: The empty bag {}.

[x_1, x_2, ... , x_n]
: The bag containing x_1, x_2, ... and x_n with the frequency they occur in the list.

items s
: The bag of items contained in the sequence s:
  ≙ { x:rng s • x↦#{i:dom s | s(i)=x} }.

Schema Notation

Schema definition: a schema groups together some declarations of variables and a predicate relating these variables. There are two ways of writing schemas: vertically, for example

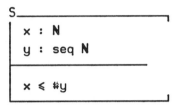

or horizontally, for the same example

$$S \triangleq [\ x: N;\ y:\ seq\ N\ |\ x{\leqslant}\#y\ ].$$

Use in signatures after $\forall$, λ, $\{\ldots\}$, etc.:

$$(\forall S \cdot y \neq [\ ]) \triangleq (\forall x:N;\ y:\ seq\ N\ |\ x{\leqslant}\#y \cdot y{\neq}[\ ]).$$

Schemas as types

> When a schema name S is used as a type it stands for the set of all objects described by the schema, $\{S\}$. e.g., w : S declares a variable w with components x (a natural number) and y (a sequence of natural numbers) such that $x \leqslant \#y$.

Projection functions

> The component names of a schema may be used as projection (or selector) functions, e.g., given w : S, x(w) is w's x component and y(w) is its y component; of course, the following predicate holds: $x(w) \leqslant \#y(w)$.
> Alternative notations for x(w) and y(w) are w.x and w.y, respectively.

tuple S   The tuple formed from a schema's variables: e.g., tuple S is (x, y). Where there is no risk of ambiguity, the word "tuple" can be omitted, so that just "S" is written for "(x, y)".

pred S   The predicate part of a schema: e.g. pred S is $x \leqslant \#y$.

Inclusion   A schema S may be included within the declarations of a schema T, in which case the declarations of S are merged with the other declarations of T (variables declared in both S and T must be of the same type) and the predicates of S and T are conjoined. For example,

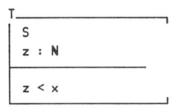

is

is

```
┌─ x, z : N ──────────────┐
│  y : seq N              │
├─────────────────────────┤
│  x ≤ #y ∧ z < x         │
└─────────────────────────┘
```

S | P   The schema S with P conjoined to its predicate part. For example,

$$(S \mid x{>}0) \quad \text{is} \quad [\, x{:}N; y{:}\text{seq } N \mid x{\leqslant}\#y \,\wedge\, x{>}0\,].$$

S ; D   The schema S with the declarations D merged with the declarations of S. For example,

$$(S \;;\; z : N) \quad \text{is} \quad [\, x, z{:}N; \; y{:}\text{seq } N \mid x{\leqslant}\#y \,].$$

S[new/old]   Renaming of components: the schema S in which the component old has been renamed to new both in the declaration and at its every free occurrence in the predicate. For example,

$$S[z/x] \quad \text{is} \quad [\ z:N;\ y:\text{seq } N\ |\ z \leqslant \#y\ ]$$
$$\text{and } S[y/x, x/y] \quad \text{is} \quad [\ y:N;\ x:\text{seq } N\ |\ y \leqslant \#x\ ]$$

In the second case above, the renaming is simultaneous. And as usual, the renaming in the predicate might entail consequential changes of bound variable.

Decoration   Decoration with subscript, superscript, prime, etc.; systematic renaming of the variables declared in the schema. For example,

$$S' \text{ is } [\ x':N;\ y':\text{seq } N\ |\ x' \leqslant \#y'\ ]$$

$\neg S$ The schema S with its predicate part negated. For example,

$$\neg S \text{ is } [\ x:N;\ y:\text{seq } N\ |\ \neg(x \leqslant \#y)\ ].$$

$S \wedge T$ The schema formed from schemas S and T by merging their declarations (see inclusion above) and conjoining (and-ing) their predicates. Given $T \triangleq [x:\ N;\ z:\ P\ N\ |\ x \in z]$, $S \wedge T$ is

$$
\begin{array}{|l}
\hline
x\ :\ N \\
y\ :\ \text{seq } N \\
z\ :\ P\ N \\
\hline
x \leqslant \#y \wedge x \in z \\
\hline
\end{array}
$$

$S \vee T$ The schema formed from schemas S and T by merging their declarations and disjoining (or-ing) their predicates. For example, $S \vee T$ is

$$
\begin{array}{|l}
\hline
x\ :\ N \\
y\ :\ \text{seq } N \\
z\ :\ P\ N \\
\hline
x \leqslant \#y \vee x \in z \\
\hline
\end{array}
$$

S $\Rightarrow$ T   The schema formed from schemas S and T by merging their declarations and taking pred S $\Rightarrow$ pred T as the predicate. For example, S $\Rightarrow$ T is

$$
\begin{array}{|l}
x : \mathbf{N} \\
y : seq\ \mathbf{N} \\
z : \mathbf{P\ N} \\
\hline
x \leqslant \#y \Rightarrow x \in z
\end{array}
$$

S $\Leftrightarrow$ T   The schema formed from schemas S and T by merging their declarations and taking pred S $\Leftrightarrow$ pred T as the predicate. For example, S $\Leftrightarrow$ T is

$$
\begin{array}{|l}
x : \mathbf{N} \\
y : seq\ \mathbf{N} \\
z : \mathbf{P\ N} \\
\hline
x \leqslant \#y \Leftrightarrow x \in z
\end{array}
$$

S \ (v$_1$, v$_2$, ... , v$_n$)

Hiding: the schema S with the variables v_1, v_2, ..., and v_n hidden: the variables listed are removed from the declarations and are existentially quantified in the predicate. For example,

S \ x   is   [y:seq $\mathbf{N}$ | ($\exists$x:$\mathbf{N}$ • x$\leqslant$#y)].

(We omit the parentheses when only one variable is hidden.) A schema may be specified instead of a list of variables; in this case the variables declared in that schema are hidden. e.g. (S $\wedge$ T)\S is

```
┌─────────────────────────────
│  z : P N
│ ─────────────────────────
│  (∃ x: N; y: seq N •
│      x ≤ #y ∧ x ∈ z)
└─────────────────────────────
```

$$S \upharpoonright (v_1, v_2, \ldots, v_n)$$

Projection: The schema S with any variables that do not occur in the list v_1, v_2, ..., v_n hidden: the variables removed from the declarations are existentially quantified in the predicate.

For example, $(S \wedge T) \upharpoonright (x, y)$ is

```
┌─────────────────────────────
│  x : N
│  y : seq N
│ ─────────────────────────
│  (∃ z : P N •
│      x ≤ #y ∧ x ∈ z)
└─────────────────────────────
```

(We omit the parentheses when only one variable is hidden.) The list of variables may be replaced by a schema as for hiding; the variables declared in the schema are used for the projection.

The following conventions are used for variable names in those schemas which represent operations - that is, which are written as descriptions of operations on some state:

undashed	state before the operation,
dashed	state after the operation,
ending in "?"	inputs to (arguments for) the operation, and
ending in "!"	outputs from (results of) the operation.

The following schema operations only apply to schemas following the above conventions.

pre S   Precondition: all the state after components (dashed) and the outputs (ending in "!") are hidden. e.g. given

```
S
┌──────────────────────────────┐
│  x?, s, s', y! : N           │
├──────────────────────────────┤
│  s' = s-x? ∧ y! = s          │
└──────────────────────────────┘
```

pre S is

```
┌──────────────────────────────┐
│  x?, s : N                   │
├──────────────────────────────┤
│  (∃ s', y! : N •             │
│     s' = s-x? ∧ y! = s)      │
└──────────────────────────────┘
```

post S   Postcondition: this is similar to precondition except all the state before components (undashed) and inputs (ending in "?") are hidden. (Note that this definition differs from some others, in which the "postcondition" is in fact the predicate relating all of initial state, inputs, outputs, and final state.)

S ⊕ T   Overriding:
              ≘ (S ∧ ¬pre T) ∨ T. For example, given S above and

```
T
┌──────────────────────────────┐
│  x?, s, s' : N               │
├──────────────────────────────┤
│  s < x? ∧ s' = s             │
└──────────────────────────────┘
```

S ⊕ T is

```
┌──────────────────────────────┐
│  x?, s, s', y! : N           │
├──────────────────────────────┤
│  (s' = s-x? ∧ y! = s ∧       │
│   ¬(∃s': N •                 │
│      s < x? ∧ s' = s))       │
│  ∨ (s < x? ∧ s' = s)         │
└──────────────────────────────┘
```

Because (given the declaration s: N above)

$$(\exists s': N \bullet s'{=}s \land s < x?) \Leftrightarrow$$
$$(s \in N \land s < x?) \Leftrightarrow$$
$$s < x?,$$

the predicate can be simplified:

```
┌─────────────────────────────┐
│  x?, s, s′, y! : N           │
├─────────────────────────────┤
│  (s′ = s−x? ∧ y! = s         │
│    ∧ s ⩾ x?)                 │
│  ∨                           │
│  (s < x? ∧ s′ = s)           │
└─────────────────────────────┘
```

S ; T   Schema composition: if we consider an intermediate state that is both the final state of the operation S and the initial state of the operation T then the composition of S and T is the operation which relates the initial state of S to the final state of T through the intermediate state. To form the composition of S and T we take the state-after components of S and the state-before components of T that have a basename[*] in common, rename both to new variables, take the schema which is the "and" ($\land$) of the resulting schemas, and hide the new variables. For example, S ; T is

```
┌─────────────────────────────┐
│  x?, s, s′, y! : N           │
├─────────────────────────────┤
│  (∃ s⁺ : N .                 │
│     s⁺ = s−x ∧ y! =      ∧   │
│     s⁺ < x? ∧ s′ = s⁺)       │
└─────────────────────────────┘
```

[*] basename is the name with any decoration ("′", "!", "?", etc.) removed.

S >> T   Piping: this schema operation is similar to schema composition; the difference is that, rather than identifying the state after components of S with the state before components of T, the output components of S (ending in "!") are identified with the input components of T (ending in "?") that have the same basename.

The logical calculi

The formal manipulations and (occasional) proofs found in the various papers of this volume make extensive use of the propositional and predicate calculi. We of course hope that the use of mathematics in program specification and development will soon be taken for granted, and that as a result these two logical calculi will be taught early, and used fluently.

But for now, we hope to give some assistance by presenting a few "important facts" — first of propositional, and then of predicate logic. These facts are actually theorems of the relevant calculi, and of course could be proved from scratch, using the basic axioms and inference rules. But it is not the aim of this brief discussion to give a thorough development of formal logic — quite the contrary: the aim of this discussion is to isolate, and to some extent motivate, the theorems which are themselves useful in deriving the results presented elsewhere in this book.

For those who do want to pursue the matter further, an introductory course on formal logic could be worthwhile. [Ham] and [End] are good texts, the former more an introduction than the latter.

We begin with the propositional calculus.

1. Some facts of the propositional calculus

We give our facts as a list of equivalences: P and Q are equivalent (written $P \Leftrightarrow Q$) if and only if their truth values always agree; that is, either they are both true or they are both false. P and Q themselves stand for arbitrary predicates, and the equivalences given below remain true no matter what predicates are put in place of them.

Commutativity of $\wedge$ and $\vee$.

1.	$P \wedge Q$	$\Leftrightarrow$	$Q \wedge P$
2.	$P \vee Q$	$\Leftrightarrow$	$Q \vee P$

Associativity of ∧ and ∨.

3.   P ∧ (Q ∧ R)   ⇔   (P ∧ Q) ∧ R
4.   P ∨ (Q ∨ R)   ⇔   (P ∨ Q) ∨ R

Together, equivalences 1-4 mean we can ignore order and parentheses in strings of conjoined (P ∧ Q ∧ R ...) and disjoined (P ∨ Q ∨ R ...) terms. Following are the "distributive laws", reminiscent of the distribution of multiplication over addition in arithmetic. Note however that in logic, the distribution goes both ways.

5.   P ∧ (Q ∨ R)   ⇔   (P ∧ Q) ∨ (P ∧ R)
6.   P ∨ (Q ∧ R)   ⇔   (P ∨ Q) ∧ (P ∨ R)

Here are "De Morgan's laws".

7.   ¬(P ∧ Q) ⇔ ¬P ∨ ¬Q
8.   ¬(P ∨ Q) ⇔ ¬P ∧ ¬Q

Laws 5-8 can be used to convert any proposition to either disjunctive or conjunctive normal form. In disjunctive normal form, the proposition is written as a disjunction ("or") of conjuncts (terms formed by "and" from elementary propositions or their negations; elementary propositions are just the individual letters). In conjunctive normal form, it's the other way around: the proposition is written as a conjunction of disjuncts. For example, we have

P ∧ ¬(Q ∧ R)
⇔   P ∧ (¬Q ∨ ¬R)   by (7),

which is in conjunctive normal form. If we go on, we have

⇔   (P ∧ ¬Q) ∨ (P ∧ ¬R)   by (4),

which is in disjunctive normal form. Disjunctive normal form is the more common of the two.

The following equivalence is useful if you are better at manipulating ∧ and ∨ than you are ⇒; it is also helpful in proceeding to normal form:

9.   P ⇒ Q   ⇔   ¬P ∨ Q

But in some cases, conjunctions and disjunctions can be removed immediately, without further expansion. These are known as the absorption laws:

10. P ∧ (P ∨ Q)   ⟷   P
11. P ∨ (P ∧ Q)   ⟷   P

The next equivalence allows several "antecedents" (P and Q) to be collected into a conjunction. The associativity and commutativity of ∧ can then be exploited.

12. P ⟹ (Q ⟹ R)   ⟷   (P ∧ Q) ⟹ R

If you can't prove an equivalence directly, try proving each direction separately:

13. (P ⟷ Q)   ⟷   (P ⟹ Q) ∧ (Q ⟹ P)

And if you can't prove an implication one way, negate its parts and go backwards:

14. P ⟹ Q   ⟷   ¬Q ⟹ ¬P

But if you're better at equivalences than implications, use these two:

15. P ⟹ Q   ⟷   (P ⟷ (P ∧ Q))
16. Q ⟹ P   ⟷   (P ⟷ (P ∨ Q))

We finish off with some basic facts about "true" and "false". In them, "true" denotes any propositional formula already known to be true; and "false" has the complementary meaning.

17. true ∧ P   ⟷   P
18. false ∧ P   ⟷   false
19. true ∨ P   ⟷   true
20. false ∨ P   ⟷   P

21. true ⟹ P   ⟷   P
22. false ⟹ P   ⟷   true
23. P ⟹ true   ⟷   true
24. P ⟹ false   ⟷   ¬P

2. Some facts of the predicate calculus

There are two main differences between propositional and predicate logic. The first is of course the presence of quantifiers. In predicate logic, we can write

$(\forall x:S \bullet P)$ for all x of type S, the predicate P holds; and

$(\exists x:S \bullet P)$ there exists and x of type S such that the predicate P holds.

The second difference is more subtle. In propositional logic, it is always possible in principle to decide the truth or falsity of a formula, no matter how complex. The rules in the previous section can be used for this, to some extent; but if they fail there is always — for example — the truth table technique. Although our rules are useful (very, for truth tables are extremely tedious), they are not absolutely necessary.

But the axioms and inference rules for predicate logic — the predicate calculus — have a grander role to play, for it is known that there is no technique which can in general tell whether a formula in predicate logic is true. (This was proved by Church in 1936.) Informally, the universal ($\forall$) and existential ($\exists$) quantifiers can be seen as a compact notation for possibly infinite conjunction and disjunction respectively, and this is why the truth table technique would not work: we would have to consider an infinite number of states.

Fortunately, it is known that if a formula is true (technically, "universally valid"), then there must be a proof that it is. (This was shown by Goedel in 1930.) Thus our proof-finding skills are very important, especially because there are no "truth tables" to back us up if we fail.

Because the predicate calculus is far richer (and more interesting) than the propositional calculus, the small set of rules below will represent even less comprehensive a selection than did their propositional counterparts in the previous section. But it seems that even this small set is useful.

We begin with a brief discussion of occurrence and substitution of variables.

2.1 Occurrence of variables in predicates

Simply speaking, we will say that a variable occurs in a predicate if we can see it written there: for example, "x" occurs in "x ≤ y". But we will ignore "inessential" occurrences such as those of "x" in

$$(\exists x : N \bullet x \leqslant y),$$

because in that formula, the "x" is just a place-holder for the quantifier "∃x". For that matter, we could just as easily have written

$$(\exists z : N \bullet z \leqslant y),$$

and the meaning would have been the same. The variable "y", however, occurs in both the formulas above.

The technical terms for these distinctions are: "free" for essential occurrences like "y"; and "bound" for inessential occurrences like "x" and "z". One speaks of "x" being bound by the quantifier "∃x" — and "free" is of course the opposite of "bound". Finally, the "scope" of a quantifier is the area between its immediately enclosing parentheses, in which any occurrence of the quantified variable would be bound.

In the following, for simplicity, we will say just "occurs in" (or doesn't) instead of "occurs free in" (or doesn't).

2.2 Substitutions of terms for variables

We write the substitution of a term "T" for a variable "x" in a predicate "P" as follows:

$$P[T/x]$$

We effect the substitution by replacing in P all (free) occurrences of x by T. Thus for example,

	$(x \leqslant y)[13+z/x]$	is	$13+z \leqslant y;$
but	$(\exists x : N \bullet x \leqslant y)[13+z/x]$	is just	$(\exists x : N \bullet x \leqslant y).$

The reason that the second substitution has no effect is that the variable "x" to be replaced does not occur (free) in the predicate. We must be careful, however, in situations like the following:

$$(\exists x:N \bullet x \leqslant y)[x-1/y] \qquad \text{is } \underline{not} \qquad (\exists x:N \bullet x \leqslant x-1).$$

The problem here is that the occurrence of "x" in "x-1" has been "captured" by the quantifier "∃x", and this is clearly not our intention. We must proceed as follows:

$$(\exists x:N \bullet x \leqslant y)[x-1/y] \qquad \text{is}$$
$$(\exists z:N \bullet z \leqslant y)[x-1/y] \qquad \text{is}$$
$$(\exists z:N \bullet z \leqslant x-1)$$

In the first step, we change the inessential "x" to a (still inessential, but no longer dangerous) "z". The substitution can then be made correctly.

2.3 The facts

We begin by relating the two quantifiers to each other. Let "x" be a variable, "S" a non-empty type in which "x" does not occur (we will always assume this), and "P" any predicate. We have

$$1. \quad \neg(\forall x:S \bullet P) \qquad \Leftrightarrow \qquad (\exists x:S \bullet \neg P)$$

The next two equivalences allow us to distribute ∀ over ∧, and ∃ over ∨. The other two possibilities, however, are given only as implications, and are not valid in the other direction.

$$2. \quad (\forall x:S \bullet P \wedge Q) \qquad \Leftrightarrow \qquad (\forall x:S \bullet P) \wedge (\forall x:S \bullet Q)$$
$$3. \quad (\exists x:S \bullet P \vee Q) \qquad \Leftrightarrow \qquad (\exists x:S \bullet P) \vee (\exists x:S \bullet Q)$$

$$4. \quad (\forall x:S \bullet P \vee Q) \quad \Leftarrow \quad (\forall x:S \bullet P) \vee (\forall x:S \bullet Q)$$
$$5. \quad (\exists x:S \bullet P \wedge Q) \quad \Rightarrow \quad (\exists x:S \bullet P) \wedge (\exists x:S \bullet Q)$$

Now suppose additionally that "N" is a predicate in which "x" does <u>not</u> occur. We have first that

$$6. \quad (\forall x:S \bullet N) \qquad \Leftrightarrow \qquad (\exists x:S \bullet N) \qquad \Leftrightarrow \qquad N$$

but we have also the following equivalences, all of which can help us to simplify
expressions containing quantifiers:

7. $(\forall x:S \cdot P \wedge N)$ $\Leftrightarrow$ $(\forall x:S \cdot P) \wedge N$
8. $(\forall x:S \cdot P \vee N)$ $\Leftrightarrow$ $(\forall x:S \cdot P) \vee N$
9. $(\exists x:S \cdot P \wedge N)$ $\Leftrightarrow$ $(\exists x:S \cdot P) \wedge N$
10. $(\exists x:S \cdot P \vee N)$ $\Leftrightarrow$ $(\exists x:S \cdot P) \vee N$

For implication, the situation is slightly more interesting. We have:

11. $(\forall x:S \cdot P \Rightarrow N)$ $\Leftrightarrow$ $(\exists x:S \cdot P) \Rightarrow N$
12. $(\forall x:S \cdot N \Rightarrow P)$ $\Leftrightarrow$ $N \Rightarrow (\forall x:S \cdot P)$
13. $(\exists x:S \cdot P \Rightarrow N)$ $\Leftrightarrow$ $(\forall x:S \cdot P) \Rightarrow N$
14. $(\exists x:S \cdot N \Rightarrow P)$ $\Leftrightarrow$ $N \Rightarrow (\exists x:S \cdot P)$

All of the equivalences 2,3,6-13 are useful in reducing the scope of a quantifier; and
this reduction is often a prelude to removing the quantifier altogether. In the following
equivalences, we will do just that.

Let "x", "S", and "P" have their usual meanings (including that "x"doesn't occur in
"S"), and let "T" be a term in which "x" doesn't occur. We have

15. $(\exists x:S \cdot x=T \wedge P)$ $\Leftrightarrow$ $(T \in S) \wedge P[T/x]$
16. $(\forall x:S \cdot x=T \Rightarrow P)$ $\Leftrightarrow$ $(T \in S) \Rightarrow P[T/x]$

Notice that we have removed the quantifier in each case, even though "x" might have
occurred in "P". These last two rules are used with great frequency, and one usually
finds that "T∈S" holds in any case, so that the final result is just "P[T/x]".

2.4 An example

We conclude with a small example in which a quantifier is removed. Suppose we have
the two schemas

```
A _____
  |    st, st', in?: N
  |_____
  |    st' = st + in?
  |_____
```

```
B _____
   |    st, st', out!: N          |
   |_____|
   |                              |
   |    st' = st - out!           |
   |_____|
                                  •
```

We calculate the schema "A $\mathsf{\,;\,}$ B" as follows:

A $\mathsf{\,;\,}$ B   =

$(A[st^+/st'] \land B[st^+/st]) \setminus st^+$ =

```
 _____
|   st, st', in?, out!: N                |
|_____|
|                                        |
|  (∃st⁺:N •  st⁺ = st  + in?            |
|             st' = st⁺ - out!)          |
|_____|
```
=

by equivalence 15,

```
 _____
|   st, st', in?, out!: N                |
|_____|
|                                        |
|  (st + in?) ∈ N                        |
|  st' = (st + in?) - out!               |
|_____|
```
=

since (st + in?) ∈ N follows from the signature,

```
 _____
|   st, st', in?, out!: N                |
|_____|
|                                        |
|   st' + out! = st + in?                |
|_____|
                                        •
```

3. References

[End]   Enderton, H.B; "A mathematical introduction to logic"; Academic Press, 1972

[Ham]   Hamilton, A.G.; "Logic for mathematicians"; Cambridge University Press, 1978

PART A — TUTORIALS

In this section we present three papers that provide tutorial introductions to the techniques used in the remainder of the book. The first introduces the notion of using mathematics for specification through examples of a symbol table, file updating and sorting. The second introduces the schema notation by way of a specification of a block-structured symbol table; it makes use of the simple symbol table specified in the first paper. The third provides a slightly more advanced example, in which both the descriptive power of mathematics and the notational compactness of schemas are well exploited.

Contents

Examples of Specification Using Mathematics

Ian Hayes

Abstract

A number of specification examples are developed in the specification language Z[1,2,3], which is based on typed set theory. Z gains its simplicity and expressive power by using directly the well developed notations of mathematics. Since it is based on set theory, it has the dual advantage of using a tried and tested notation and of being widely accessible - especially to those with some mathematical training.

This paper is intended for people experienced in programming but not necessarily in specification. It introduces specification using mathematics with the aid of a few simple examples:

- a symbol table with operations to look up, update, and delete symbols,

- a file update, and

- sorting.

This paper does not address the area of specifying large systems nor does it use that part of Z designed to deal with building large specifications.

As many readers will have some background in logic and basic set operations, these will be treated sparingly. Readers without such background are advised to refer to an introductory book[4] that covers these areas.

A Symbol Table

The first example specifies a simple symbol table. Symbol tables are used by compilers, for example, to record during the compilation of a program the attributes of the symbols defined there. Our specification will demonstrate the use of a mathematical function to specify such a data type, and we will treat the operations which update, lookup, and delete entries in the symbol table.

We describe our table by a partial function from symbols (SYM) to values (VAL)

$$st \ : \ SYM \ \twoheadrightarrow \ VAL$$

The arrow $\twoheadrightarrow$ indicates a function from SYM to VAL that is not necessarily defined for all elements of SYM (hence "partial"). The subset of SYM for which it is defined is its domain of definition

$$dom(st)$$

If a symbol s is in the domain of definition of st ($s \in dom(st)$) then $st(s)$ is the unique value associated with s ($st(s) \in VAL$). The notation $\{ \ s \mapsto v \ \}$ describes a function which is only defined for that particular s

$$dom(\{ \ s \mapsto v \ \}) = \{ \ s \ \}$$

and which maps that s onto v

$$\{ \ s \mapsto v \ \}(s) = v$$

More generally we can use the notation

$$\{ \ x_1 \mapsto y_1, \ x_2 \mapsto y_2, \ \ldots \ , \ x_n \mapsto y_n \ \}$$

where all the x_k's are distinct, to define a function whose domain is

$$\{ \ x_1, \ x_2, \ \ldots, \ x_n \ \}$$

and whose value for each x_k is the corresponding y_k. For example, if we let our symbols be names and values be ages we have the following mapping

$$st = \{ \text{ "John" } \mapsto 23, \text{ "Mary" } \mapsto 19 \}$$

which maps "John" onto 23 and "Mary" onto 19, then the domain of st is the set

$$dom(st) = \{ \text{ "John", "Mary" } \}$$

and

$$st(\text{"John"}) = 23$$
$$st(\text{"Mary"}) = 19$$

The range of st, rng(st), is the set of values that are associated with a symbol in the table. For the example above

$$rng(st) = \{ 19, 23 \}$$

The notation {} is used to denote the empty function whose domain of definition is the empty set.

Initially the symbol table will be empty

$$st = \{\}$$

We are describing a symbol table by modelling it as a partial function. This use of a function is quite different to the normal use of functions in computing, where an algorithm is given to compute the value of the function for a given argument. Here instead we use it to describe a data structure.

There may be many possible models that we can use to describe the same object. Other models of a symbol table could be a list of pairs of symbol and value, or a binary tree containing a symbol and value in each node. But these other models are not as abstract, because many different lists (or trees) can represent the same function. And we would like two symbol tables to be equal if they give the same values for the same symbols.

It is possible to distinguish between two unordered list representations which, if regarded as symbol tables, are equal; on the other hand, for the function representation different functions represent different symbol tables. Thus the list and tree models of a symbol table tend to bias an implementor, working from the specification, towards a particular implementation. Of course, both lists and trees could be used to implement such a symbol table. But any reasoning we wish to perform which involves symbol tables is far easier if we use the partial function model rather than either the list or the tree models.

As some operations can change the symbol table we represent the effect of an operation by the relationship between the symbol table before the operation and the symbol table after the operation. We use

$$st, \ st' \ : \ SYM \nrightarrow VAL$$

where by convention we use the undecorated symbol table (st) to represent the state before the operation and the dashed symbol table (st') the state after. The operation to update an entry in the table is described by the following schema

```
Update
    st, st' : SYM ⇸ VAL
    s? : SYM
    v? : VAL

    st' = st ⊕ { s? ↦ v? }
```

A schema consists of two parts: the declarations (above the centre line) in which variables to be used in the schema are declared, and a predicate (below the centre line) containing predicates giving properties of and relating those variables. In the schema Update the second line declares a variable with name "s?" which is the symbol to be updated. The third line declares a variable with name "v?" which is the value to be associated with s? in the symbol table. By convention names in the declarations ending in "?" are inputs and names ending in "!" will be outputs; the "?" and "!" are otherwise just part of the name.

The predicate part of the schema states that it updates the symbol table (st) to give a new symbol table (st') in which the symbol s? is associated with the value v?. Any previous value associated with s? (if there was one) is lost.

The operator ⊕ (function overriding) combines two functions of the same type to give a new function. The new function f ⊕ g is defined at x if either f or g are defined at x, and will have value $g(x)$ if g is defined at x, otherwise it will have value $f(x)$

$$\text{dom}(f \oplus g) = \text{dom}(f) \cup \text{dom}(g)$$

$$x \in \text{dom}(g) \qquad\qquad \Rightarrow (f \oplus g)(x) = g(x)$$

$$x \notin \text{dom}(g) \wedge x \in \text{dom}(f) \Rightarrow (f \oplus g)(x) = f(x)$$

For example

$$\{ \text{``Mary''} \mapsto 19, \text{``John''} \mapsto 23 \} \oplus \{ \text{``John''} \mapsto 25, \text{``George''} \mapsto 62 \}$$
$$= \{ \text{``Mary''} \mapsto 19, \text{``John''} \mapsto 25, \text{``George''} \mapsto 62 \}$$

For the operation Update above the value of $st'(x)$ is $v?$ if $x = s?$, otherwise it is $st(x)$ provided x is in the domain of st. In our example we are only using $\oplus$ to override one value in our symbol table function; the operator $\oplus$ is, however, more general: its arguments may both be any functions of the same type.

The following schema describes the operation to look up an identifier in the symbol table

```
LookUp_____
    st, st' : SYM ↠ VAL
    s? : SYM
    v! : VAL
  _____
    s? ∈ dom(st) ∧
    v! = st(s?) ∧
    st' = st
  _____
```

The second line of the signature declares a variable with name "s?" which is the symbol to be looked up. The third line of the signature declares a variable with name "v!" which is the value that is associated with s? in the symbol table.

The first line of the predicate states that the identifier being looked up should be in the symbol table before the operation is performed; the above schema does not define the effect of looking up an identifier which is not in the table. The second line states that the output value is the value associated with s? in the symbol table st. The final line states that the contents of the symbol table is not changed by a LookUp operation.

The operation to delete an entry in the symbol table is given by

```
Delete
    st, st' : SYM ⇸ VAL
    s? : SYM
    _____

    s? ∈ dom(st) ∧
    st' = { s? } ◁ st
```

To delete the entry for s? from the symbol table it must be in the table to start with (s? ∈ dom(st)). The resultant symbol table st' is the symbol table st with s? deleted from its domain. We use the domain subtraction operator ◁ where

$$dom(s ◁ f) = dom(f) - s$$

$$x ∈ dom(s ◁ f) ⟹ (s ◁ f)(x) = f(x)$$

where f is a function and s is a set of elements of the same type as the domain of f. For example

$$\{ \text{"Mary", "John"} \} ◁ \{ \text{"Mary"} ↦ 19, \text{"John"} ↦ 25, \text{"George"} ↦ 62 \}$$
$$= \{ \text{"George"} ↦ 62 \}$$

Exercise: In place of a single Update operation define two separate operations: Add, to add a symbol and value if the symbol is not already in the table, and Replace, to replace the value associated with a symbol already in the table. ☐

File Update

The second example is a specification of a simple file update. It uses sets and functions to model the file update operation.

Each record in the file is indexed by a particular key. We will model the file as a partial function from keys to records

$$f \;:\; Key \nrightarrow Record$$

A transaction may either delete an existing record or provide a new record which either replaces an existing record or is added to the file. The transactions for an update of a file will be specified as a set of keys d? which are to be deleted from the file, and a partial function u? giving the keys to be updated and their corresponding new records. We add the further restriction that we cannot both delete a record with a given key and provide a new record for that key. For example, if

$$f \;=\; \{ \, k_1 \mapsto r_1, \; k_2 \mapsto r_2, \; k_3 \mapsto r_3, \; k_4 \mapsto r_4 \, \}$$

$$d? \;=\; \{ \, k_2, \; k_4 \, \}$$

$$u? \;=\; \{ \, k_3 \mapsto r_5, \; k_5 \mapsto r_6 \, \}$$

then the resultant file f' will be

$$f' \;=\; \{ \, k_1 \mapsto r_1, \; k_3 \mapsto r_5, \; k_5 \mapsto r_6 \, \}$$

Our specification is

```
File Update ───────────────────────────────┐
  f, f' : Key ⇸ Record
  d? : P Key
  u? : Key ⇸ Record
 ───────────────────────────────
  d? ⊆ dom(f) ∧
  d? ∩ dom(u?) = {} ∧
  f' = (d? ⩤ f) ⊕ u?
```

The original file f and the updated file f' are modelled by partial functions from keys to records. The keys to be deleted (d?) are a subset of Key. Hence d? is an element of the powerset of Key (the set of all subsets of Key); the notation **P** Key is used to denote the powerset of Key. The updates u? are specified as a partial function from Key to Record.

We can only delete records already in the file f. Hence the set of keys to be deleted $d?$ must be a subset of the domain of the original file ($d? \subseteq \text{dom}(f)$). We are precluded from trying both to delete a key and add a new record for the same key since the intersection of the deletions with the domain of the updates must be empty ($d? \cap \text{dom}(u?) = \{\}$). The resultant file f' is the original file f with all records corresponding to keys in $d?$ deleted ($d? \triangleleft f$), overridden by the new records $u?$.

The last line of File Update could have equivalently been written

$$f' = d? \triangleleft (f \oplus u?)$$

Although it is not always the case that these two lines are equivalent, the extra condition that the intersection of $d?$ and $\text{dom}(u?)$ is empty ensures their equivalence in this case.

Lemma: Given $d? \cap \text{dom}(u?) = \{\}$ the following identity holds

$$d? \triangleleft (f \oplus u?) = (d? \triangleleft f) \oplus u?$$

Proof: Firstly we show that the domains of the two sides are equal

$$\text{dom}(d? \triangleleft (f \oplus u?)) = \text{dom}(f \oplus u?) - d?$$

$$= (\text{dom}(f) \cup \text{dom}(u?)) - d?$$

$$= (\text{dom}(f) - d?) \cup (\text{dom}(u?) - d?)$$

$$= (\text{dom}(f) - d?) \cup \text{dom}(u?)$$
$$\text{since } d? \cap \text{dom}(u?) = \{\}$$

$$= \text{dom}(d? \triangleleft f) \cup \text{dom}(u?)$$

$$= \text{dom}((d? \triangleleft f) \oplus u?)$$

Secondly, for any key k in the domain, the two sides are equal. We prove this for the two cases: $k \in \text{dom}(u?)$ and $k \notin \text{dom}(u?)$.

(a) If $k \in dom(u?)$ then

$$k \notin d? \qquad\qquad \text{as } dom(u?) \cap d? = \{\}$$

$$(d? \lhd (f \oplus u?))(k) = (f \oplus u?)(k) \quad \text{as } k \notin d?$$

$$= u?(k) \qquad \text{as } k \in dom(u?)$$

and $\quad ((d? \lhd f) \oplus u?)(k) = u?(k) \qquad \text{as } k \in dom(u?)$

(b) If $k \notin dom(u?)$ then

$$(d? \lhd (f \oplus u?))(k) = (f \oplus u?)(k) \quad \text{as } k \in dom(d? \lhd (f \oplus u?))$$

$$= f(k) \qquad \text{as } k \notin dom(u?)$$

and $\quad ((d? \lhd f) \oplus u?)(k) = (d? \lhd f)(k) \quad \text{as } k \notin dom(u?)$

$$= f(k) \qquad \text{as } k \in dom(d? \lhd (f \oplus u?)) \quad \square$$

If in the specification of File Update we were not given the extra restriction then, as specified in the last line, the updating of records would have precedence over deletions. If the alternative specification were used then deletions would have precedence over updates. It is sensible to include the extra restriction in the specification as it allows the most freedom in implementation without any real loss of generality.

Exercise: Define an operation (File Add) to add a number of keys with associated records to a file. The keys should not already be contained in the file. $\square$

Sorting

The third example specifies sorting a sequence into non-decreasing order; it uses bags (multi-sets) and sequences.

The input and the output to Sort are sequences of items of a given type X which has a total order "$<_X$" defined on it. Recall that $<_X$ is a (strict) total order on X iff for all $x, y, z : X$ the following are true:

1. $\neg(x <_X x)$;   and

2. $(x <_X y) \lor (x = y) \lor (y <_X x)$;   and

3. $(x <_X y) \land (y <_X z) \implies (x <_X z)$.

We model a sequence as a partial function from the positive natural numbers (N^+) to the base type X as follows

$$\text{seq } X \triangleq \{ s : N^+ \nrightarrow X \mid (\exists n: N \bullet dom(s) = 1..n) \}$$

where #s is the number of entries in the mapping s (which is also the length of the sequence s). The notation of enclosing a list of items in square brackets can be used to construct a sequence consisting of the list of items. For example

$$t = [a, b, c]$$

$$= \{ 1 \mapsto a, 2 \mapsto b, 3 \mapsto c \}$$

We can select an item in a sequence by indexing the sequence with the position of the item

$$t(2) = b$$

$$s = [s(1), s(2), \ldots, s(\#s)]$$

The empty sequence is denoted by [].

The output of Sort must be in non-decreasing order. We define

```
Non-Decreasing────────────────────────┐
   s : seq X
   ─────────────────────
   ∀ i, j : dom(s) •
              (i < j) ⇒ ¬(s(j) <ₓ s(i))
└──────────────────────────────────────┘
```

The output of Sort must contain the same values as the input, with the same frequency. We can state this property using bags. A bag is similar to a set except that multiple occurrences of an element in a bag are significant. We can model a bag as a partial function from the base type X of the bag to the positive integers (N^+) where for each element in the bag the value of the function is the number of times that element occurs in the bag

$$\text{bag } X \;\; \triangleq \;\; X \rightarrowtail N^+$$

We use the notation **[** ... **]** to construct a bag. For example

$$\textbf{[} 1, \; 2, \; 2, \; 2 \textbf{]} \;\; = \;\; \{ \; 1 \mapsto 1, \; 2 \mapsto 3 \; \}$$

The following gives some examples of how sets, bags, and sequences (in this case, of natural numbers) are related

$$\{1, 2, 2, 2\} = \{1, 2, 2\} = \{2, 1, 2\} = \{1, 2\} = \{2, 1\}$$

$$\textbf{[}1, 2, 2, 2\textbf{]} \neq \textbf{[}1, 2, 2\textbf{]} = \textbf{[}2, 1, 2\textbf{]} \neq \textbf{[}1, 2\textbf{]} = \textbf{[}2, 1\textbf{]}$$

$$[1, 2, 2, 2] \neq [1, 2, 2] \neq [2, 1, 2] \neq [1, 2] \neq [2, 1]$$

In specifying Sort we would like to say that the bag formed from all the items in the output sequence is the same as the bag of items in the input sequence. We introduce the function items which forms the bag of all the elements in a sequence. For example

$$\text{items}([\,]) \qquad = \textbf{[]}$$

$$\text{items}([1]) \qquad = \textbf{[}1\textbf{]}$$

$$\text{items}([1, 2, 2]) = \text{items}([2, 1, 2]) = \textbf{[}1, 2, 2\textbf{]}$$

$$\text{items}([1, 2, 3]) = \text{items}([2, 1, 3]) = \textbf{[}1, 2, 3\textbf{]}$$

More precisely

$$\text{items } : \text{ seq } X \;\rightarrow\; \text{bag } X$$

$$\forall \; s: \text{ seq } X \;\bullet$$
$$\text{items}(s) = \{ \; x : \text{rng}(s) \;\bullet$$
$$x \mapsto \#\{ \; i : \text{dom}(s) \mid s(i) = x \; \}$$
$$\}$$

Each element x that occurs in the sequence is mapped onto its frequency of occurrence in the sequence (i.e. the size of the set of positions in the sequence that have value x).

The specification of sorting is given by

```
Sort
    in?,
    out! : seq X

    Non-Decreasing[out!/s] ∧
    items(out!) = items(in?)
```

The output of the sort is non-decreasing (in the use of Non-Decreasing above the variable s has been renamed to out! so that the predicate of Non-Decreasing applies to the output of the sort). The output sequence must contain the same items as the input, with the same frequency.

Sort is an example of a non-algorithmic specification. It specifies what Sort should achieve but not how to go about achieving it. The advantage of a non-algorithmic specification is that its meaning may be more obvious than one which contains the extra detail necessary for it to be algorithmic. The specification is given in terms of the (defining) properties of the problem without biasing the implementor towards a particular form of algorithm. There are many possible sorting algorithms. The implementor should be allowed the freedom to choose the most appropriate.

Exercise: Rewrite the sort specification for the case of sorting a sequence with no duplicates into strictly ascending order. □

References

1. J.-R. Abrial, Programming as a mathematical exercise. In *Mathematical Logic and Programming Languages (eds. C.A.R. Hoare and J.C. Shepherdson)*, Prentice-Hall, 1985.

2. C. C. Morgan and B. A. Sufrin, Specification of the UNIX file system. *IEEE Transactions on Software Engineering, Vol. 10, No. 2*, (March 1984), pp. 128-142 (and in part B of this monograph).

3. B. A. Sufrin, Mathematics for system specification. *University of Oxford Programming Research Group lecture notes*, 1983-84.

4. P. Halmos, *Naive Set Theory*. Springer-Verlag, 1974.

Solutions to Exercises

Symbol table

```
Add_____
┌─────────────────────────────────────────┐
│   st, st' : SYM ↛ VAL                    │
│   s? : SYM                               │
│   v? : VAL                               │
│  ──────────────                          │
│   s? ∉ dom(st) ∧                         │
│   st' = st ∪ { s? ↦ v? }                 │
└─────────────────────────────────────────┘
```

```
Replace_____
┌─────────────────────────────────────────┐
│   st, st' : SYM ↛ VAL                    │
│   s? : SYM                               │
│   v? : VAL                               │
│  ──────────────                          │
│   s? ∈ dom(st) ∧                         │
│   st' = st ⊕ { s? ↦ v? }                 │
└─────────────────────────────────────────┘
```

File add

```
┌─ File Add ─────────────────────────────────┐
│   f, f' : Key ⇸ Record                      │
│   a?     : Key ⇸ Record                     │
├─────────────────────────────────           │
│   dom(a?) ∩ dom(f) = {} ∧                   │
│   f' = f ∪ a?                               │
└─────────────────────────────────────────────┘
```

Sorting

```
┌─ NoDuplicates ─────────────────────────────┐
│   s : seq X                                 │
├─────────────────────                        │
│   ∀ i, j : dom(s) •                         │
│             (i ≠ j) ⟹ (s(i) ≠ s(j))         │
└─────────────────────────────────────────────┘
```

```
┌─ Ascending ────────────────────────────────┐
│   s : seq X                                 │
├─────────────────────                        │
│   ∀ i, j : dom(s) •                         │
│             (i < j) ⟹ (s(i) <_X s(j))       │
└─────────────────────────────────────────────┘
```

```
┌─ Sort ─────────────────────────────────────┐
│   in?, out! : seq X                         │
├─────────────────────                        │
│   NoDuplicates[in?/s] ∧                     │
│   Ascending[out!/s] ∧                       │
│   rng(in?) = rng(out!)                      │
└─────────────────────────────────────────────┘
```

Block-Structured Symbol Table

Ian Hayes

Abstract

A specification of a symbol table suitable for processing a block structured language is given. This specification is intended to demonstrate how, using the specification notation $Z^{1,2,3}$, a specification can be built from components.

A simple symbol table suitable for a single block is described first; it has operations to look up, update, and delete entries. This simple symbol table is the same as that given in the paper entitled "Examples of Specification Using Mathematics"[4] preceding this paper. The treatment given here differs from that in the earlier paper in that it emphasises how such a specification can be built using the schema notation of Z[5] and includes a treatment of error conditions not given in the earlier paper. Readers not familiar with the mathematics used in this specification should consult the earlier paper for a more detailed explanation.

The second part of this paper specifies a block structured symbol table in terms of a sequence of simple symbol tables; one for each nested block. Operations are given to search the *environment* for a symbol, and to start and finish nested blocks; the operations on a simple symbol table are upgraded appropriately to work on the symbol table corresponding to the smallest enclosing block.

Symbol Table

A symbol table associates a unique value (from the set VAL) with a symbol (from the set SYM). The operations allowed on a symbol table are to:

- update the value associated with a symbol in the table, adding the symbol if it is not already there;

- look up the value associated with a symbol in the table;

- delete a symbol and its associated value from the table.

To specify our symbol table we first give a model of its state and a description of its initial state, then we specify each of the operations in terms of the relationship between the state before an operation, the inputs to the operation, the outputs from the operation, and the state after the operation.

The State

The state of a symbol table can be modelled by a partial function from symbols to values

$$ST \;\hat{=}\; SYM \nrightarrow VAL$$

Initially the symbol table is empty

$$st_{INIT} \;\hat{=}\; \{\}$$

Operations

Each operation on a symbol table transforms a symbol table before (st) into a symbol table after (st ′).

$$\Delta ST \;\hat{=}\; [\; st,\; st' \,:\, ST \;]$$

The definition of each operation must include declarations of the before and after states of the operation; rather than write out these declarations in full in each definition, we introduce a schema ΔST that contains just these declarations and include this schema in the definition of each operation as an abbreviation for the declarations. The "Δ" (for "change") in "ΔST" is just part of the name of the schema; we allow Greek letters in names. By convention names beginning with "Δ" are used for schemas that contain before and after state components.

Error handling and the operation to look up a symbol do not modify the symbol table.

$$\equiv\!ST \quad \hat{=} \quad [\ \Delta ST \ | \ st' = st \ ]$$

The schema ≡ST declares the before and after states (in ΔST) and constrains them to be equal; this schema describes the effect on the state of inquiry-like operations (such as looking up a symbol in the symbol table) and error handling; neither of these modifies the state. The "≡" (for no change) in "≡ST" is again just part of the name. By convention names beginning with "≡" are used for schemas which are written to express that there is no change.

An extra constraint may be added to the predicate part of a schema by following the schema with a "|" followed by the predicate. The additional predicate is conjoined with the existing predicate of the schema to form the predicate of the resulting schema; in the case of ≡ST the existing predicate is true (the default when no predicate is given as in ΔST). Expanding the definition of ≡ST we get

$$\equiv\!ST \quad \hat{=}$$

```
┌─────────────────────────────┐
│  st, st' : ST               │
│─────────────────────────────│
│  st' = st                   │
└─────────────────────────────┘
```

To look up the value v! associated with a symbol s? we use

```
┌─LookUp──────────────────────┐
│  ≡ST                        │
│  s? : SYM                   │
│  v! : VAL                   │
│─────────────────────────────│
│  s? ∈ dom(st) ∧             │
│  v! = st(s?)                │
└─────────────────────────────┘
```

The schema ≡ST *is used in the definition of* LookUp *to declare the before and after states (*st *and* st'*) and to constrain them to be equal. The convention of using the* ≡ST *schema saves writing out all the state components and the equality constraint explicitly.*

A schema may be included in the declaration part of a schema; the declarations of the included schema are merged with the other declarations and its predicates are conjoined with the predicates of the schema.

LookUp
≜

```
┌─────────────────────────────────────
│   st, st' : ST
│   s?   : SYM
│   v!   : VAL
│   ─────────────────────────
│   st' = st ∧
│   s?  ∈ dom(st) ∧
│   v!  = st(s?)
└─────────────────────────────────────
```

To update the value associated with a symbol we use

```
Update ──────────────────────────────
│   ΔST
│   s? : SYM
│   v? : VAL
│   ─────────────────────────
│   st' = st ⊕ { s? ↦ v? }
└─────────────────────────────────────
```

This schema uses ΔST *to include the declarations of the before and after states.*

If the symbol was already in the table, its old value is replaced by v?; if it was not in the table, it is added.

To delete an entry in the symbol table we use

```
Delete_____
   ΔST
   s? : SYM
  _____
   s?  ∈ dom(st) ∧
   st' = {s?} ⊲ st
```

Errors

LookUp and Delete are only defined if the symbol is present in the table. If the symbol is not present an error is reported and the symbol table is not modified.

```
NotPresent!_____
   ≡ST
   s?   : SYM
   rep! : Report
  _____
   s? ∉ dom(st) ∧
   rep! = "Symbol not present"
```

The schema ≡ST *is included in the above schema to introduce the declarations of the before and after states and to constrain them to be equal.*

A convention used within this specification is that schemas denoting errors have names ending in "!"; the "!" is just part of the name.

Successful operations return a report of "OK".

$$\text{Success} \quad \hat{=} \quad [\ \text{rep!} : \text{Report}\ |\ \text{rep!} = \text{"OK"}\ ]$$

The operations with error handling are

STLookUp   ≙   (LookUp ∧ Success) ∨ NotPresent!

STUpdate   ≙   Update ∧ Success

STDelete   ≙   (Delete ∧ Success) ∨ NotPresent!

Either a LookUp operation can be successfully performed (if s? ∈ dom(st)*), in which case a report of "OK" is given, or the LookUp cannot be performed (if* s? ∉ dom(st)*), in which case an error report of "Symbol not present" is given.*

The conjunction (∧) of two schemas is formed by merging their declarations (variables common to both declarations must have the same type) and conjoining their predicates. Below we give expanded versions of the LookUp operation. We do not normally find it necessary to expand such definitions to understand the specification but the expansions are intended to help those who are not familiar with the notation.

LookUp ∧ Success
≙

```
┌─────────────────────────────────────┐
│ ≡ST                                  │
│ s?   : SYM                           │
│ v!   : VAL                           │
│ rep! : Report                        │
├──────────────────────────────        │
│ s?   ∈ dom(st) ∧                     │
│ v!   = st(s?) ∧                      │
│ rep! = "OK"                          │
└─────────────────────────────────────┘
```

In this example there are no common variables.

The disjunction (∨) of two schemas is formed by merging their declarations (variables common to both must have the same type) and disjoining their predicate parts.

STLookUp
≙

```
┌─────────────────────────────────────────┐
│  ≡ST                                     │
│  s?   : SYM                              │
│  v!   : VAL                              │
│  rep! : Report                           │
│ ├───────────────────────────────────     │
│   (s? ∈ dom(st) ∧                        │
│    v! = st(s?) ∧                         │
│    rep! = "OK")                          │
│  ∨                                       │
│   (s? ∉ dom(st) ∧                        │
│    rep! = "Symbol not present")          │
└─────────────────────────────────────────┘
```

In this example the declarations in ≡ST and the declarations of s? and rep! are common and have the same types, and hence can be merged. Note that no constraint is placed on the value of v! returned in the error case.

Exercise 1: Give expanded forms of the schemas STUpdate and STDelete. ☐

Block-Structured Symbol Table

We will now describe a symbol table suitable for use in processing (e.g., compiling) a block-structured language such as Algol 60. In such languages each variable declaration is associated with a block and a variable may be referred to only from within the block with which it is associated. Blocks may be nested within other blocks to an arbitrary level; each nested block must be completely enclosed by the block in which it is included. For example, consider the following fragment of Algol 60

```
begin A
    integer x, y;
    . . .
    x := 2; y := 3;                         (1)
    . . .
    begin B
        real y; integer z;
        . . .
        y := 0.5;  x := z;                  (2)
        . . .
    end B;
    . . .
    y := x;                                 (3)
    . . .
end A
```

The outer block A declares variables x and y of type integer. These variables may be referred to anywhere within block A, except that the variable y of block A may not be referred to within block B because there is a variable with the same name declared in block B; within block B the outer (block A) declaration of y is "hidden" by the declaration of y in block B. We refer to those parts of the program in which a variable may be referred to as being within the "scope" of that variable.

A symbol table suitable for sequential processing of a block-structured language should support the scoping rules of block-structured languages; it should have operations for starting and finishing blocks as well as operations to access, update, and delete entries in the table.

The State

The simple symbol table described in the earlier part of this paper is suitable only for keeping track of the variables of a single block. At a given point in a program we need to keep track of all the variables declared in all the blocks enclosing that point; this can be done by associating a simple symbol table with each block enclosing the point. To keep track of the order in which the blocks are nested we will arrange the symbol tables into a sequence so that, if a block A encloses another block B, the symbol table for A will precede the symbol table for B in the sequence. We can model a block-structured symbol table by

$$BST \; \triangleq \; seq \; ST$$

The first symbol table in the sequence is for the outermost block enclosing a point.

In the example given above, the block-structured symbol table within block A but excluding block B (e.g., at the positions marked (1) and (3)) will be a sequence containing a single symbol table

$$[\; \{ \; x \mapsto integer, \quad y \mapsto integer \; \} \;]$$

Within block B (e.g., at the position marked (2)) the sequence contains two symbol tables

$$[\; \{ \; x \mapsto integer, \; y \mapsto integer \; \}, \; \{ \; y \mapsto real, \; z \mapsto integer \; \} \;]$$

At any point within a program at most one variable of a given name may be referenced. We will refer to the variables that may be referenced at a given point, along with their associated information, as the "environment" of that point. An environment may be represented as a simple symbol table. In the example above, the environment within block A but excluding block B (viz. (1) and (3)) is

$$\{ \; x \mapsto integer, \; y \mapsto integer \; \}$$

and within block B it is equal to the symbol table for block A overridden by the symbol table for block B

$$\{ \; x \mapsto integer, \; y \mapsto integer \; \} \oplus \{ \; y \mapsto real, \; z \mapsto integer \; \}$$

$$= \{ \; x \mapsto integer, \; y \mapsto real, \; z \mapsto integer \; \}$$

In general, if we have a block-structured symbol table consisting of a sequence of symbol tables the environment is given by overriding the symbol tables in sequence. For example, for the sequence

$$[\ st_1, \quad st_2, \quad \ldots \ , \quad st_n \ ]$$

the environment is

$$st_1 \oplus st_2 \oplus \ldots \oplus st_n.$$

We can define the distributed override operator $\oplus/$ which extracts the environment from a sequence of symbol tables by

$$\oplus/ \ : \ seq \ ST \ \rightarrow \ ST$$

$$\oplus/[\ ] \ = \ \{\}$$

$$\oplus/(s \ \frown \ [t]) \ = \ (\oplus/s) \oplus t$$

Initially no blocks have been entered; hence the block structured symbol table is the empty sequence

$$bst_{INIT} \ \hat{=} \ [\ ]$$

Operations

The operations on a block-structured symbol table transform a state before (bst) to a state after (bst').

$$\Delta BST \triangleq [\ bst,\ bst'\ :\ BST\ ]$$

Some operations leave the state unchanged.

$$\equiv BST \triangleq [\ \Delta BST\ |\ bst'\ =\ bst\ ]$$

There are two operations which retrieve information about a symbol from a block-structured symbol table: BLookUp and BSearch. BLookUp looks in the most nested symbol table only; it will be defined in terms of STLookUp. BSearch searches for a symbol in the environment (i.e., the most nested occurrence of the symbol in the block structured symbol table).

```
BSearch₀
    ≡BST
    s? : SYM
    v! : VAL
    _____
    s? ∈ dom(⊕/bst) ∧
    v! = (⊕/bst)(s?)
```

When the start of a block is encountered a new (empty) symbol table is appended to the sequence

```
BStart₀
    ΔBST
    _____
    bst' = bst ⌢ [st_INIT]
```

When the end of a block is encountered the last symbol table in the sequence is deleted

```
┌─ BEnd₀ ──────────────────────────────────┐
│  ΔBST                                     │
│ ─────────────────────────────            │
│                                           │
│  bst  ≠ []    ∧                           │
│  bst' = front(bst)                        │
└───────────────────────────────────────────┘
```

We want to be able to perform the simple symbol table operations (STLookUp, STUpdate and STDelete) on the most nested (last) symbol table in the sequence. These operations can only be performed provided the sequence is non-empty, and they change only the last symbol table in the sequence. The relationship between the before and after values of the last symbol table in the sequence is determined by the simple symbol table operations.

The common part of the three upgraded operations is given by

```
┌─ Upgrade ────────────────────────────────┐
│  ΔBST                                     │
│  ΔST                                      │
│ ─────────────────────────────            │
│                                           │
│  bst ≠ []    ∧                            │
│  front(bst') = front(bst) ∧               │
│  st  = last(bst) ∧                        │
│  st' = last(bst')                         │
└───────────────────────────────────────────┘
```

The above description does not specify the relationship between the last symbol table in the sequence before (st) and after (st') an operation; we have already described these relationships in our definitions of the simple symbol table operations. We can now define the upgraded symbol table operations in terms of the definitions of the simple symbol table operations given earlier.

The upgraded operations are given by

$$\text{BLookUp}_0 \;\;\hat{=}\;\; (\text{STLookUp} \wedge \text{Upgrade}) \setminus \Delta\text{ST}$$

$$\text{BUpdate}_0 \;\;\hat{=}\;\; (\text{STUpdate} \wedge \text{Upgrade}) \setminus \Delta\text{ST}$$

$$\text{BDelete}_0 \;\;\hat{=}\;\; (\text{STDelete} \wedge \text{Upgrade}) \setminus \Delta\text{ST}$$

A schema may have a list of its components hidden by use of schema hiding ("\"). The declarations of the hidden variables are removed from the declaration part of the schema and are existentially quantified in the predicate part. If the second operand to "\" is a schema then all the variables in the declaration part of the second schema are hidden in the first schema.

The components of ΔST (st and st') are hidden in the above definitions because we wish to define the operations as working on before and after states which are of type BST; the ΔST components are only used to make the link between the specifications of the operations on the simple symbol table and the part of the BST state that the simple operations are to be performed on. The reason for introducing Upgrade is to allow the definitions of the operations on simple symbol tables to be used directly in the definitions of the operations on block structured symbol tables.

BUpdate_0
$\hat{=}$

```
┌─────────────────────────────────────────────
│  ΔBST
│  s?   : SYM
│  v?   : VAL
│  rep! : Report
├─────────────────────────────────────────────
│  (∃ st, st' : ST •
│     bst ≠ [] ∧
│     front(bst') = front(bst) ∧
│     st  = last(bst) ∧
│     st' = st ⊕ { s? ↦ v? } ∧
│     rep! = "OK" ∧
│     st' = last(bst')
│  )
└─────────────────────────────────────────────
```

$BUpdate_0$ *may be simplified to*

```
┌─────────────────────────────────────────────────────┐
│ ΔBST                                                  │
│ s?    : SYM                                           │
│ v?    : VAL                                           │
│ rep!  : Report                                        │
│ ─────────────────────────────────────────────────    │
│ bst ≠ [] ∧                                            │
│ front(bst') = front(bst) ∧                            │
│ last(bst') = last(bst) ⊕ { s? ↦ v? } ∧               │
│ rep! = "OK"                                           │
└─────────────────────────────────────────────────────┘
```

Errors

The upgraded operations and BEnd will fail if the sequence is empty

```
Empty!
    ≡BST
    rep! : Report
    _____
    bst  = []  ∧
    rep! = "Not within any block"
```

The BSearch operation will fail if the symbol is not in the environment. If the
sequence is empty we give preference to the Empty! error. Hence, for this error, we
require that the sequence is non-empty.

```
NotFound!
    ≡BST
    s?   : SYM
    rep! : Report
    _____
    bst ≠ [] ∧
    s? ∉ dom(⊕/bst) ∧
    rep! = "Symbol not found"
```

The final definitions of the operations are

$$BSearch \triangleq (BSearch_0 \wedge Success) \vee NotFound! \vee Empty!$$

$$BStart \triangleq BStart_0 \wedge Success$$

$$BEnd \triangleq (BEnd_0 \wedge Success) \vee Empty!$$

$$BLookUp \triangleq BLookUp_0 \vee Empty!$$

$$BUpdate \triangleq BUpdate_0 \vee Empty!$$

$$BDelete \triangleq BDelete_0 \vee Empty!$$

An expanded and simplified definition of BSearch *is*

```
≡BST
s? : SYM
v! : VAL
rep! : Report
─────────────────────────────
  (s? ∈ dom(⊕/bst) ∧
   v! = (⊕/bst)(s?) ∧
   rep! = "OK")
∨
  (bst ≠ [] ∧
   s? ∉ dom(⊕/bst) ∧
   rep! = "Symbol not found")
∨
  (bst = []  ∧
   rep! = "Not within any block")
```

Here is a different expansion and simplification of BSearch. *It is logically equivalent to the one above, but achieves a different emphasis:*

```
≡BST
s? : SYM
v! : VAL
rep! : Report
─────────────────────────────
  (bst = []  ⟹
      rep! = "Not within any block")
  ∧
  (bst ≠ []  ⟹
    (s? ∈ dom(⊕/bst)  ⟹
      v! = (⊕/bst)(s?) ∧
      rep! = "OK")
    ∧
    (s? ∉ dom(⊕/bst)  ⟹
      rep! = "Symbol not found"))
```

<u>Exercise   2:</u> Give an expansion of BDelete. []

<u>Exercise   3:</u> Define a search operation BLocate that returns not only the value associated with a symbol but also the level of the innermost block in which it is declared. []

References

1. Abrial, J.-R. The specification language Z: Basic library. *Oxford University Programming Research Group internal report*, (April 1980).

2. Morgan, C. C., and Sufrin, B. A. Specification of the UNIX file system. *IEEE Transactions on Software Engineering, Vol. 10, No. 2*, (March 1984), pp. 128-142 (and in part B of this monograph).

3. Sufrin, B. A.   Mathematics for system specification. *University of Oxford Programming Research Group lecture notes*, 1983-84.

4. Hayes, I. J.   Examples of specification using mathematics. *The preceding paper in this monograph.*

5. Morgan, C. C.   Schemas in Z: A preliminary reference manual. *Oxford University Programming Research Group Distributed Computing Project report*, (March 1984).

Solutions to Exercises

1. STUpdate
    > ΔST
    > s? : SYM
    > v? : VAL
    > rep! : Report
    >
    > ---
    >
    > st' = st $\oplus$ { s? $\mapsto$ v? } $\wedge$
    > rep! = "OK"

    STDelete
    > ΔST
    > s? : SYM
    > rep! : Report
    >
    > ---
    >
    > (s? $\in$ dom(st) $\wedge$
    > st' = { s? } $\lhd$ st $\wedge$
    > rep! = "OK")
    > $\vee$
    > (s? $\notin$ dom(st) $\wedge$
    > st' = st $\wedge$
    > rep! = "Symbol not found")

2.   BDelete_____

> ΔBST
> s? : SYM
> rep! : Report
>
> ---
>
> (∃ st, st′ : ST •
>   bst ≠ [] ∧
>   front(bst′) = front(bst) ∧
>   st = last(bst) ∧
>   ((s? ∈ dom(st) ∧ st′ = { s? } ⩤ st ∧ rep! = "OK")
>   ∨(s? ∉ dom(st) ∧ st′ = st ∧ rep! = "Symbol not found")
>   ) ∧
>   st′ = last(bst′))
> ∨
> (bst = [] ∧
> bst′ = bst ∧
> rep! = "Not within any block")

This is equivalent to

BDelete_____

> ΔBST
> s? : SYM
> rep! : Report
>
> ---
>
> (bst ≠ [] ∧ s? ∈ dom(last(bst)) ∧
> front(bst′) = front(bst) ∧
> last(bst′) = { s? } ⩤ last(bst) ∧
> rep! = "OK")
> ∨
> (bst ≠ [] ∧ s? ∉ dom(last(bst)) ∧
> bst′ = bst ∧
> rep! = "Symbol not found")
> ∨
> (bst = [] ∧
> bst′ = bst ∧
> rep! = "Not within any block")

3.

```
┌─ BLocate₀ ─────────────────────────────────────────────┐
│   ≡BST                                                  │
│   s? : SYM                                              │
│   v! : VAL                                              │
│   level! : N                                            │
├────────────────────────                                │
│   bst ≠ [] ∧                                            │
│   s? ∈ dom(⊕/bst) ∧                                     │
│   level! = max { i : dom(bst) | s? ∈ dom(bst(i)) } ∧    │
│   v! = bst(level!)(s?)                                  │
└────────────────────────────────────────────────────────┘
```

$\text{BLocate} \;\widehat{=}\; (\text{BLocate}_0 \land \text{Success}) \lor \text{NotFound!} \lor \text{Empty!}$

Telephone Network

Carroll Morgan

Abstract

The specification of a simple telephone system is used to illustrate two general features of specifications in Z:

- how the use of *schemas* can drastically reduce the amount of rewriting required when developing specifications; and

- how the direct use of mathematics makes it possible to describe desired properties of an implementation without constraining the implementor's choice of algorithm.

Exercises and solutions to them are included.

A similar but more comprehensive specification is given in [1].

1. Introduction

We choose as our example a simple *telephone network* in which connections may be established between pairs of telephones. A request may be made for the connection of a given phone to any other; if the request cannot be satisfied immediately, it will be stored by the network and satisfied if possible at some later time (for example, the other phone might be engaged).

We describe only three network operations; they are

Call   -   request a connection between two telephones.

Hangup -   terminate a connection.

Engaged -   indicate whether a given telephone is currently engaged, and if so, with which phone.

2. The specification

Let the set of telephones be PHONE. We define a connection to be a set of PHONEs:

CON ≙ **P** PHONE

This definition allows the possibility of "conference calls" (connections c such that #c>2), as well as "test calls" perhaps made by maintenance staff (#c=1). Even the "empty call" is possible (but perhaps pointless).

The state of the telephone network will be described by two variables:

reqs: **P** CON   -   the set of connections requested but not yet terminated; and

cons: **P** CON   -   the set of connections currently active,

and these variables will satisfy the two invariants:

cons ⊆ reqs   -   only requested connections are active; and

disjoint cons   -   no phone may engage in more than one
                             connection at any time.

We have applied disjoint to a set of sets as follows (in contrast to the glossary) :

$$\text{disjoint cons} \iff (\forall c1, c2 : \text{cons} \cdot c1 \neq c2 \implies c1 \cap c2 = \{\}).$$

Our state is described by the schema TN:

```
┌─ TN ──────────────────────────────────┐
│       reqs, cons: P CON               │
│ ──────────────────────                │
│       cons ⊆ reqs                     │
│       disjoint cons                   │
└───────────────────────────────────────┘
```

An *efficient* network, however, would at any time have activated as many connections as possible. We describe it with the following schema efficient TN:

```
┌─ efficient TN ────────────────────────┐
│       TN                              │
│ ──────────────────────                │
│    ¬(∃ cons⁰: P CON ·                 │
│       cons ⊂ cons⁰                    │
│       TN [cons⁰/cons])                │
└───────────────────────────────────────┘
```

efficient TN requires the set of connections cons to be *maximal* with respect to TN; that is, at any time it must not be possible to augment the set while continuing to satisfy the TN invariant.

Notice that it is not necessary to select an algorithm for achieving maximality: it is sufficient simply to state that it is required.

The definition of efficientTN is, in full:

```
efficientTN_____
      reqs, cons: P CON
   _____

      cons ⊆ reqs
      disjoint cons

       ¬(∃ cons⁰: P CON •
          cons ⊂ cons⁰
          cons⁰ ⊆ reqs
          disjoint cons⁰)

```

Each of the three operations on the network will be described in terms of the state before (efficientTN) and after (efficientTN'), and the phone from which it is initiated:

ph: PHONE

We collect these in the schema ΔTN, but impose the additional constraint that a connection will never be terminated unless such termination is necessary to preserve the invariant:

```
ΔTN_____
      efficientTN
      efficientTN'

      ph: PHONE
   _____

       ¬(∃ cons¹: P CON •
          (cons - cons¹) ⊂ (cons - cons')
          efficientTN' [cons¹/cons'])
```

ΔTN requires the set of connections terminated as an effect of the operation (cons - cons') to be *minimal* with respect to efficient TN'. That is, it must not be possible to diminish that set while maintaining the efficient TN' invariant.

Each of the three operations is expressed in terms of the ΔTN schema above, and any additional variables it requires individually:

Call

> The call operation requests a connection between the initiating phone ph and the phone dialled. The request {ph, dialled} is added to the set reqs of requests; the maximality constraint of efficient TN' ensures that if the request can be satisfied immediately, it will be; and the minimality constraint of ΔTN ensures that no other change will occur in cons.

```
Call
    ΔTN
    dialled: PHONE

    reqs' = reqs ∪ {ph, dialled}
```

HangUp

> The hangup operation terminates any connection in which the initiating phone is engaged; any such connection c is removed from the set of requests (which therefore forces it to be removed from the set of connections also).

```
HangUp
    ΔTN

    reqs' = reqs - {c: cons | ph ∈ c}
```

Engaged

The engaged operation indicates whether a phone is connected or not.

```
Engaged_____
 |    ΔTN
 |    engaged': { Yes, No }
 |    other'   : PHONE
 |    _____
 |
 |    TN' = TN
 |
 |    (engaged' = Yes) ⟹ ({ph, other'} ∈ cons)
 |    (engaged' = No ) ⟹ ph ∉ (U cons)
```

3. Exercises

1. "A connection is not terminated unless terminating it is necessary to preserve the invariant". Justify the formulation of ΔTN by showing that

$$\Delta TN \implies (\forall c: \text{cons} \bullet c \in \text{reqs}' \implies c \in \text{cons}')$$

That is, any connection which

   (i) was active before an operation (∈ cons), and
   (ii) is still requested after the operation (∈ reqs')

remains active (∈ cons').

2. Show that it is possible for HangUp to activate a connection. That is, prove the following:

$$(\exists \text{HangUp} \bullet (\text{cons}' - \text{cons}) \neq \{\})$$

3. Add a variable

avail: **P** PHONE

to the telephone network state; avail is to be, at any time, the set of phones which are *available* for connection (i.e., are in working order). Leave aside for the moment just what determines the value of avail itself; concentrate instead on what changes must be made to ensure that only available phones can be used (to initiate an operation) or engaged.

Hint: consider the effect of "dynamic binding" when one schema is included within another. Extending TN *would then* automatically *extend* efficientTN, ΔTN, *etc.*

4. Specify two operations for updating the variable avail. That is, define

```
AV
    avail: P PHONE
```

and two operations

```
Break
    ΔAV
    phone: PHONE

    ?????
```

```
Fix
    ΔAV
    phone: PHONE

    ?????
```

where Break makes a phone unavailable, and Fix makes it available again.

5. Extend the operations Break and Fix (introduced in question 4) so that they operate on the network state efficientTN, but do not change reqs (cons may *have* to change). Add to Call, HangUp, and Engaged the constraint that they do not change avail. Finally, present the entire specification as it now stands.

4. Answers

1.   Since from efficient TN' we have cons' $\subseteq$ reqs', it follows that

$$(cons - reqs') \subseteq (cons - cons')$$

But $(cons - reqs') = cons - (reqs' \cap cons)$, and so

$$cons - (reqs' \cap cons) \subseteq cons - cons' \qquad (1)$$

Now if for some c,

$$(c \in cons \wedge c \in reqs') \Rightarrow c \in cons' \qquad (2)$$

were not true, then we would have both of the following

(i) $c \notin (cons - (reqs' \cap cons))$, and
(ii) $c \in (cons - cons')$,

which together would show that the inclusion (1) was strict:

$$cons - (reqs' \cap cons) \subset cons - cons'$$

Letting $cons^1$ be reqs' $\cap$ cons, this contradicts ΔTN, and so we have established (2).

□

2.   We assume that the set PHONES is big enough to contain at least 3 distinct elements; let them be a, b, and c. Then

$$\text{Hangup} \mid \begin{aligned} reqs &= \{\{a, b\}, \{a, c\}\} \quad \wedge \\ cons &= \{\{a, b\}\} \qquad\qquad \wedge \\ ph &= a \end{aligned}$$

$$\Rightarrow \quad \begin{aligned} reqs' &= \{\{a, c\}\} \\ cons' &= \{\{a, c\}\} \end{aligned}$$

$$\Rightarrow \quad (cons' - cons) \neq \{\}$$

□

3. First extend the *original* TN (before efficient TN), specifying that only available phones can be engaged in a connection:

```
TN_____
   |  TN
   |  avail: P PHONE
   |_____
   |
   |  (U cons) ⊆ avail
   |_____
```

The use of TN within its own definition is not recursive; the sub-schema name TN refers to its *previous* definition, and so the above is strictly an extension. We have redefined TN to be:

```
TN_____
   |     reqs, cons: P CON
   |     avail:      P PHONE
   |     _____
   |
   |     cons ⊆ reqs
   |     (U cons) ⊆ avail
   |_____
```

If we consider the definitions of efficient TN and ΔTN to include their sub-schemas *dynamically* (i.e., a dynamic binding), they are automatically extended also. In particular, the efficiency extension takes the new variable avail into account.

We now extend the (already implicitly extended) ΔTN by adding the constraint that only available phones can initiate an operation:

```
ΔTN_____
   |  ΔTN
   |  _____
   |
   |  ph ∈ avail
   |_____
```

Again, by considering schema inclusion to be dynamic, the definitions of Call, HangUp, and Engaged are automatically extended.

4. First define

```
AV
    avail: P PHONE
```

and the straightforward

```
ΔAV
    AV
    AV'
```

The two operations are then

```
Break
    ΔAV
    phone: PHONE

    phone  ∈ avail
    avail' = avail - {phone}
```

and

```
Fix
    ΔAV
    phone: PHONE

    phone  ∉ avail
    avail' = avail ∪ {phone}
```

5.   We again exploit dynamic binding by redefining ΔAV to achieve an implicit extension of Break and Fix:

```
ΔAV
┌──────────────────────────────────────────┐
│        ΔTN                                │
│                                           │
├──────────────────────────────────────────┤
│                                           │
│        reqs' = reqs                       │
└──────────────────────────────────────────┘
```

and we redefine Call, HangUp, and Engaged explicitly:

$$
\begin{aligned}
\text{Call}   &\;\hat{=}\; \text{Call}   &&\wedge\; (\text{avail}' = \text{avail}) \\
\text{Hangup} &\;\hat{=}\; \text{HangUp} &&\wedge\; (\text{avail}' = \text{avail}) \\
\text{Engaged} &\;\hat{=}\; \text{Engaged} &&\wedge\; (\text{avail}' = \text{avail})
\end{aligned}
$$

The complete specification is now

The state

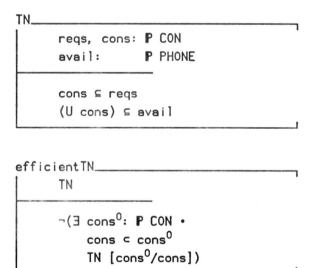

```
TN
┌──────────────────────────────────────────┐
│        reqs, cons:  P CON                 │
│        avail:       P PHONE               │
├──────────────────────────────────────────┤
│        cons ⊆ reqs                        │
│        (U cons) ⊆ avail                    │
└──────────────────────────────────────────┘
```

```
efficient TN
┌──────────────────────────────────────────┐
│        TN                                 │
├──────────────────────────────────────────┤
│     ¬(∃ cons⁰: P CON •                     │
│          cons ⊂ cons⁰                      │
│          TN [cons⁰/cons])                  │
└──────────────────────────────────────────┘
```

General properties of the operations

```
ΔTN
┌──────────────────────────────────────────────────┐
│        efficientTN
│        efficientTN'
│
│        ph: PHONE
│  ──────────────────────
│        ph ∈ avail
│
│        ¬(∃ cons¹: P CON •
│            (cons - cons¹) ⊂ (cons - cons')
│            efficientTN' [cons¹/cons'])
└──────────────────────────────────────────────────┘
```

The operations

Request a connection

```
Call
┌────────────────────────────────────────┐
│        ΔTN
│        dialled: PHONE
│  ──────────────────────
│        reqs'  = reqs ∪ {ph, dialled}
│        avail' = avail
└────────────────────────────────────────┘
```

Terminate a connection

```
HangUp
┌────────────────────────────────────────────┐
│        ΔTN
│  ──────────────────────
│        reqs'  = reqs - {c: cons | ph ∈ c}
│        avail' = avail
└────────────────────────────────────────────┘
```

Determine telephone status

```
Engaged_____
    │   ΔTN
    │   engaged': Yes | No
    │   other'   : PHONE
    │  _____
    │   TN' = TN
    │
    │   (engaged' = Yes) ⟹ ({ph, other'} ∈ cons)
    │   (engaged' = No ) ⟹ ph ∉ (U cons)
    └_____
```

Break a telephone

```
Break_____
    │   ΔAV
    │   phone: PHONE
    │  _____
    │   phone  ∈ avail
    │   avail' = avail - {phone}
    │   reqs'  = reqs
    └_____
```

Fix a telephone

```
Fix_____
    │   ΔAV
    │   phone: PHONE
    │  _____
    │   phone  ∉ avail
    │   avail' = avail ∪ {phone}
    │   reqs'  = reqs
    └_____
```

5. Supplementary exercises

6.   Can a telephone call itself? If so, what is the effect of a subsequent Engaged?

7.   If an engaged telephone is suddenly broken, does the connection remain active? Is the request lost? What happens when the telephone is fixed?

8.   The system state is capable of describing conference calls, in which more than two telephones may be connected together, but some of the operations as now specified are inappropriate for this. Why? Modify those operations so that conference calls are supported.

References

1.   Carroll Morgan, "Specification of a communication system," in *Distributed computing systems: synchronisation, control, and communication*, Y. Paker, J.-P. Verjus (ed.), Academic Press, 1983.

PART B — SOFTWARE ENGINEERING

The software engineering project has been the mainstay of the work on specification within the Programming Research Group. The work dates from 1979-80 when both Jean-Raymond Abrial and Cliff Jones were visiting the group at the invitation of Tony Hoare. In that year the seeds were sown for the work that is reported in this book.

The major part of the work done within the project has involved the application of techniques for mathematical specification to real systems, and a significant part of that work has involved industrial collaboration. The software engineering project spawned the project to study the formalisation of transaction processing reported in part D, and has worked closely with the distributed computing project reported in part C.

The specification of UNIX filing system was the first published paper to use the schema notation as a mechanism for presenting mathematical specifications. It gives a gentle introduction to both the use of the notation and to the UNIX filing system; as such it provides a more tutorial introduction to specification than the papers that follow. The version presented here is slightly changed from that originally published in the March 1984 issue of the IEEE Transactions on Software Engineering.

The early work on specification included a project with STL on a Computer Aided Visitor Information And Control system (CAVIAR). The result of this work was an unpublished specification and an implementation. At the stage the work was done the schema notation had not been developed; the CAVIAR specification has since been reworked using the schema notation and has now been consolidated into the second paper presented in this section. The work makes extensive use of generic specifications to factor out the common components of the subsystems which go together to make up the CAVIAR system.

A collaboration with ICL produced the third paper in this section. It describes an existing ICL product — the ICL Data Dictionary. The paper carefully builds a mathematical model of a data dictionary, which provides the reader with an insight into its logical structure. The precision of mathematics allows one to deduce properties that are not at all made clear in the user manual for the system.

The fourth paper describes a flexitime system, and it provides a good example of the descriptive power of set theory. The specification makes use of a state which is richer than that necessary for an implementation; and this has its rewards in an overall simplification. This specification describes a simplified version of a flexitime system suggested by a contact at GEC.

The fifth paper presents a specification of a simple assembler. It gives a good example of how such specifications should be based on the fundamental properties of the system, rather than on a particular implementation strategy. A first-level design is sketched - mathematically - which turns out to be very like the conventional two-pass-with-symbol-table strategy. And a justification is given that this design satisfies the specification.

Contents

Specification of the UNIX Filing System

Carroll Morgan

Bernard Sufrin

Abstract

A specification of the UNIX filing system is given using a notation based on elementary mathematical set theory. The notation used involves very few special constructs of its own.

The specification is detailed enough to capture the filing system's behaviour at the system call level, yet abstracts from issues of data representation, whether within programs or on the storage medium, and from the description of any algorithms which might be used to implement the system.

The presentation of the specification is in several stages, each new stage building on its predecessors; major concepts are introduced separately so that they may be easily understood. The notation used allows these separate stages to be joined together to give a complete description of each filing system operation — including its error conditions.

1. Introduction

The UNIX [1] operating system is widely known, and its filing system is well understood. Why, then, do we present a formal specification of it here? It is because the idea of formalising the specification of computer-based systems has yet to receive widespread acceptance among computing practitioners, and in our view this is because very few realistic examples have been published. Publishing a *post hoc* specification of aspects of the UNIX filestore offered us the possibility of showing how to use a mathematically based notation to capture important aspects of the behaviour of a system which is clearly not just a toy.

The use of natural language — *without* supporting mathematics — has serious limitations as a vehicle for the description of computer systems. As anyone who has ever used an operating system will confirm, the manuals cannot tell the whole story about the behaviour of a system. Indeed, almost every programmer who starts to use a new operating system sets up a number of *experiments*, by which she attempts to discover how it "really" behaves. It is a commonplace observation that large computer systems, operating systems in particular, accumulate around themselves a body of folklore — necessary knowledge for anybody who wishes to use them effectively — and a number of "gurus" — people who understand the hidden secrets of the system because they have read ... the source code!

In our approach to the description of computer systems we use natural language *together with* the formal language of mathematics. And our particular style is simply a means of presenting the formal part of the description in a way which can be easily manipulated and understood. The formal descriptions themselves are given in elementary mathematical set theory, which is convenient for this purpose because programs are themselves mathematical objects [2,3]. The difference between a mathematical specification and a program is only of degree: they are objects drawn from the same continuum. This uniformity allows, for example, the refinement of formal specifications into programs to be mathematically verified [4].

By using a mixture of natural language and elementary set theory we have enabled ourselves to give a description which is comprehensive enough to describe the essential aspects of the system's behaviour, but is sufficiently abstract that it will not burden the reader with the kind of detail that appears in the source code. In particular, it has allowed us to avoid describing the representation of data on external media and within programs and to refrain from presenting details of the algorithms which are used to implement the filestore operations. Thus the specification here might occur midway along the path from a more abstract but informal specification — a description such as is given in [1] — to a more concrete one — the source code itself [5]. This intermediate level of abstraction is one which conveniently captures the behaviour of the system at the system call level, without being concerned with representational matters.

At each stage of presentation, the static (invariant) properties of the system are characterised by *naming* the observations which can be made of it, attributing a (set theoretical) *type* to each observation, and recording the invariant relationships between these observations as a collection of predicates.

The dynamic behaviour of the system is characterised by giving — for each of the operations under which the system evolves — the names of the observations which can be made *before* the operation, the names of those which can be made *after* the operation, and a collection of predicates which relate these two sets of observations. The operations in question in this case are just the UNIX system calls, and the observations we are interested in may include components of the system state, and the "arguments" and "results" of system calls.

When providing a specification (such as this one) which is a "tutorial" exercise rather than a reference manual, the concepts must be introduced gradually so as not to overwhelm the reader with immediate detail. The specification begins with the definition of a file alone, but ultimately includes channels (file descriptors), file identifiers (i-numbers), and even the abstract format of a directory file. Error conditions are treated last of all, so that they do not complicate the description of what usually happens with the problems of what might happen.

One novel aspect of the specification style is the use of a *homogeneous* framework — *schemas* — to characterise both dynamic and static properties. Schemas supplement the notation of set theory by providing notations for naming and combining groups of observations and predicates, and methods of reasoning about the combinations; this is exactly what is needed to present the specification gradually. Moreover, since the tutorial style of the specification is based on mathematics, it is necessary when providing a reference manual only to collect its definitions into one unit — a summary, in effect — using the laws of combination of schemas.

The value of a specification such as this is that it defines the system in question, so that its properties may be determined by reasoning rather than by performing experiments on the system itself — these could be difficult (if the system is complex) and costly (if it has not yet been built). Since several specifications can be constructed for one system, each may take a point of view, or adopt a level of abstraction, which is appropriate to the questions it is required to answer. And if these specifications are presented within a formal framework, the question of their meaning and consistency is only a mathematical one, and so can be answered by mathematical means rather than by armwaving. But of course the *real* payoff is that when the system is built and in use, all those painful — and perplexing — visits to the guru can be avoided.

2. Scope of the specification

The system described is UNIX Level 6. The operations covered include the system calls

```
read            write           create
seek            open            close
fstat           link            unlink
```

and the commands

```
ls              move.
```

Some of the features not treated are

```
special files
pipes
file access permissions
```

Some of the more practical considerations, such as storage device size, are examined in an appendix. The treatment of errors covers only a few examples, but illustrates the technique which would apply to them all.

3. The specification

3.1 Bytes and files

The ultimate constituent of the filing system is the *byte*; the set of all bytes is called

BYTE

A *file* is a finite *sequence* of bytes of any length[1] (including the null sequence [ ] of length 0).

FILE $\triangleq$ seq BYTE

In general, a sequence of X is a partial function from the natural numbers (N) into X; for any sequence s and natural number n, s(n) is the nth element of s (if defined). Thus for any f of type FILE,

f(1)

is the first byte of the file. The function # gives the length of any sequence; hence #f is the size of the file, and

f(#f)

is its last byte.

3.2 Reading and writing

When a file is read the file itself is not changed; if file' is the file's value after the operation, and file is its value before, then

file' = file

The result of *reading* a file is a sequence data! of bytes

data!: seq BYTE

1: See appendix to this paper, note 1

The value of data! is determined by an offset into the file and a length to be read; both are natural numbers (that is, non-negative integers)

$$\text{offset?, length?: } \mathbb{N}$$

and in fact

$$\text{data!} = 1..\text{length?} \lhd (\text{file}\circ\text{suc}^{\text{offset?}})$$

The function suc^k is the successor function (over the natural numbers) composed with itself k times;

$$\text{suc}^k(n) = n+k$$

and so

$$(\text{file}\circ\text{suc}^{\text{offset?}})(n) =$$

$$\text{file}(\text{suc}^{\text{offset?}}(n)) =$$

$$\text{file}(n+\text{offset?})$$

Therefore

$$(\text{file}\circ\text{suc}^{\text{offset?}})$$

is a formalisation of

"file after the first offset? bytes"

This means that the first byte of the file has offset 0.

The domain restriction operator ($\lhd$) here excludes any element whose index is not in the set 1..length?; data! is therefore

"file, after offset?, for no more than length?"

For example, if

```
file    = [XANFRED]
offset? = 2
length? = 3
```

then

$$suc^{offset?} = suc^2 = suc \circ suc$$

and so

$$
\begin{aligned}
(\text{file} \circ suc^2)\,(n) &= \\
\text{file}(suc(suc(n))) &= \\
\text{file}(n+2)
\end{aligned}
$$

That is,

$$\text{file} \circ suc^{offset?} = [NFRED]$$

and therefore

$$\text{data!} = 1..3 \triangleleft [NFRED] = [NFR]$$

All of these properties may be collected in a *schema* which defines the reading operation

```
┌─────────────────────────────────────────────┐
│  file, file':      FILE                       │
│  offset?, length?: N                          │
│  data!:            seq BYTE                    │
├─────────────────────────────────────────────┤
│  file' = file                                 │
│  data! = 1..length? ◁ (file∘suc^offset?)      │
└─────────────────────────────────────────────┘
```

When a schema is used (as it is here) to characterise an operation, its *signature*

```
file, file':      FILE
offset?, length?: N
data!:            seq BYTE
```

gives names and types to the observations which can be made before and after the operation. The *predicate*

```
file' = file
data! = 1..length? ◁ (file∘suc^offset?)
```

relates these observations to one another.

Naming a schema allows it to be referred to within subsequent definitions; the name is written as part of the enclosing "box":

```
┌─ readFILE ──────────────────────────────────┐
│    file, file':      FILE                    │
│    offset?, length?: N                       │
│    data!:            seq BYTE                 │
│ ─────────────────────────                    │
│    file' = file                              │
│    data! = 1..length? ◁ (file∘suc^offset?)   │
└──────────────────────────────────────────────┘
```

The definition above can be read:

> "The readFILE operation does not change the file. It expects an offset and length as parameters, and returns as its result the data read. The value returned is the longest sequence of bytes, of length not greater than that requested, which begins at the given offset in the file."

To define the writeFILE operation, a similar schema is used; this time, however, the file *is* changed.

The byte ZERO is used in the definition of writeFILE; it is a distinguished element of BYTE (that is, ZERO ∈ BYTE).

Writing with an offset greater than the file length leaves ZERO bytes between the previous end of the file and the newly-written data.

```
┌─── writeFILE ──────────────────────────────────────────────┐
│   file, file':  FILE                                        │
│   offset?:      N                                           │
│   data?:        seq BYTE                                    │
├─────────────────────────────────────────────────────────── │
│   file' = zero offset? ⊕ file ⊕ (data?∘pred^offset?)        │
│                                                             │
│   where zero_k = (λn:N | 1≤n≤k • ZERO)                      │
└─────────────────────────────────────────────────────────────┘
```

$zero_k$ is a sequence of length k containing only ZERO bytes. ⊕ is the function overriding operator: f⊕g behaves like g except where g is undefined, in which case it behaves like f. pred is the predecessor function, defined for all strictly positive integers. Thus the value of any byte in the file

$$\text{zero}_{offset?} \oplus \text{file} \oplus (\text{data?} \circ \text{pred}^{offset?})$$

is determined first by the written data, then by the previous contents of the file, and finally is ZERO otherwise. The length of the new file is

$$\max(\#file, offset? + \#data?)$$

Thus
```
        file    = [XANFRED]
        offset? = 8
        data?   = [NUNIBAD]
```
⟹
```
        file'   = [        ] ⊕ [XANFRED] ⊕ ([NUNIBAD]∘pred^8)
```
⟹
```
        file'   = [XANFRED ] ⊕ ([NUNIBAD]∘pred^8)
```
⟹
```
        file'   = [XANFRED NUNIBAD]
```

(The byte ZERO is here represented by a blank.)

A consequence of this definition is that writeFILE is possible for all values of file, offset?, and data? (subject to any limitation on the maximum size of files in general); formally, this is shown by proving that there is always a value for file', consistent with its type FILE (seq BYTE), such that the predicate

$$\texttt{file}' = \texttt{zero}_{\texttt{offset?}} \oplus \texttt{file} \oplus (\texttt{data?} \circ \texttt{pred}^{\texttt{offset?}})$$

holds.

3.3 File storage

The *file storage* system allows files to be stored and retrieved using *file identifiers*; the set of all file identifiers is called

> FID

The storage system is characterised by a single observation: a partial function[2] from FID to FILE.

```
┌─ SS ─────────────────────────────┐
│   fstore: FID ↦ FILE             │
└──────────────────────────────────┘
```

An empty file may be *created* in the storage system by supplying its identifier as a parameter to an operation which changes an *old* storage system

> SS

into a *new* one which contains the created file

> SS′

SS is textually equivalent to

> fstore: FID ↦ FILE

so SS′ is equivalent to

> fstore′: FID ↦ FILE

2: See appendix to this paper, notes 2,3

Thus, the effect of decorating a schema name is to decorate the names of its observation(s).

The operation which creates an empty file is defined by the schema

```
┌─ createSS ──────────────────────────┐
│  SS                                  │
│  SS'                                 │
│  fid: FID                            │
│ ────────────────────                 │
│                                      │
│  fstore' = fstore ⊕ {fid ↦ []}       │
└──────────────────────────────────────┘
```

The new store fstore' is identical to the old except that fid now refers to the empty file [] — *whether or not it referred to a file previously.* Thus creating an existing file empties it.

We do not write "fid?" because later it will be seen that these file identifiers are in fact not visible to the user. And it must be emphasised that the "?" and "!" convention is entirely syntactic: the presence or absence of these symbols in names has no effect on the meaning of this specification. (In fact, it is only the piping operator >> which is sensitive to ? and ! — and this specification does not use >>.) Even the "dashed" and "undashed" convention is almost always just an aid to the reader, helping him to remember which names refer to observations "before", and which to "after".

Destroying a file is defined

```
┌─ destroySS ─────────────────────────┐
│  SS                                  │
│  SS'                                 │
│  fid: FID                            │
│ ────────────────────                 │
│                                      │
│  fid ∈ dom fstore                    │
│  fstore' = {fid} ◁ fstore            │
└──────────────────────────────────────┘
```

Naturally, a file must exist (∈ dom fstore) to be destroyed. The new fstore' is identical to the old except that there is no file referred to by fid:

```
fid ∉ dom fstore'
```

3.4 Reading and writing stored files — framing

Reading a *stored* file is defined by the schema

```
┌─────────────────────────────────────────────────┐
│  SS                                             │
│  SS'                                            │
│  fid:               FID                         │
│  offset?, length?: ℕ                            │
│  data!:             seq BYTE                     │
│                                                 │
│  file, file':       FILE                        │
│ ────────────────────────────────               │
│  file    = fstore (fid)                         │
│                                                 │
│  data!   = 1..length? ◁ (file∘suc^{offset?})    │
│  file'   = file                                 │
│                                                 │
│  fstore' = fstore ⊕ {fid ↦ file'}               │
└─────────────────────────────────────────────────┘
```

The file read is that referred to by `fid`, the data output is from `offset?` for `length?` (as before), and the file is not changed.

This long-winded definition of reading a stored file shows that it is in fact a combination of the definitions given above for

   reading a file (`readFILE`) and

   the storage system (`SS`)

This kind of combination is called *framing*, because it involves specifying

   which file is read or written, and

   that the *other* files are unaffected

That is, a frame is supplied within which the operation occurs. The following schema states this framing combination generally

```
┌─ φSS ─────────────────────────────────────┐
│  SS                                        │
│  SS′                                       │
│  file, file′: FILE                         │
│  fid:          FID                         │
│ ──────────────────────────────────────    │
│  file   = fstore (fid)                     │
│  fstore′ = fstore ⊕ {fid ↦ file′}          │
└────────────────────────────────────────────┘
```

fid denotes the file affected in fstore — namely (file, file′) — and no other file is changed. φ is conventionally used as the first letter of framing schemas (φ for *frame*).

Although the definition given above of reading a stored file could have stated explicitly that the filestore is not changed — "fstore′ = fstore" — this is really a *consequence* of the fact that the file itself is not changed. And the framing schema φSS makes it much easier to write such definitions generally — for example, the operation above could be defined as follows:

```
┌─ readSS ──────┐
│  φSS          │
│  readFILE     │
└───────────────┘
```

The signatures and predicates of the two schemas are combined separately and then joined to form the new schema. Where the two schemas *share* a named observation in their signatures, it appears only once in the new schema. Thus, although file and file′ occur in both readFILE and φSS, they appear only once in readSS.

Writing a stored file is defined similarly

```
┌─ writeSS ───────┐
│  φSS            │
│  writeFILE      │
└─────────────────┘
```

Its definition may be expanded:

```
┌─────────────────────────────────────────────────────────────┐
│  SS                                                          │
│  SS'                                                         │
│  fid:     FID                                                │
│  offset?: N                                                  │
│  data?:   seq BYTE                                           │
│                                                             │
│  file, file': FILE                                          │
├─────────────────────────────────────────────────────────────│
│  file = fstore fid                                          │
│                                                             │
│  file' = zero_{offset?} ⊕ file ⊕ (data?∘pred^{offset?})     │
│                                                             │
│  fstore' = fstore ⊕ {fid ↦ file'}                          │
│                                                             │
│  where zero_k = (λn:N | 1≤n≤k • ZERO)                       │
└─────────────────────────────────────────────────────────────┘
```

As in readSS, file and file' appear only once in this combination.

3.5 Hiding and simplification

In the schema readSS the observations file and file' are entirely determined in value by the other observations of the schema. Unless it is necessary to observe the *whole file* involved in a read or write operation, these observations have become inessential to the specification. Observations such as these are called *auxiliary*.

Hiding auxiliary observations can allow simplification of the schema in which they occur. Components are hidden by removing them from the signature of the schema and by existentially quantifying them in the predicate part. readSS, with file and file' hidden, is written

$$readSS\backslash (file,\ file')$$

and is in full

```
┌────────────────────────────────────────────┐
│  SS                                         │
│  SS'                                        │
│  fid:              FID                       │
│  offset?, length?: N                         │
│  data!:            seq BYTE                   │
├────────────────────────────────────────────│
│  (∃file,file': FILE •                        │
│                                              │
│    file    = fstore fid                      │
│                                              │
│    data!   = 1..length? ◁ (file∘suc^offset?) │
│    file'   = file                            │
│                                              │
│    fstore' = fstore ⊕ {fid ↦ file'})         │
└────────────────────────────────────────────┘
```

This schema can be simplified using basic predicate calculus:

```
┌────────────────────────────────────────────┐
│  SS                                         │
│  SS'                                        │
│  fid:              FID                       │
│  offset?, length?: N                         │
│  data!:            seq BYTE                   │
├────────────────────────────────────────────│
│  fstore' = fstore                            │
│  data!   = 1..length? ◁ ((fstore fid)∘suc^offset?) │
└────────────────────────────────────────────┘
```

Writing may be treated similarly.

3.6 Sequential access to files

The read and write operations described so far support random access; in order to allow easy sequential use of these operations, a *channel* is defined which remembers the current position in the file.

```
┌─── CHAN ──────────┐
│  fid:  FID        │
│  posn: N          │
│                   │
└───────────────────┘
```

A channel has a file identifier f id — which may refer to a file in f store — and a position posn within the file. As usual, operations involving the channel take the form of a predicate relating the observations of

CHAN

to those of

CHAN'

They have the additional property that the f id of a channel is never changed. The schema ΔCHAN expresses the general properties of any operation on a channel (Δ for *change*)

```
┌─── ΔCHAN ──────────┐
│  CHAN              │
│  CHAN'             │
├───────────────     │
│  fid' = fid        │
└────────────────────┘
```

Sequential reading and writing using channels is easily characterised by combining the previous definitions

```
┌─── readCHAN ──────────┐
│  readSS               │
│  ΔCHAN                │
├─────────────          │
│  offset? = posn       │
│  posn'   = posn + #data! │
└───────────────────────┘
```

```
┌── writeCHAN ──────────────┐
│ writeSS
│ ΔCHAN
├───────────────────────────
│ offset? = posn
│ posn'    = posn + #data?
└────────────────────────────┘
```

In addition, there is an operation seekCHAN which changes only the position[3]

```
┌── seekCHAN ──────────┐
│ SS
│ SS'
│ ΔCHAN
│ newposn?: N
├──────────────────────
│ fstore' = fstore
│ posn'    = newposn?
└───────────────────────┘
```

The new position is not constrained to be within the file[4].

3.7 Channel system

A *channel storage* system may be defined which is analogous to the file storage system; it allows channels to be stored and retrieved using channel identifiers[5] CID

```
┌── CS ──────────────────┐
│ cstore: CID ↦ CHAN
└────────────────────────┘
```

3: See appendix to this paper, note 4
4: See appendix to this paper, note 5
5: A channel identifier is a "file descriptor"

Operations on the channel system have the general form

```
┌─── ΔCS ───┐
│  CS        │
│  CS'       │
└───────────┘
```

These operations are defined below.

```
┌─── openCS ────────────────────────────────────┐
│  ΔCS                                            │
│  CHAN                                           │
│  cid': CID                                      │
│ ──────────────────                              │
│                                                 │
│  cid'    ∉ dom cstore                           │
│  posn = 0                                       │
│  cstore' = cstore ⊕ {cid' ↦ CHAN}               │
└─────────────────────────────────────────────────┘
```

openCS creates a new channel and returns a new identifier which refers to it; the new channel's position is 0.

```
┌─── closeCS ──────────────────┐
│  ΔCS                          │
│  cid: CID                     │
│ ──────────────                │
│                               │
│  cid    ∈ dom cstore          │
│  cstore' = {cid} ◁ cstore    │
└───────────────────────────────┘
```

closeCS removes a channel from the channel system.

3.8 The access system

The storage and channel systems together form the *access* system

```
___ AS _____
  SS
  CS
 _____
  ran(fid∘cstore) ⊆ dom fstore
_____
```

The *function* fid is the projection function of type CHAN ⇸ FID — it is an abbreviation for (λCHAN•fid). That is, fid(c) is the fid observation of channel c.

The predicate in the above schema requires that every channel must refer to an existing file. This property is an *invariant* of the access system and is preserved by all operations on it. The schema ΔAS automatically includes the invariant of both the initial (AS) and final (AS′) state.

```
___ ΔAS ___
  AS
  AS′
_____
```

Reading, writing, and seeking in the access subsystem are defined with the assistance of a framing schema

```
___ φAS _____
  ΔAS
  ΔCHAN
  cid: CID
 _____
  CHAN    = cstore cid
  cstore′ = cstore ⊕ {cid ↦ CHAN′}
_____
```

CHAN in the predicate part is the channel with components fid and posn as they appear in ΔCHAN; CHAN′ is similar.

Reading, writing, and seeking in the access system are now defined by combination of previous definitions and the framing schema φAS; as usual, some auxiliary variables will be hidden.

The operator ∧ when applied to two schemas is shorthand for writing the two together; that is,

φAS ∧ readCHAN

is just

```
┌─────────────────────
│   φAS
│   readCHAN
└─────────────────────
```

The definitions are

$$readAS \triangleq (\phi AS \wedge readCHAN) \setminus (offset?, fid', posn', file')$$
$$writeAS \triangleq (\phi AS \wedge writeCHAN) \setminus (offset?, fid', posn')$$
$$seekAS \triangleq (\phi AS \wedge seekCHAN) \setminus (fid, fid', posn, posn')$$

which when expanded and simplified give

```
┌─ readAS ─────────────────────────────────────────────
│  ΔAS
│  cid:      CID
│  length?:  N
│  data!:    seq BYTE
│
│  CHAN
│  file: FILE
├──────────────────────
│  cid   ∈ dom cstore
│  CHAN  = cstore cid
│  file  = fstore fid
│
│  fstore' = fstore
│  (∃ CHAN'• posn'  = posn + #data!
│            cid'    = cid
│            cstore' = cstore ⊕ {cid ↦ CHAN'})
│
│  data'    = 1..length ◁ (file∘suc^{posn})
└──────────────────────
```

and

```
┌─ writeAS ────────────────────────────────────────────┐
│ ΔAS                                                    │
│ cid:  CID                                              │
│ data: seq BYTE                                         │
│                                                        │
│ fid:  FID                                              │
│ posn: N                                                │
│ file: FILE                                             │
├────────────────────                                    │
│ cid ∈ dom cstore                                       │
│ CHAN = cstore cid                                      │
│ file = fstore fid                                      │
│                                                        │
│ file'    = zero_posn ⊕ file ⊕ (data∘pred^posn)        │
│                                                        │
│ fstore' = fstore ⊕ {fid ↦ file'}                      │
│ (∃ CHAN'• posn'   = posn + #data!                     │
│           cid'    = cid                                │
│           cstore' = cstore ⊕ {cid ↦ CHAN'})           │
│                                                        │
│ where zero _k = (λn:N | 1⩽n⩽k • ZERO)                 │
└────────────────────────────────────────────────────────┘
```

and

```
┌─ seekAS ─────────────────────────────────────────────┐
│ ΔAS                                                    │
│ cid:     CID                                           │
│ newposn?: N                                            │
├────────────────────────                                │
│ cid ∈ dom cstore                                       │
│                                                        │
│ fstore' = fstore                                       │
│ (∃ CHAN'• posn'   = newposn?                           │
│           cid'    = cid                                │
│           cstore' = cstore ⊕ {cid ↦ CHAN'})           │
└────────────────────────────────────────────────────────┘
```

In addition to the three operations above, the fstat operation, which returns the size of the file accessed with a given CID, can be defined by

```
┌─ fstat ─────────────────────────────────────┐
│ ΔAS                                          │
│ cid:   CID                                   │
│ size!: N                                     │
├──────────────────────                        │
│ cid ∈ dom cstore                             │
│                                              │
│ fstore′ = fstore                             │
│ cstore′ = cstore                             │
│                                              │
│ size! = #(fstore∘fid∘cstore(cid))            │
└─────────────────────────────────────────────┘
```

3.9 A file naming system

The naming system associates file names NAME with file identifiers FID; these file names will normally be chosen by the users of the file system

```
┌─ NS ────────────────────────────┐
│ nstore: NAME ↦ FID               │
└─────────────────────────────────┘
```

To create an association in the naming system, a name and fid are supplied; the new association *overrides any existing association for that name*

```
┌─ createNS ─────────────────────────┐
│ ΔNS                                 │
│ name?: NAME                         │
│ fid:   FID                          │
├────────────────────                 │
│ nstore′ = nstore ⊕ {name? ↦ fid}    │
└────────────────────────────────────┘
```

Given a name, its fid may be discovered

```
┌──── lookupNS ──────────────┐
│ ΔNS                        │
│ name?: NAME                │
│ fid':   FID                │
│ ──────────────             │
│ name? ∈ dom nstore         │
│ fid'  = nstore name        │
│                            │
│ nstore' = nstore           │
└────────────────────────────┘
```

Finally, given a name?, any association it has may be destroyed (this is the *unlink* operation)

```
┌──── destroyNS ─────────────┐
│ ΔNS                        │
│ name?: NAME                │
│ ──────────────             │
│ name?    ∈ dom nstore      │
│ nstore' = {name?} ⩤ nstore │
└────────────────────────────┘
```

3.10 Pathnames and directories

By further revealing file names to be sequences of *syllables*

$$\text{NAME} \triangleq \text{seq SYL}$$

it is possible to provide more structure in the name space as a whole (the name space is dom nstore). The naming system is augmented by a set of *directory* names dnames

```
┌──── NS ────────────────────┐
│ NS                         │
│ dnames: ℙ NAME             │
│ ──────────────             │
│ front⦅dnames ∪ dom nstore⦆ ⊆ dnames │
└────────────────────────────┘
```

ℙ is the *powerset* constructor. The fat brackets ⦅⦆ denote application of the function (front in this case) to a *set* of arguments to yield a *set* of results. That is,

$$\text{front}(\![S]\!) = \{s:S \cdot \text{front}(s)\}$$

NS within its own definition is textually equivalent to its *previous* value; the redefinition above is strictly an extension.

front of a sequence is obtained by removing its last element; only the empty sequence ("root") has no front. The predicate states that the front of every (file or directory) name must itself be a directory name (that is, every file or directory — except root — must appear in some directory). For example, if dom nstore included

```
/Carroll/Unix/paper
/dev/sanders
/Bernard/IEEE/Unixpaper
/Bernard/Mumble
```

(where syllables are preceded by /) then dnames would necessarily include

```
/
/Carroll
/dev
/Bernard
/Carroll/Unix
/Bernard/IEEE
```

Given a directory name dir?, the operation lsNS reveals its "contents".

```
┌─ lsNS ──────────────────────────────────────────────────┐
│  ΔNS                                                      │
│  dir?:        NAME                                        │
│  contents!:  ℙ SYL                                        │
│  ──────────────────────────                               │
│                                                           │
│  dir? ∈ dnames                                            │
│                                                           │
│  contents! = last(\![{n: dom nstore | front n = dir?}]\!)  │
│                                                           │
│  nstore' = nstore                                         │
└───────────────────────────────────────────────────────────┘
```

last of a sequence is its final element.

3.11 Directories are files

An additional constraint on the Unix system is that directories are in fact stored as files; they can be read (but not written) by users. That is

> dnames ⊆ dom nstore

and the content of each directory file is determined by the system in accordance with the requirement that

> nstore =
>
> (λn:NAME • (dirformat∘fstore∘nstore(front n))(last n))
> ∪ {[] ↦ RootFid}

dirformat is a function which maps a FILE to the directory structure it represents

> dirformat: FILE ↠ (SYL ↠ FID)

The mathematical definition of dirformat *would be* the definition of the format of a directory file — but such a definition need not be given here. RootFid is the FID of the root directory []. The constraint above may be paraphrased as follows:

> "The association of names and file identifiers (nstore) is found by taking for any name (λn:NAME...) all of its syllables except the last (front n); finding the file identifier so referred to (nstore...); finding the contents of that file (fstore...); interpreting those contents as a directory (dirformat...); and finally using the last syllable of the original name (last n) to obtain a file identifier from that directory — unless the original name is empty, in which case its file identifier is RootFid".

3.12 The complete filing system

The complete filing system is described by combining the descriptions of the three separate systems above: the storage systems SS, the channel system CS, and the name system NS.

```
┌─ FS ──────────────────────────────────────────┐
│  SS                                            │
│  CS                                            │
│  NS                                            │
│                                                │
│  usedfids: P FID                               │
├────────────────────────┐                       │
│  usedfids = ran nstore ∪ ran (fid∘cstore)      │
│                                                │
│  usedfids ⊆ dom fstore                         │
└────────────────────────────────────────────────┘
```

The auxiliary observation usedfids is introduced; it is the set of file identifiers in use at any time, either in the channel store or the name store. The predicate states that all file identifiers in use must refer to an existing file in the file store; members of (dom fstore - usedfids) are the fids of files which may be destroyed (since they are not referred to).

The filing system operations can be specified by combining the definitions of their effects on each separate subsystem. The create operation, for example, makes an empty file in the storage system, a new channel referring to it in the channel system, and associates a name with it in the naming system

```
┌─ create ──────────────────────────────────────┐
│  createSS                                      │
│  createCS                                      │
│  createNS                                      │
├────────────────────────┐                       │
│  name? ∈ dom nstore  ⟹  fid = nstore name?     │
│  name? ∉ dom nstore  ⟹  fid ∉ usedfids         │
└────────────────────────────────────────────────┘
```

If an *existing* name is created, the file it refers to is emptied — that is, it is simply replaced with an empty file, and its previous contents are lost. If the name does not exist in the naming system, a new fid is chosen which is not currently in use.

The channel identifier of a channel referring to the new (or newly truncated) file is returned (cid' is a observation of createCS).

open returns the channel identifier of an existing file.

```
┌──── open ──────┐
│ ≡SS
│ openCS
│ lookupNS
│ ────────────────
│ fid = fid'
└────────────────┘
```

The fid' returned by lookupNS is equal to the fid supplied to openCS (and both fid' and fid are good candidates for hiding). The schema ≡SS expresses the observation that the storage system is unaffected; its definition is

```
┌──── ≡SS ────────┐
│ SS
│ SS'
│ ─────────────────
│ fstore' = fstore
└─────────────────┘
```

≡CS and ≡NS are defined similarly.

close removes the association between a channel name and the channel it refers to

```
┌──── close ─────┐
│ ≡SS
│ closeCS
│ ≡NS
└────────────────┘
```

unlink removes a name from the naming system, but it does *not* destroy the associated file.

```
┌──── unlink ─────┐
│ ≡SS
│ ≡CS
│ destroyNS
└─────────────────┘
```

Destroy removes a file from the filing system.

```
┌─── destroy ────┐
│  destroySS     │
│  ≡CS           │
│  ≡NS           │
└────────────────┘
```

But can a file be destroyed while it's in use? The FS′ invariant requires that

$$usedfids' \subseteq dom\ fstore' \qquad (1)$$

and from ≡CS and ≡NS it follows that

$$usedfids = usedfids' \qquad (2)$$

and so, from (1) and (2),

$$usedfids \subseteq dom\ fstore' \qquad (3)$$

But

$$destroySS \Rightarrow fid \notin dom\ fstore' \qquad (4)$$

and (3) and (4) give

$$destroySS \Rightarrow fid \notin usedfids \qquad (5)$$

That is, a file cannot be destroyed while it is in use.

3.13 Honesty of definitions

The constraint on the destroy operation

$$fid \notin usedfids$$

is not immediately obvious from its definition above. Because the constraint is implicit, the above definition could be said to be dishonest.

An honest definition is one for which the conditions of applicability are explicit. In general, a schema which describes an operation can be expanded to have the form

```
┌─── operation ────────────────────────┐
│  STATE                                 │
│  STATE'                                │
│  IN?                                   │
│  OUT!                                  │
├────────────────────────┘              │
│                                        │
│    inv    (STATE)                      │
│    pre    (STATE, IN?)                 │
│                                        │
│    trans (STATE, IN?, OUT!, STATE')    │
│                                        │
│    post  (STATE', OUT!)                │
│    inv    (STATE')                     │
└────────────────────────────────────────┘
```

where P(S) denotes a predicate in which the observations of S may occur free.

STATE, STATE', IN?, and OUT! are schemas with no predicates — they are just signatures.

inv is the state invariant, pre and post are the pre- and post-conditions respectively, and trans is the predicate expressing the relationship between the initial state, inputs, outputs, and final state. The conjunction of the five predicates forms the definition of the operation, but the definition is said to be *honest* only if

$$\text{inv} \wedge \text{pre} \Rightarrow (\exists \text{OUT!}; \text{STATE}' \bullet \text{trans} \wedge \text{post} \wedge \text{inv})$$

If the invariant holds, and the input satisfies its precondition, then the operation should have at least one defined result. Thus, in an honest definition, applicability can be determined by considering the precondition alone (if all operations preserve the invariant). This is an honest definition of destroy

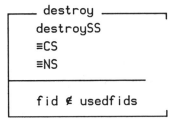

It is, however, *mathematically* equivalent to its original definition above.

For any schema describing an operation, a suitably honest precondition can be discovered by hiding the OUT! and STATE′ observations, and simplifying the resulting predicate.

3.14 Observation renaming and schema composition

It may be necessary at times to rename the observations of a schema to avoid name clashes with other schemas. Writing

$$\text{schema}[\text{name2}/\text{name1}]$$

denotes the result of systematically substituting name2 for name1 throughout schema (with suitable renaming of bound variables if necessary). For example,

createNS[newname?/name?] ≜

```
┌─────────────────────────────────────────┐
│  ΔNS                                      │
│  newname?: NAME                           │
│  fid:       FID                           │
├─────────────────────────────────────────┘
│  nstore′ = nstore ⊕ {newname? ↦ fid}     │
└─────────────────────────────────────────┘
```

and

lookupNS[oldname?/name?] ≜

```
┌─────────────────────────────────────────┐
│  ΔNS                                      │
│  oldname?: NAME                           │
│  fid′:      FID                           │
├─────────────────────────────────────────┘
│  oldname? ∈ dom nstore                    │
│  fid′     = nstore oldname?               │
│  nstore′  = nstore                        │
└─────────────────────────────────────────┘
```

The *composition* of two schemas, written

```
schema1 ; schema2
```

is intended to capture the effect of "schema1 then schema2". It is formed by

1. Determining all of the dashed observations of schema1 which correspond with undashed observations of schema2 (name' corresponds with name).

2. Renaming each corresponding pair to a single new name

$$\text{schema1}\,[\text{name}^+/\text{name}'\,]$$

$$\text{schema2}\,[\text{name}^+/\text{name}\;\,]$$

3. Combining the schemas, and hiding the new observations

```
schema1 ; schema2 ≙
```

$$(\quad \text{schema1}\,[\text{name}^+/\text{name}''\,]$$
$$\wedge\;\text{schema2}\,[\text{name}^+/\text{name}\;\;]\;)\;\backslash\;(\text{name}^+)$$

This operation allows schemas to be combined in a way suggestive of forward functional composition: the final state of schema1 becomes the initial state of schema2. For example,

```
linkNS ≙ lookupNS[oldname?/name?] ;
          createNS[newname?/name?]
```

gives in full

```
┌─ linkNS ──────────────────────────────────────────────────┐
│  ΔNS                                                        │
│  oldname?, newname?: NAME                                   │
│ ──────────────────────────────────────────                 │
│  oldname ∈ dom nstore                                       │
│  nstore' = nstore ⊕ {newname? ↦ (nstore oldname?)}          │
└────────────────────────────────────────────────────────────┘
```

The hidden observations are nstore and fid. linkNS makes the filename newname refer to the same file as does oldname.

A similar construction defines moveNS

$$\text{moveNS} \triangleq \text{linkNS}; \text{destroyNS}[\text{oldname?/name?}]$$

That is,

```
┌─ moveNS ──────────────────────────────────────────────────┐
│  ΔNS                                                        │
│  oldname?, newname?: NAME                                   │
│ ──────────────────────────────────────────                 │
│  oldname? ∈ dom nstore                                      │
│                                                             │
│  nstore' =  {oldname?} ◁ (nstore ⊕                          │
│                     {newname? ↦ (nstore oldname?)})         │
└────────────────────────────────────────────────────────────┘
```

moveNS renames a file from oldname? to newname?.

It is important that the two occurrences of oldname? — in linkNS and destroyNS[oldname?/name?] — are merged, and so only one file is referred to. However, oldname? appears only once in the signature of moveNS.

Combining the definitions of linkNS and moveNs above, with ≡SS and ≡CS, gives their definitions in the complete file system FS

$$\text{link} \triangleq \text{≡SS} \wedge \text{≡CS} \wedge \text{linkNS}$$

$$\text{move} \triangleq \text{≡SS} \wedge \text{≡CS} \wedge \text{moveNS}$$

3.15 Definition of error conditions

The definitions given so far describe only *successful* operations. For example, the schema

```
┌─── lookupNS ──────────────────────────────┐
│ ≡NS                                        
│ name?: NAME
│ fid' : FID
│ ───────────────────────────────
│ name? ∈ dom nstore
│ fid'  = nstore name
└──────────────────────────────────────┘
```

gives no indication of the result of looking up a name which is *not* in the name store. In fact, the definition explicitly states that the name must be there

name? ∈ dom nstore

It is to that extent unrealistic.

To describe unsuccessful as well as successful operations, a schema is introduced below which includes an *error report* observation

```
┌─── ΔFS ─────────────────────────────────┐
│ FS
│ FS'
│ report!: REPORT
│ ───────────────────────────────
│ report! ≠ Ok ⟹ (FS' = FS)
└──────────────────────────────────────┘
```

The predicate states that in the event of an unsuccessful report (report! ≠ Ok) the system's state is unaltered (FS' = FS).

Successful operations are described by the schema below

```
┌─── success ──────────────┐
│ ΔFS                      │
│                          │
├──────────────────────    │
│                          │
│ report! = Ok             │
└──────────────────────────┘
```

The following schemas define typical failures

```
┌─── Cid! ─────────────────┐
│ ΔFS                      │
│ cid: CID                 │
├──────────────────────    │
│                          │
│ cid      ∉ dom cstore    │
│ report! = NoSuchCid      │
└──────────────────────────┘
```

Cid! describes an attempt to use a non-existent channel identifier. Two other common errors are

```
┌─── Name! ─────────────────┐
│ ΔFS                       │
│ name?: NAME               │
├──────────────────────     │
│                           │
│ name?    ∉ dom nstore     │
│ report! = NoSuchName      │
└───────────────────────────┘
```

```
┌─── Chan! ─────────────────┐
│ ΔFS                       │
│                           │
├──────────────────────     │
│                           │
│ dom cstore = CID          │
│ report!    = NoFreeCids   │
└───────────────────────────┘
```

Name! describes an attempt to use a non-existent file name; Chan! describes an unsuccessful attempt to obtain a new channel identifier[6].

6: See appendix to this paper, note 6

These error descriptions should be associated with the operations which can give rise to them; this is accomplished by schema *disjunction*:

schema1 ∨ schema2

This is the schema formed by merging the two schemas' signatures (as for conjunction ∧) and forming the disjunction of their predicate parts (where, in contrast, ∧ forms their conjunction).

Thus the schemas read and open, for example, can be redefined (in terms of their previous definitions)

$$read \; \hat{=} \; (read \wedge success) \vee Cid!$$

$$open \; \hat{=} \; (open \wedge success) \vee Name!$$
$$\vee \; Chan!$$

The other operations may be similarly treated once their error conditions have been defined.

The two schemas below are the expansions of read and open

```
┌─ read ────────────────────────────────────────────────────┐
│  FS                                                        │
│  FS'                                                       │
│  cid:       CID                                            │
│  length?:   ℕ                                              │
│  data!:     seq BYTE                                       │
│  report!:   REPORT                                         │
│                                                            │
│  CHAN                                                      │
│  file: FILE                                                │
├────────────────────────────────                           │
│                                                            │
│  (report! = Ok ∧                                           │
│                                                            │
│      cid  ∈ dom cstore                                     │
│      CHAN = cstore cid                                     │
│      file = fstore fid                                     │
│                                                            │
│      fstore' = fstore                                      │
│      (∃ CHAN'• posn'   = posn + #data!                     │
│              cid'    = cid                                 │
│              cstore' = cstore ⊕ {cid ↦ CHAN'})            │
│      nstore' = nstore                                      │
│                                                            │
│      data! = 1..length? ◁ (file∘suc$^{posn}$))            │
│                                                            │
│                                                            │
│  ∨ (report! = NoSuchCid ∧                                  │
│                                                            │
│      cid ∉ dom cstore                                      │
│      FS' = FS)                                             │
│                                                            │
└────────────────────────────────────────────────────────────┘
```

```
┌─ open ──────────────────────────────────────────────┐
│  FS                                                   │
│  FS′                                                  │
│  name?:   NAME                                        │
│  cid′:    CID                                         │
│  report!: REPORT                                      │
│                                                       │
│  fid, fid′: FID                                       │
├───────────────────────────────────────────────────── │
│  (report! = Ok ∧                                      │
│                                                       │
│      name ∈ dom nstore                                │
│      fid = fid′ = nstore name                         │
│                                                       │
│      fstore′ = fstore                                 │
│      (∃ CHAN′• posn′   = 0                            │
│                 cid′    = cid                          │
│                 cstore′ = cstore ⊕ {cid′ ↦ CHAN′})    │
│      nstore′ = nstore                                 │
│      cid′ ∉ dom cstore)                               │
│                                                       │
│                                                       │
│  ∨ (report! = NoSuchName ∧                            │
│                                                       │
│      name ∉ dom nstore                                │
│      FS′ = FS)                                        │
│                                                       │
│                                                       │
│  ∨ (report! = NoFreeCids ∧                            │
│                                                       │
│      dom cstore = CID                                 │
│      FS′ = FS)                                        │
└───────────────────────────────────────────────────── ┘
```

4. Summary

The schema approach to the incremental presentation of large system specifications has been illustrated by using it to describe the UNIX filestore. This technique has been used elsewhere to present, and reason about, specifications of other large-scale systems [6, 7, 8, 9]. It has also proved useful in presenting the behaviour of systems from a *variety* of points of view, drawing these together by showing how they are related from an "Olympian" point of view.

However, because of the generality of the underlying theory (set theory), and in particular because of the unrestricted nature of the predicates which can be written to characterise operations, there is no a *priori* guarantee that a system specified in this style is implementable, nor is there any "automatic" way of checking even its internal consistency. The best that can be done is to demonstrate a constructive model at a suitably high level of abstraction. Fortunately, the provision of such a model is usually the first step to be taken in the development of an implementation.

This specification technique is not yet a *development method*; it is simply a step on the way to one. In particular, the usual criteria for deciding on correctness of representations and of algorithms have yet to be adapted to this style of presentation.

Once suitable mathematical types have been discovered for the *observations* to be made of a system (i.e., once suitable mathematical theories have been found and decided upon), the *narrative* part of the top-level views of a system is relatively easy to formulate.

Appendix — Differences from UNIX

1. File size

There is an upper bound on the size of files; if a file could contain no more than FileSizeLimit bytes, then FILE would be defined

```
┌─ FILE ──────────────────┐
│  f: seq BYTE            │
│ ────────────────────── │
│  #f ⩽ FileSizeLimit     │
└─────────────────────────┘
```

2. Directory size

There is an upper bound on the number of files in the storage system (that is, the number of "inodes" is limited).

```
┌─ SS ──────────────────────────────────────────┐
│   fstore: FID ↠ FILE                           │
│   ─────────────────                            │
│                                                │
│   #fstore ⩽ FileNumberLimit                    │
│                                                │
└────────────────────────────────────────────────┘
```

3. Storage medium capacity

The storage medium used to implement the filing system has finite capacity.

```
┌─ SS ──────────────────────────────────────────┐
│   fstore: FID ↠ FILE                           │
│   ─────────────────                            │
│                                                │
│   #fstore ⩽ FileNumberLimit                    │
│                                                │
│                                                │
│   DeviceCapacity ⩾ Σ minbytes∘fstore (fid)     │
│                      fid ∈                      │
│                    dom fstore                   │
│                                                │
└────────────────────────────────────────────────┘
```

$minbytes$ is some function $FILE \rightarrow N$ which maps a file into the minimum number of bytes required to represent it in the storage system.

Because in the storage system it's possible to represent a file in more than one way (small, large, huge — also, totally zero blocks may or may not be allocated), all that can be said about the system's capacity is that it must be at least as large as the minimum required to represent the files within it. Similarly, all that can be said of the device-full condition is that it *cannot* occur while the capacity is sufficient for the *maximum* required; that is,

$$\sum_{\substack{fid \in \\ dom\ \underline{fstore}}} maxbytes \circ \underline{fstore}\ (fid) > DeviceCapacity$$

is a *necessary* condition for a device full error (where <u>fstore</u> is the storage system which would have resulted from the attempted operation).

4. Seek

seek as defined in UNIX has several options, which automatically calculate the desired new offset depending, for example, on the file's current length. These may be described separately

```
┌── seekoffset ──────────────────────────────┐
│ SS                                          
│ CHAN                                        
│ n?, p?: N                                   
│                                             
│ offset?,                                    
│ size:   N                                   
├─────────────────────────────────           
│ size = #(fstore fid)                        
│                                             
│ p?=0 ⟹ offset? = n?                        
│ p?=1 ⟹ offset? = posn + n?                 
│ p?=2 ⟹ offset? = size + n?                 
│ p?=3 ⟹ offset? = 512  * n?                 
│ p?=4 ⟹ offset? = posn + 512*n?             
│ p?=5 ⟹ offset? = size + 512*n?             
└─────────────────────────────────────────────┘
```

offset? and size are now auxiliary components.

The above schema could be combined with the schema for seek to give the full definition of the seek system call.

5. Representation of numbers

The new position of the file is in fact limited by the ability of the computer to represent numbers.

In this and other cases this limitation could be expressed, for example, as

$$24bit ≙ 0..2^{24}-1$$

Such sets would then be used, where appropriate, instead of N:

```
        CHAN
      fid:   FID
      posn: 24bit
```

6. Limited number of channels

This is "out of file descriptors"; in UNIX, however, this error occurs on a per-user basis.

References

[1]   D. M. Ritchie and K. Thompson, "The UNIX Time-Sharing System," *Comm. ACM, Vol. 17, No. 7 (July 1974).*

[2]   J.-R. Abrial, "Formal Programming," *Private manuscript, Paris, 1982.*

[3]   C. A. R. Hoare, "Specifications, Programs and Implementations," *Technical Monograph PRG-29, Oxford University Programming Research Group, 1982.*

[4]   C. B. Jones, *Software Development: A Rigorous Approach.* Prentice-Hall International 1980.

[5]   J. Lions, "UNIX Operating System Source Code Level 6," *University of N.S.W., 1977.*

[6]   C. C. Morgan, "Specification of the Cambridge Model Distributed System Name Service," *Distributed Computing Working Paper, Oxford University Programming Research Group, 1982.*

[7]   C. C. Morgan, "Mailbox Communication in Pascal-M," *Distributed Computing Working Paper, Oxford University Programming Research Group, 1982.*

[8]   B. Sufrin, "Formal Specification of an Electronic Mail System," *Software Engineering Working Paper, Oxford University Programming Research Group, 1983.*

[9]   B. Sufrin, "Formal Specification of a Display-Oriented Text Editor," *Science of Computer Programming, Vol. 1, May 1982.*

Acknowledgement

The use of set theory to specify the behaviour of computer systems was first explained to us by Jean-Raymond Abrial. This specification has been developed from the original attempt by Richard Miller. We have benefited from collaboration with many of our colleagues, especially Ib Sørensen, Steve Schumann, Tony Hoare, Ian Hayes, Roger Gimson, and Tim Clement. The continuing financial support of the UK Science and Engineering Research Council is gratefully appreciated.

Index of schemas and components

Following is an index of schema and component names. The first column gives the name of the schema or component; the second column, when present, gives the schema within which the name occurs; and the third column gives the page number of the occurrence.

NAME	WITHIN	PAGE
====	======	====
≡CS	destroy	118
	unlink	117
≡NS	close	117
	destroy	118
≡SS	...	117
	close	117
	open	117
	unlink	117
ΔAS	...	109
	φAS	109
	fstat	112
	readAS	110
	seekAS	111
	writeAS	111
ΔCHAN	...	106
	φAS	109
	readCHAN	106
	seekCHAN	107
	writeCHAN	107
ΔCS	...	108
	closeCS	108
	openCS	108
ΔFS	...	123
	Chan!	124
	Cid!	124
	Name!	124

NAME	WITHIN	PAGE
====	======	====
ΔNS	createNS	112
	destroyNS	113
	linkNS	122
	lookupNS	113
	moveNS	122
	NS	114
φAS	...	109
φSS	...	103
	readSS	103
	writeSS	103
AS	...	109
	ΔAS	109
AS'	ΔAS	109
BYTE	...	95
CHAN	...	106, 131
	ΔCHAN	106
	openCS	108
	read	126
	readAS	110
	seekoffset	130
Chan!	...	124
CHAN'	ΔCHAN	106
cid	φAS	109
	Cid!	124
	closeCS	108
	fstat	112
	read	126
	readAS	110
	seekAS	111
	writeAS	111
Cid!	...	124
cid'	open	127
	openCS	108
close	...	117

NAME	WITHIN	PAGE
====	======	====
size!	fstat	112
SS	...	100, 129
	≡SS	117
	φSS	103
	AS	109
	createSS	101
	destroySS	101
	FS	116
	seekCHAN	107
	seekoffset	130
SS'	≡SS	117
	φSS	103
	createSS	101
	destroySS	101
	seekCHAN	107
success	...	124
SYL	...	113
unlink	...	117
usedfids	FS	116
writeAS	...	111
writeCHAN	...	107
writeFILE	...	99
	writeSS	103
writeSS	...	103, 104
	writeCHAN	107
ZERO	...	98

CAVIAR: A Case Study in Specification

Bill Flinn and Ib Holm Sørensen

Abstract

This paper describes the specification in Z of a reasonably complex software system. Important features of the Z approach which are highlighted in this paper include the interleaving of mathematical text with informal prose, the creation of parameterised specifications, and use of the Z schema calculus to construct descriptions of large systems from simpler components.

Contents

0. Introduction

1. The Case Study

2. Identification of the Basic Sets

3. The Subsystems of CAVIAR

4. A General Resource-User System

5. Specialisation of the General R-U System
   5.1 An R-U system where resources cannot be shared
   5.2 An R-U system where each user may occupy at most one resource
   5.3 An R-U system where a user occupies
                              at most one non-shareable resource
   5.4 The specification library

6. Classification and Instantiation
   6.1 Some laws for CAVIAR
   6.2 Matching system with models
   6.3 The hotel reservation subsystem - HR-V
   6.4 The transport reservation subsystem - TR-V

7. The Meeting Attendance Subsystem
   7.1 A pool system
   7.2 The meeting - visitor subsystem

0. Introduction

We view a specification as having a two-fold purpose: firstly, to give a formal (mathematical) system description which provides a basis from which to construct a design. Such a mathematical description is essential if we are to prove formally that a design meets its specification. Secondly, to give an informal statement of the system's properties, in order that the specification can be tested (validated) against the (usually informal) statement of requirements. Thus the Z approach is to construct a specification document which consists of a judicious mix of informal prose with precise mathematical statements. The two parts of the document are complementary in that the informal text can be viewed as commentary for the formal text. It can be consulted to find out what aspects of the real world are being described and how they relate to the informally stated requirements. The formal text on the other hand provides the precise definition of the system and hence can be used to resolve any ambiguities present in the informal text. A beneficial side effect for practitioners writing such documents is that their understanding of the system in question is greatly helped by the process of constructing both the formal and the informal descriptions.

It is often the case that the process of abstraction used to construct a specification results in structures which are more general than those actually required for the system being considered. It is part of the Z approach to identify and describe such general structures. These descriptions can be placed in a specification library. Particular cases of these general components can then be used later, either as part of the current system or in subsequent projects.

This specification case study develops a number of general systems which are subsequently constrained and combined to form the complete system description.

1. The Case Study

This specification of a Computer Aided Visitor Information And Retrieval system resulted from the analysis of a manual system concerned with the recording and retrieval of data about arrangements for visitors and meetings at a large industrial site. Standard Telecommunications Laboratories (U.K.) sponsored the study in order to investigate the feasibility of converting to a computer based solution. Of particular concern were the interrelationships of the stored information, the quality of the user interface and the volume of data which was required to be processed. The customer provided as input to the study an informal requirements document. We attempt to provide in this paper an outline of the steps involved in development of the eventual formal specification. It is important to stress at the outset that we view the task of constructing such a specification to be an iterative process, involving several attempts at construction of a model for the system interspersed with frequent dialogues with the customer to clarify details which are ambiguous or undefined in the initial requirements document, and frequent redrafting to clarify the structure of the document.

At an early stage in the analysis it became clear that the CAVIAR system consisted of several highly independent subsystems. Each subsystem records important relationships within the complete system and these separate subsystems are themselves related according to some simple rules. Most of the operations to be provided in the user interface can be explained as functions which transform one particular subsystem only, leaving the others invariant. These observations led to the decision to first define the subsystems in isolation and then to describe the complete system by combining the definitions of the subsystems. Once this decision had been taken, it also became clear that each of the individual subsystems, when viewed at an appropriate level of abstraction, was a particular instance of a general structure. From this vantage point it was natural to specify each of the subsystems by "refining" a specification which describes the underlying general system.

The process of analysis as presented here begins with an identification of the sets which appear to be important from the customer's point of view. Next the relationships between these sets are investigated and a preliminary classification of the subsystems follows. The third phase consists of developing an appropriate general mathematical structure in which to place these subsystems. Various ways of *specialising* (restricting) the general structure are then investigated and particular subsystems are modelled by *instantiation*. Finally the subsystem models are combined.

2. Identification of the Basic Sets

We now present a brief account of the existing system, emphasising the important concepts in boldface. **Visitors** come to the site to attend **meetings** and/or consult Company employees. A visitor may require a **hotel reservation** and/or **transport reservation**. Each meeting is also required to take place in a designated **conference room**, at a certain **time**. A meeting may require the use of a **dining room** for lunch, on a particular date. Booking a dining room requires **lunch information** including the number of places needed. Each conference room booking requires **session information** about resources required for use in the meeting, e.g., viewgraphs, projectors. The main operations required at the user interface can briefly be described as facilities for booking, changing and cancelling the use of resources. We list below the sets together with the names that we shall adopt for referring to them.

Set	Name
Meetings	M
Visitors	V
Conference Rooms	CR
Dining Rooms	DR
Lunch Information	LI
Session Information	SI
Hotel Reservation	HR
Transport Reservation	TR

The informal interpretation of these sets is straightforward, and for the purpose of this specification no further detail is necessary. Note that the question of modelling time remains to be resolved; at this point we simply observe that hotel reservations are made for particular *dates*, transport reservations are made for certain *times* on particular dates, and conference room bookings are made for *sessions* on particular dates. We shall not specify the term *session* further, apart from noting that a date is always associated with a session; it could, for example, denote complete mornings or afternoons, or hourly or half-hourly intervals, depending on the way conference rooms are allocated.

The notion of time and the relationship between the different units of time used within the system can be formalised by asserting the existence of three sets as follows:

```
Date
Session
Time
```

together with two total functions

```
date-of-session : Session → Date
date-of-time    : Time    → Date.
```

3. The Subsystems of CAVIAR

The first approach to a mathematical model stems from the realisation that several of the sets listed above can be viewed as *resources* and other sets can be viewed as *users* of those resources. We can identify the following subsystems of CAVIAR in this framework (i. e., Resource-User systems). Observe that in different subsystems the same set may appear in different roles.

System	Resources	Users
CR-M	Conference Rooms	Meetings
DR-M	Dining Rooms	Meetings
M-V	Meetings	Visitors
HR-V	Hotel Reservations	Visitors
TR-V	Transport Reservations	Visitors

Once we have made this mathematical abstraction it seems worthwhile, for the following reasons, to develop a general theory of such resource-user systems:

1. A specification of such a general system would be more useful as part of a "specification library" than a specific instance of such a system. Re-usability is much more likely to be achieved by having *generic* specifications available which can be *instantiated* to provide particular systems.

2. Particular subsystems of the general system can be constructed as *special cases* of the general specification in various ways. This will amply repay care and time spent on the general case. Furthermore, such instantiation may well result in a more compact implementation.

4. A General Resource-User System

We consider a system parameterised over three sets;

$$[\ T, \ R, \ U \ ]$$

Informally, T is to be thought of as a set of *time slots*, R is a set of *resources* and U is a set of *users*. We describe a general resource-user system as a function from T to the set of relations between R and U. Thus we have a rather general framework: for each time slot t ∈ T, some users are occupying or using some resources. The set T will later be instantiated with different sets in the various applications. Notice that considering *relations* between R and U allows us the possibility of a user occupying several different resources simultaneously, as is shown informally in the following diagram:

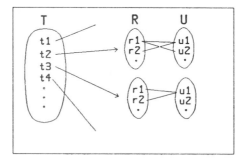

Formally, the structure we are describing is captured by a function of type

$$T \rightarrow (R \leftrightarrow U)$$

We shall now incorporate this into a *schema definition*. This schema is parameterised over the sets T, R and U, and contains some useful ancillary concepts in addition to the function ru above which will be useful in later analysis. In Z specifications it is common to introduce such derived components: as specifiers of software we are neither in the position of a pure mathematician looking for a particularly sparse set of concepts and axioms with which to define a mathematical structure, nor are we in the position of an implementor trying to minimise storage. The component in-use, which gives the set of resources in use at any instant, will be useful in contexts where we are not concerned with the user component of the system state. The function users, which gives the users occupying resources at any instant, will be used in situations where we do not require the information about resources. We also note that there may be occasions when we wish to consider the set of *inverse* relations generated by ru; we call this function ur.

```
┌─ R-U ─────────────────────────────────────────────┐
│   ru       : T → (R ↔ U)                           │
│   in-use : T → P R                                 │
│   users   : T → P U                                │
│   ur        : T → (U ↔ R)                          │
│ ──────────────────────────────────────────────     │
│                                                     │
│   ∀t: T •                                           │
│         in-use(t) = dom(ru(t)) ∧                    │
│         users(t)  = rng(ru(t)) ∧                    │
│         ur(t) = (ru(t))⁻¹                           │
└─────────────────────────────────────────────────────┘
```

The *initial state* of this system is defined by making ru(t) the empty relation for each t.

$$\text{Init-R-U} \triangleq [\text{ R-U } | \text{ rng(ru)} = \{ \{\} \}]$$

Our first theorem proves that such an initial state is reasonable and assures us of the consistency of the definition of R-U.

Theorem 1.
⊢ ∃ R-U • Init-R-U

In the interests of readability we have not given proofs of theorems stated in this paper.

We continue by defining the appropriate operations for this structure. The first step is to identify *commonalities*. For our purposes, the operations that we wish to consider on this structure are concerned with making a new booking, i. e., adding a new pair (r, u) to an existing relation at some time t, cancelling an existing booking, i. e., removing such an (r, u) pair, or modifying in some other way the relation that exists at some particular time. In fact we shall be a little more general and define a class of operations on R-U which allows the image of a *set* of time values to be altered. This is because we anticipate such operations as booking a conference room for a meeting which lasts for several time slots. Of course a booking which involves only a single time slot is a particular case.

Thus we may summarise the common part of all the operations as follows. Their description involves: a state before, R-U, which introduces ru, in-use, users and ur; a state after, R-U', which introduces ru', in-use', users' and ur'; a set of time values, t? which denotes an input. The operations always leave the function ru unchanged except for times in t?. Formally this is captured by

```
┌─ ΔR-U ─────────────────────────────────┐
│ R-U                                     │
│ R-U'                                    │
│ t? : P T                                │
├─────────────────────                    │
│ t? ◁ ru'  =  t? ◁ ru                    │
└─────────────────────────────────────────┘
```

We now have a successful *booking* operation defined as follows

```
┌─ R-U-Book ─────────────────────────────┐
│ ΔR-U                                    │
│ r? : R                                  │
│ u? : U                                  │
├─────────────────────                    │
│ ∀ t : t? •                              │
│     (r?,u?) ∉ ru(t) ∧                   │
│     ru'(t) = ru(t) ∪ {r? ↦ u?}          │
└─────────────────────────────────────────┘
```

Thus R-U-Book inherits all the properties of ΔR-U. Furthermore, it takes two additional (input) parameters r?:R and u?:U, and is constrained by a predicate which imposes a requirement on the input parameters and also further relates the before and after states.

Notice that we are making the predicate

$$\forall\ t:\ t?\ \bullet\ (r?,u?)\ \notin\ ru(t)$$

a pre-condition for a successful booking. In fact, we can show that this condition is sufficient for performing a successful booking; that is, if we are in a valid system state with the required input parameters of the correct type available and if furthermore the above condition holds, then there exists a resulting valid system state which is related to the starting state according to the R–U–Book schema. Formally, this is the content of the following result:

Theorem 2

R–U $\wedge$ [t?: $\mathbb{P}$ T; r?: R; u?: U | $\forall$ t: t? $\bullet$ (r?,u?) $\notin$ ru(t)]

$\vdash$

$\exists$ R–U′ $\bullet$ R–U–Book

A successful *cancellation* operation may be defined via

```
  ┌─ R-U-Cancel ─────────────────────────┐
  │ ΔR-U                                   │
  │ r? : R                                 │
  │ u? : U                                 │
  ├────────────────────                    │
  │ ∀ t : t? •                             │
  │     (r?,u?) ∈ ru(t) ∧                   │
  │     ru'(t) = ru(t) - { (r?,u?) }        │
  └────────────────────────────────────────┘
```

The pre-condition for successful cancellation is that the pair $(r?,u?)$ is related by $ru(t)$ for all time values t in t?; i. e., the following theorem holds.

Theorem 3

R–U $\wedge$ [t? : $\mathbb{P}$ T; r? : R; u? : U | $\forall$ t: t? $\bullet$ (r?,u?) $\in$ ru(t)]

$\vdash$

$\exists$ R–U′ $\bullet$ R–U–Cancel

So far we have only specified successful operations; thus these descriptions are incomplete. We could at this stage define robust operations by introducing appropriate error recovery machinery. In the interests of simplicity we shall not give a general treatment of errors; however we shall indicate in a later section (9.2.1) how the descriptions of the operations at the user interface can be completed.

We shall define two further operations on this structure. The first involves deleting a resource and all use of that resource. This is an operation to be treated with caution: see Theorem 7 below.

```
┌─ R-U-Del-Res ──────────────────────────┐
│  ΔR-U                                   │
│  r? : R                                 │
│  ─────────────────────────             │
│  ∀ t : t? •                            │
│       r? ∈ dom ru(t) ∧                 │
│       ru'(t) = { r? } ◁ ru(t)          │
└─────────────────────────────────────────┘
```

Informally, this operation may be described as follows. Consider, in turn, each element t in t? and the corresponding relation ru(t). All elements (r?, u) are to be removed from ru(t).

Theorem 4
$$R\text{-}U \wedge [\ t? : \mathbb{P}\ T;\ r? : R\ |\ \forall\ t: t? \bullet r? \in dom\ ru(t)\ ]$$
$$\vdash$$
$$\exists\ R\text{-}U' \bullet R\text{-}U\text{-}Del\text{-}Res$$

Corresponding to the deletion of a resource there is an operation which, given a user value u?, deletes all pairs (r, u?) from the relations associated with time values in t?. This is defined as follows:

```
┌─ R-U-Del-User ─────────────────────────┐
│  ΔR-U                                   │
│  u? : U                                 │
│  ─────────────────────────             │
│  ∀ t : t? •                            │
│       u? ∈ rng ru(t) ∧                 │
│       ru'(t) = ru(t) ▷ { u? }          │
└─────────────────────────────────────────┘
```

Theorem 5

R-U ∧ [t? : **P** T; u? : U | ∀ t : t? • u? ∈ rng ru(t)]
⊢
∃ R-U′ • R-U-Del-User

So far we have listed theorems that a specifier is obliged to prove; viz the result that the initial state satisfies the required definition (and therefore that the specification is consistent), and in addition the theorems that explicitly give the pre-conditions for each operation.

For the specifications that we shall develop from now on these theorems have been omitted in the interests of brevity.

In addition to these obligatory results, there are other "optional" theorems that are satisfied by the specification, and which often give insight into the structure being developed.

Two such results for our system are as follows:

Theorem 6

R-U-Book ; R-U-Cancel   ⊢   ru′ = ru.

Informally, this theorem states that if we make a booking and follow it immediately by a cancellation using the same input parameters, then the state of the system does not change.

Theorem 7

R-U-Del-Res
⊢
in-use′ = in-use ⊕ (λt:t? • in-use(t) − { r? }) ∧
users′ = users ⊕
          (λt:t? • (users(t) − {u : U | ur(t)(｛u｝) = {r?}}))

This theorem makes precise the informal comment made earlier about the need for caution with the R-U-Del-Res operation. It shows that, as expected, resources are removed from the system structures, but that in addition the operation can remove existing users — namely, those using the deleted resource.

There is a similar result concerning the R-U-Del-User operation.

5. Specialisation of the General R-U System

We shall now *specialise* the general R-U system into particular classes of the system. These specialisations are motivated by the observation that for some of the instances listed earlier, a resource may at any given time be related to only one user, or a user may occupy only one resource, or both.

5.1 An R-U system where resources cannot be shared

The first case we define is the class where each resource may be utilised by at most one user, but each user may occupy several resources. We denote this system by R⟩U (where "⟩" is just a character in the name) and define it formally by

$$\text{R⟩U} \triangleq [\text{ R–U} \mid rng(ru) \subseteq \text{R⇸U}]$$

The initial state of this system is given by the same condition as for Init-R-U; thus we have

$$\text{Init–R⟩U} \triangleq [\text{ R⟩U} \mid rng(ru) = \{ \{\} \}]$$

All operations are described in terms of

$$\Delta\text{R⟩U} \triangleq \text{R⟩U} \wedge \text{R⟩U}'$$

The operations on this system may be defined as special cases of the general operations for R-U. We first consider the booking operation.

$$\text{R⟩U–Book} \triangleq \Delta\text{R⟩U} \wedge [\text{ R–U–Book} \mid \forall t: t? \bullet r? \notin dom\ ru(t)]$$

The qualifying predicate is included to indicate that there is a further pre-condition for booking a resource in a R⟩U system.

We now have two parts to the pre-condition for this operation; firstly this qualifying predicate, and secondly the pre-condition arising from R-U-Book. In fact the former implies the latter, as is easily checked.

The cancellation operation is defined as follows:

$$\text{R⟩U–Cancel} \triangleq \Delta\text{R⟩U} \wedge \text{R–U–Cancel}$$

On considering the two deletion operations defined for R–U, we observe that R–U–Del–Res is equivalent to a cancellation in our present context, because the resource is associated with only one user. We therefore need only the operation which deletes a user.

$$R\!\rangle\!U\text{-Del-User} \triangleq \Delta R\!\rangle\!U \wedge R\text{-U-Del-User}$$

5.2 An R–U system where each user may occupy at most one resource

The second case we define is the class where each user may occupy at most one resource but resources may be shared amongst users. We denote this system by $R\!\langle\!U$ and define it formally by

$$R\!\langle\!U \triangleq [\ R\text{-U}\ |\ rng(ur) \subseteq U\twoheadrightarrow R\ ]$$

The initial state of this system is also given by the predicate for Init–R–U. We have

$$\text{Init-}R\!\langle\!U \triangleq [\ R\!\langle\!U\ |\ rng(ru) = \{\ \{\}\ \}\ ]$$

The operations are described in terms of

$$\Delta R\!\langle\!U \triangleq R\!\langle\!U \wedge R\!\langle\!U'$$

We now define the booking operation for the system.

$$R\!\langle\!U\text{-Book} \triangleq \Delta R\!\langle\!U \wedge [\ R\text{-U-Book}\ |\ \forall\ t\ :\ t?\ \bullet\ u?\notin rng(ru(t))\ ]$$

As before, a qualifying predicate is needed and again as before the constraint given here implies the earlier pre-condition for the general R–U–Book operation.

The cancellation operation is defined as follows:

$$R\!\langle\!U\text{-Cancel} \triangleq R\text{-U-Cancel} \wedge \Delta R\!\langle\!U$$

On considering the two deletion operations defined for R–U, we observe that this time R–U–Del–User is equivalent to a cancellation in our present context, because a user may be associated with only one resource. We therefore need only the operation which deletes a resource.

$$R\!\langle\!U\text{-Del-Res} \triangleq R\text{-U-Del-Res} \wedge \Delta R\!\langle\!U$$

5.3 An R-U system where a user occupies at most one nonsharable resource

The third and last specialisation we define shares all of the properties of the systems defined in the preceding two sections. It is therefore defined as the *conjunction* of the two schemas above. In this system each user may occupy at most one resource and each resource may be occupied by at most one user. Formally we have

$$R{\equiv}U \quad \triangleq \quad R{>}U \wedge R{<}U$$

The initial state of this system is clearly defined by

$$\mathtt{Init\text{-}R{\equiv}U} \quad \triangleq \quad [\ R{\equiv}U \mid \mathtt{rng(ru)} = \{\ \{\}\ \}\ ]$$

The operations of this system are given by the conjunction of the operations defined for each of the two earlier systems. For this system we require only the booking and cancellation operations. Thus we have

$$R{\equiv}U\text{-}Book \quad \triangleq \quad R{>}U\text{-}Book \quad \wedge \quad R{<}U\text{-}Book$$

$$R{\equiv}U\text{-}Cancel \quad \triangleq \quad R{>}U\text{-}Cancel \wedge R{<}U\text{-}Cancel$$

5.4 The specification library

We have now constructed four specifications which might be considered to form the nucleus of a specification library for resource-user systems. We may summarise the relationships between the four classes of system schematically as follows:

6. Classification and Instantiation

6.1 Some laws for CAVIAR

In this section, in order to illustrate the clarification process which took place during requirements analysis, we list some observations about the CAVIAR system which emerged during dialogue with the customer. We formalise the important constraints as *laws* which need to be taken into account in the development which follows.

1. At any time a conference room is associated with only one meeting.

2. At any time a meeting may be associated with *more than one* conference room.

Law 1 is reasonably obvious: it would be difficult to hold more than one meeting in a given room. Law 2 is not obvious: it was unclear from the informal description whether or not a meeting could occupy more than one room. In fact the customer believed initially that a meeting could only take up one room, but a counter-example was found amongst the supporting documentation.

3. At any time a meeting is associated with only one dining room.

4. At any time participants from several meetings can occupy the same dining room.

These laws followed from the informal information provided that all visitors in a particular meeting would go to lunch in the same dining room. It was further established that all seats in a dining room were treated as indistinguishable, so further meetings could be accommodated if enough seats were available. Further clarification was necessary regarding lunch times: it transpired that there were "early" and "late" lunches; however this was handled by "doubling up" each dining room. For example, a booking would be made for "DR 1, early" and this was a different dining room from "DR 1, late."

5. At any time a visitor is associated with only one meeting.

6. At any time a meeting may involve several visitors.

Law 5 had to be checked out with the customer.

7. At any time a hotel room is associated with only one visitor and vice versa.

8. At any time a transport reservation is associated with only one visitor and vice versa.

Law 7 was natural, but law 8 was less so. It was established that even if the transport department decided to use a minibus, a separate transport reservation would be issued to each visitor.

6.2 Matching system with models

In this section we first consider each **CAVIAR** subsystem in turn and match it to the appropriate model. In fact we have enough structure available to define two subsystems directly and we do this in the remainder of this section.

(1) We first consider the conference room - meeting system CR-M.

From laws 1 and 2 we see that CR-M is an instance of the R⟩U subsystem.

(2) The dining room - meeting subsystem DR-M.

Applying laws 3 and 4 we find that DR-M is an instance of R⟨U.

However this system does not contain any information about numbers of seats or the lunch details, so we will need to extend this system later.

(3) The meeting - visitor subsystem M-V.

From laws 5 and 6 M-V is an instance of R⟨U.

However we have not documented the fact that meetings have to be created before visitors can be attached to them; this will also be done later.

(4) The hotel reservation - visitor subsystem HR-V, and the transport reservation - visitor subsystem TR-V, both have the property that each resource is occupied by only one user and vice versa. Therefore both these systems are instances of R⊒U.

In fact this model is sufficient to define HR-V and TR-V completely, by *instantiation*, as we now show.

6.3 The hotel reservation subsystem - HR-V

We define HR-V as follows:

$$HR-V \ \hat{=} \ R \bar{=} U_{HR-V}[Date, HR, V]$$

This object is a *decorated* instance of the $R\bar{=}U$ schema, with its parameter sets instantiated by the sets Date, HR and V introduced in section 2. To be more explicit, the definition above is shorthand for the following:

```
┌─ HR-V ─────────────────────────────────────────────┐
│  ru_{HR-V}      : Date → (HR ↔ V)                   │
│  in-use_{HR-V} : Date → P HR                        │
│  users_{HR-V}  : Date → P V                         │
│  ur_{HR-V}      : Date → (V ↔ HR)                   │
│────────────────────────────────────────────────────│
│  rng(ru_{HR-V}) ⊆ HR↠V ∧                            │
│  rng(ur_{HR-V}) ⊆ V↠HR ∧                            │
│  (∀t: Date; r: HR •                                 │
│        r ∈ in-use_{HR-V}(t)  ⟺  r ∈ dom(ru_{HR-V}(t)) ) ∧ │
│  (∀t: Date; u: V •                                  │
│        u ∈ users_{HR-V}(t)  ⟺  u ∈ ran(ru_{HR-V}(t)) ) ∧ │
│  (∀t: Date  •  ur_{HR-V}(t) = (ru_{HR-V}(t))^{-1})  │
└────────────────────────────────────────────────────┘
```

Thus each component of the schema is given the decoration in the definition, and each occurrence of the parameterised sets is instantiated as shown above. From now on we shall use such decoration without further comment.

The initial state of HR-V is given by

$$Init-HR-V \ \hat{=} \ Init-R\bar{=}U_{HR-V}[Date, HR, V]$$

and the operations are given by

$$Book-Hotel-Room_0 \ \hat{=} \ R\bar{=}U-Book_{HR-V}[Date, HR, V]$$

and

$$Cancel-Hotel-Room_0 \ \hat{=} \ R\bar{=}U-Cancel_{HR-V}[Date, HR, V]$$

6.4 The transport reservation subsystem - TR-V

This subsystem is essentially the same as the HR-V subsystem except for the parameterisation. The instances of the parameters are denoted respectively Time, TR and V, where once again the sets TR and V are as in section 2. We shall not specify the set Time further, except to repeat that it contains a Date component (see section 2). Thus we have

$$TR\text{-}V \quad \triangleq \quad R\Xi U_{TR\text{-}V}[Time, TR, V]$$

with initial state given by

$$Init\text{-}TR\text{-}V \quad \triangleq \quad Init\text{-}R\Xi U_{TR\text{-}V}[Time, TR, V]$$

and operations given by

$$Book\text{-}Transport_0 \quad \triangleq \quad R\Xi U\text{-}Book_{TR\text{-}V}[Time, TR, V]$$

and

$$Cancel\text{-}Transport_0 \quad \triangleq \quad R\Xi U\text{-}Cancel_{TR\text{-}V}[Time, TR, V]$$

7. The Meeting Attendance Subsystem

We now turn our attention to what is necessary in order to complete a model for M-V. Booking and cancelling operations have been defined already but so far we have not taken account of the fact that before bookings can be made the system has to "create" meetings. The question of exactly which objects are "currently defined" at any particular time is important because in several cases only those objects known to the system (i. e., those objects that have been created but not yet destroyed) can book resources, etc.

7.1 A pool system

We can model this situation with a simple structure which we term a Pool. This schema is parameterised over the set T and an arbitrary set X. There are only two operations to be defined; namely those that add an object to, and delete an object from, the pool, over a specified time period.

Formally we have

$$[\ T, \ X \ ]$$

```
 ┌─ Pool ──────────────────────────────────┐
 │   exists : T → P X                        │
 └──────────────────────────────────────────┘
```

with initial state given by

$$Init-Pool \ \triangleq \ [\ Pool \ | \ rng(exists) = \{ \ \{\} \ \} \ ]$$

For later use we define

$$\equiv Pool \ \triangleq \ [\ \Delta Pool \ | \ Pool' = Pool \ ]$$

Given

$$\Delta Pool \ \triangleq \ Pool \wedge Pool'$$

The operations are given by

```
┌─ Create ──────────────────────────────────────────────────────────┐
│ ΔPool                                                               │
│ t? : P T                                                            │
│ x? : X                                                              │
│ ────────────────────                                                │
│ exists' = exists ⊕ (λ t : t? • exists(t) ∪ { x? } )                 │
└────────────────────────────────────────────────────────────────────┘
```

and

```
┌─ Destroy ─────────────────────────────────────────────────────────┐
│ ΔPool                                                               │
│ t? : P T                                                            │
│ x? : X                                                              │
│ ────────────────────                                                │
│ exists' = exists ⊕ (λ t : t? • exists(t) - { x? } )                 │
└────────────────────────────────────────────────────────────────────┘
```

We could have included in the Create operation the pre-condition that the object x? must not already exist for any of the times in t?. However we make a deliberate decision here to omit this — having in mind the situation where an object may already exist for some of the times in t? and its existence needs to be extended to all of t?. A similar remark applies to the Destroy operation.

7.2 The meeting - visitor subsystem

To construct the model for the M-V system we combine the Pool and R≼U structures.

```
┌─ M-V ─────────────────────────────────────────────────────────────┐
│ R≼U_{M-V}[Session, M, V]                                            │
│ Pool_M[Session, M]                                                  │
│ ────────────────────                                                │
│ ∀t : Session •                                                      │
│    in-use_{M-V}(t) ⊆ exists_M(t)                                    │
└────────────────────────────────────────────────────────────────────┘
```

Thus we have combined an M-V instance of an R≪U system and a meeting instantiation of a Pool system (with the parameter sets as shown). The predicate assures that visitors can only attend existing meetings.

The initial state is given by

$$\text{Init-M-V} \; \triangleq \; \text{Init-R≪U}_{M-V}[\text{Session}, M, V] \; \wedge \; \text{Init-Pool}_M[\text{Session}, M]$$

We now define the operations on M-V in terms of

$$\Delta\text{M-V} \; \triangleq \; \text{M-V} \wedge \text{M-V}'$$

The first operation is concerned with adding a visitor to a meeting.

$$\text{Add-Visitor-to-Meeting}_0 \; \triangleq$$
$$\Delta\text{M-V} \wedge \equiv\text{Pool}_M[\text{Session}, M] \wedge \text{R≪U-Book}_{M-V}[\text{Session}, M, V]$$

When an operation is "promoted" in this way, its new pre-condition is determined as follows: the "old" pre-condition (i. e., that arising from its definition) must be conjoined with a further predicate which arises from the new invariant of the larger state. Here, for example, the pre-condition for the earlier booking operation is given in section 5.2: namely

$$\forall \, t \; : \; t?_{M-V} \bullet u?_{M-V} \notin \text{rng}(\text{ru}_{M-V}(t))$$

and this must be conjoined with

$$\forall \, t \; : \; t?_{M-V} \bullet r?_{M-V} \in \text{exists}_M(t).$$

This second predicate is a consequence of the M-V invariant.

Thus the complete pre-condition for the Add-Visitor-to-Meeting operation is given by

$$\forall \, t \; : \; t?_{M-V} \bullet u?_{M-V} \notin \text{rng}(\text{ru}_{M-V}(t)) \wedge r?_{M-V} \in \text{exists}_M(t)$$

which states that the visitor $(u?_{M-V})$ is not already attending a meeting at that time and that the meeting he is going to attend actually exists.

The second operation removes a visitor from a meeting.

$$\text{Remove-Visitor-from-Meeting}_0 \ \triangleq$$
$$\Delta\text{M-V} \ \wedge \ \equiv\text{Pool}_M[\text{Session, M}] \ \wedge \ \text{R\small<\normalsize U-Cancel}_{M-V}[\text{Session, M, V}]$$

It is easy to check that the pre-condition for the Remove-Visitor-from-Meeting operation is simply inherited from the initial R-U-Cancel operation; namely

$$\forall \ t \ : \ t?_{M-V} \ \bullet \ (r?_{M-V}, u?_{M-V}) \ \in \ ru_{M-V}(t)$$

We now define the operations which create and cancel meetings as follows:

$$\text{Create-Meeting}_0 \ \triangleq$$
$$\Delta\text{M-V} \ \wedge \ \equiv\text{R\small<\normalsize U}_{M-V}[\text{Session, M, V}] \ \wedge \ \text{Create}_M[\text{Session, M}]$$

For the creation there is no pre-condition.

$$
\boxed{\begin{array}{l}
\text{Cancel-Meeting}_0 \\[2pt]
\Delta\text{M-V} \\
\text{R\small<\normalsize U-Del-Res}_{M-V}[\text{Session, M, V}] \\
\text{Destroy}_M[\text{Session, M}] \\
\hline
t?_M = t?_{M-V} \ \wedge \\
x?_M = r?_{M-V}
\end{array}}
$$

The pre-conditions for cancelling a meeting arise firstly from the original R-U-Del-Res operation, i. e., that

$$\forall \ t \ : \ t?_{M-V} \ \bullet \ r?_{M-V} \ \in \ \text{dom}(ru_{M-V}(t))$$

and secondly from the identifications required for the input parameters.

8. The Meeting Resource Subsystems

We are left with the task of defining the systems CR–M and DR–M. We observe that both of these have further information associated with the resource-user relationship; so in order to capture this facet in our model, we introduce the concept of a *diary* system.

8.1 A diary system

The diary required is to record information about some elements of a set. We denote the set in question by X and the associated information by I_X. For each t, the set of elements of X for which we have information is defined as $recorded(t)$. Once again this system is dependent on time, T.

$$[\ T, \ X, \ I_X \ ]$$

```
┌─ Diary ──────────────────────────────────┐
│   info      : T → (X ⇸ I_X)               │
│   recorded : T → P X                      │
│ ─────────────────────────────────────────│
│   ∀ t : T • recorded(t) = dom(info(t))    │
└───────────────────────────────────────────┘
```

with initial state given by

$$\text{Init-Diary} \ \triangleq \ [\ \text{Diary} \mid rng(info) = \{ \ \{\} \ \} \ ]$$

The two operations to be defined both involve a change over a particular time period. Note that we are motivated to make this definition in order to maintain compatibility with existing systems. Formally we define

$$\Delta \text{Diary} \ \triangleq \ \text{Diary} \wedge \text{Diary}' \wedge [\ t? : P \ T \ ]$$

```
┌─ Add ─────────────────────────────────────────────┐
│   ΔDiary                                           │
│   x? : X                                           │
│   i? : I_X                                         │
│ ──────────────────────────────────────────────────│
│   (∀ t : t? • x? ∉ recorded(t)) ∧                 │
│   info' = info ⊕ (λ t : t? • info(t) ⊕ { x? ↦ i? }) │
└────────────────────────────────────────────────────┘
```

The complementary erasure operation should remove one element (and the information associated with it) from $\mathrm{info}(t)$. However we note that this is a special case of the following more powerful operation.

```
┌─ Erase ─────────────────────────────────────────────────────────────┐
│ ΔDiary                                                               │
│ x? : T ↦ P X                                                         │
├─────────────────────────                                            │
│ dom(x?) = t? ∧                                                       │
│ (∀ t : t? • x?(t) ⊆ recorded(t?)) ∧                                 │
│ info' = info ⊕ (λ t : t? • x?(t) ◁ info(t))                        │
└─────────────────────────────────────────────────────────────────────┘
```

8.2 The conference room booking subsystem

We are now in a position to fully specify the subsystem CR-M, by instantiation as follows:

```
┌─ CR-M ──────────────────────────────────┐
│ R⋊U_CR-M[Session, CR, M]                 │
│ Diary_CR[Session, CR, SI]                │
├─────────────────────────                │
│ in-use_CR-M = recorded_CR                │
└──────────────────────────────────────────┘
```

with initial state given by

$$\mathrm{Init\text{-}CR\text{-}M} \;\;\triangleq\;\; \mathrm{Init\text{-}R{\rtimes}U_{CR\text{-}M}[Session, CR, M]}$$
$$\wedge \; \mathrm{Init\text{-}Diary_{CR}[Session, CR, SI]}$$

It would be more correct to regard the session information SI as being related to a meeting rather than a conference room. The reason for associating SI with conference rooms is that it contains information which is issued to the department supplying equipment for meetings, and they are concerned with the venue rather than what is to take place there.

The operations that we require for CR-M are given below. Information is recorded about each resource when it is booked, and must be erased when a cancellation takes place. The definitions use

$$\Delta\text{CR-M} \triangleq \text{CR-M} \wedge \text{CR-M}'$$

```
┌─ Book-Conf-Room₀ ──────────────────────────────┐
│ ΔCR-M                                           │
│ R≫U-Book_CR-M[Session, CR, M]                   │
│ Add_CR[Session, CR, SI]                         │
│─────────────────────────────────────────────── │
│ t?_CR-M = t?_CR ∧                               │
│ r?_CR-M = x?_CR                                 │
└─────────────────────────────────────────────────┘
```

```
┌─ Cancel-Conf-Rooms₀ ───────────────────────────┐
│ ΔCR-M                                           │
│ R≫U-Del-User_CR-M[Session, CR, M]               │
│ Erase_CR[Session, CR, SI]                       │
│─────────────────────────────────────────────── │
│ t?_CR-M = t?_CR ∧                               │
│ (∀t: t?_CR-M • x?_CR(t) = ur_CR-M(t)({u?_CR-M})) │
└─────────────────────────────────────────────────┘
```

The cancellation operation here deletes all conference rooms associated with a particular meeting over the specified time period. This is the operation which is most compatible with the Cancel-Meeting operation defined for M-V. However, if required, we could also define the operation that cancels just one conference room - meeting pairing.

8.3 The dining room booking subsystem

The final subsystem that we need to consider is DR-M.

The analysis so far does not take account of the fact that dining rooms have a finite capacity, so we need to extend our model. We suppose that we have been given a function

$$\text{max-no} : DR \rightarrow N$$

which records this capacity and we record the number of seats in each dining room which have been reserved already.

The DR-M system is defined formally as follows:

```
┌─ DR-M ─────────────────────────────────────────────────┐
│ R≪U_{DR-M}[Date, DR, M]                                  │
│ Diary_{DR}[Date, M, LI]                                  │
│ rsvd : T → (DR ↠ N)                                      │
├─────────────────────────────────────────────────────────┤
│ users_{DR-M} = recorded_{DR} ∧                          │
│ (∀t:Date • dom(rsvd(t)) = in-use_{DR-M}(t) ∧            │
│     (∀r:in-use_{DR-M}(t) • rsvd(t)(r) ⩽ max-no(r))     │
│ )                                                        │
└─────────────────────────────────────────────────────────┘
```

Observe that in this case information is associated with each *user*, and therefore the diary system takes M as its main parameter. Dining rooms that are in use have a number of seats reserved, and this number has to be within the dining room's capacity.

The initial state of DR-M is given by

$$\text{Init-DR-M} \triangleq \text{Init-R≪U}_{DR-M}[\text{Date}, DR, M] \wedge \text{Init-Diary}_{DR}[\text{Date}, M, LI]$$

The two operations that we require for this structure are *booking* a (number of seats in a) dining room and *cancelling* a lunch booking for a particular meeting. In normal circumstances, a resource (dining room) will not be subject to being taken out of service (although clearly this occurrence is easy to model if required).

Both of these operations leave rsvd unchanged for time values outside the period in question; we make this part of the operation invariant.

$$
\begin{array}{|l}
\hline \text{ADR-M} \\
\hline \Delta R \!\!\gg\!\! U_{DR-M}[\text{Date, DR, M}] \\
\Delta \text{Diary}_{DR}[\text{Date, M, LI}] \\
\text{amount?} : T \twoheadrightarrow N \\
\hline
t?_{DR-M} = t?_{DR} \; \wedge \\
\text{dom(amount?)} = t?_{DR-M} \; \wedge \\
t?_{DR-M} \;\lhd\!\!\!- \; \text{rsvd}' = t?_{DR-M} \;\lhd\!\!\!- \; \text{rsvd} \\
\hline
\end{array}
$$

$$
\begin{array}{|l}
\hline \text{Book-Dining-Room}_0 \\
\hline \Delta \text{DR-M} \\
R \!\!\gg\!\! U\text{-Book}_{DR-M}[\text{Date, DR, M}] \\
\text{Add}_{DR}[\text{Date, M, LI}] \\
\hline
x?_{DR} = u?_{DR-M} \; \wedge \\
(\forall t : t?_{DR-M} \; \bullet \\
\quad \text{rsvd}(t)(r?_{DR-M}) + \text{amount?}(t) \leqslant \text{max-no}(r?_{DR-M}) \; \wedge \\
\quad \text{rsvd}'(t) = \text{rsvd}(t) \\
\qquad\qquad \oplus \{ \, r?_{DR-M} \mapsto \text{rsvd}(t)(r?_{DR-M}) + \text{amount?}(t) \, \} \\
) \\
\hline
\end{array}
$$

$$
\begin{array}{|l}
\hline \text{Cancel-Dining-Room}_0 \\
\hline \Delta \text{DR-M} \\
R \!\!\gg\!\! U\text{-Cancel}_{DR-M}[\text{Date, DR, M}] \\
\text{Erase}_{DR}[\text{Date, M, LI}] \\
\hline
(\forall t : t?_{DR-M} \; \bullet \\
\quad x?_{DR}(t) = \{ \, u?_{DR-M} \, \} \; \wedge \\
\quad \text{rsvd}'(t) = \text{rsvd}(t) \\
\qquad\qquad \oplus \{ \, r?_{DR-M} \mapsto \text{rsvd}(t)(r?_{DR-M}) - \text{amount?}(t) \, \} \\
) \\
\hline
\end{array}
$$

8.4 The visitor pool - V-P

From the informal requirements we find that visitors must be "legitimate" before they are allowed to attend meetings or have resources booked on their behalf. This requirement is easily met by introducing a visitor Pool structure, with actual parameters Date and V. Thus we define V-P as

$$V-P \quad \triangleq \quad Pool_V[Date, V]$$

with initial state given by

$$Init-V-P \quad \triangleq \quad Init-Pool_V[Date, V]$$

The operations that we require for this system are simply those of creation and destruction of visitors. Formally we have

$$Create-Visitor_0 \quad \triangleq \quad Create_V[Date, V]$$
and
$$Destroy-Visitor_0 \quad \triangleq \quad Destroy_V[Date, V]$$

8.5 The construction process

In this section we summarise the constructions we have used to build the individual **CAVIAR** components.

In sections 7 and 8 we added *pool* and *diary* components to our basic library in section 5.4. We now have a library which consists of the 6 components R-U, R$\geqslant$U, R$\leqslant$U, R$\doteq$U, Pool and Diary. We indicate in the following diagram how each subsystem has been constructed using components from the library.

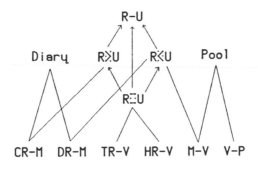

9. The Complete CAVIAR System

We have now achieved our first goal of specifying all constituent subsystems of CAVIAR. We have yet to combine the subsystems into a coherent whole. This is now a comparatively easy task, once we have observed a few extra constraints.

9.1 Combining subsystems to form the system state

We define the visitor part of the system as follows:

```
┌─ V-SYS ──────────────────────────────────────────────────┐
│  V-P                                                      │
│  HR-V                                                     │
│  TR-V                                                     │
│  ────────────────                                         │
│  (∀d : Date • users_HR-V(d) ⊆ exists_V(d) ) ∧            │
│  (∀t : Time • users_TR-V(t) ⊆ exists_V(date-of-time(t)) ) │
└───────────────────────────────────────────────────────────┘
```

The invariant states that visitors that have hotel or transport reservations must be known.

The meeting part of the system is defined by

```
┌─M-SYS──────────────────────────────────────────────────────┐
│  M-V                                                        │
│  CR-M                                                       │
│  DR-M                                                       │
│  ────────────────                                           │
│  (∀s:Session • users_CR-M(s) ⊆ exists_M(s) ) ∧             │
│  (∀d:Date •                                                 │
│      users_DR-M(d) ⊆                                        │
│      U { s:Session | date-of-session(s) = d • exists_M(s) } │
│  )                                                          │
└─────────────────────────────────────────────────────────────┘
```

The invariant states that meetings which are occupying conference rooms or dining rooms must be known to the system at that time.

These two subsystems are now combined to form the **CAVIAR** system.

```
┌─ CAVIAR ──────────────────────────────────────────────────┐
│  V-SYS                                                     │
│  M-SYS                                                     │
│ ─────────────────────                                     │
│                                                            │
│  ∀s : Session • users_{M-V}(s) ⊆ exists_V(date-of-session(s)) │
└────────────────────────────────────────────────────────────┘
```

Informally, the invariant states that all visitors who are attending meetings must be known to the system.

The initial state of the system is given by the conjunction of all the initialisations. It is easy to verify that this conjunction satisfies the invariant.

$$\text{Init-CAVIAR} \;\triangleq\; \text{Init-HR-V} \wedge \text{Init-TR-V} \wedge \text{Init-M-V} \wedge$$
$$\text{Init-CR-M} \wedge \text{Init-DR-M} \wedge \text{Init-V-P}$$

9.2 Operations on CAVIAR

The operations on **CAVIAR** may be divided naturally into three groups.

9.2.1 Operations which involve meetings only

These operations are concerned with M-SYS only and leave V-SYS unchanged. We denote this by

$$\text{M-OP} \;\triangleq\; \Delta\text{CAVIAR} \wedge \equiv\text{V-SYS}$$

where

$$\Delta\text{CAVIAR} \;\triangleq\; \text{CAVIAR} \wedge \text{CAVIAR}'$$

and

$$\equiv\text{V-SYS} \;\triangleq\; [\; \text{V-SYS} \wedge \text{V-SYS}' \mid \text{V-SYS} = \text{V-SYS}' \;]$$

(Note: in the following similar definitions of ≡CR-M, ≡DR-M, etc. are omitted.)

The first operation is to construct a meeting

$$\text{Create-Meeting} \; \triangleq \; \text{M-OP} \wedge \text{Create-Meeting}_0 \wedge \equiv\text{CR-M} \wedge \equiv\text{DR-M}$$

This operation has no pre-condition (there is no pre-condition for Create-Meeting_0), so it is total.

The next operation is to cancel a meeting.

$$\text{Cancel-Meeting}_1 \; \triangleq \; \text{M-OP} \wedge \text{Cancel-Meeting}_0 \wedge \equiv\text{CR-M} \wedge \equiv\text{DR-M}$$

We can determine the pre-condition for this operation as follows: first we establish the constraint arising from the system invariant. The operation removes an element from exists_M so this element cannot be a user in CR-M or DR-M during the period $t?_M$. Formally, we require that

$$\forall \; t \; : \; t?_M \bullet r?_{M-V} \notin \text{users}_{CR-M}(t) \cup \text{users}_{DR-M}(\text{date-of-session}(t))$$

The second part of the pre-condition arises from the earlier pre-condition for Cancel-Meeting_0. This is precisely

$$t?_M = t?_{M-V} \; \wedge \; x?_M = r?_{M-V} \wedge (\forall t:t?_{M-V} \bullet r?_{M-V} \in \text{dom}(ru_{M-V}(t)) \;).$$

We shall at this point fulfil the promise made in section 4.1, *viz.*, indicating how to define the corresponding total operation. This is formed by the *disjunction* of the successful operation with the schema which takes as its qualifying predicate the *negation* of the pre-condition established above.

```
┌─ Cancel-Meeting-Fail ──────────────────────────────────────────┐
│  ≡CAVIAR
│  t?_{M-V} : P Session
│  t?_M : P Session
│  x?_M : M
│  r?_{M-V} : M
│ ─────────────────────────────────────
│  (∃ t : t?_M •
│        r?_{M-V} ∈ (users_{CR-M}(t) ∪ users_{DR-M}(date-of-session(t))))
│  ∨ t?_M ≠ t?_{M-V}
│  ∨ x?_M ≠ r?_{M-V}
│  ∨ (∃t:t?_{M-V} • r?_{M-V} ∉ dom(ru_{M-V}(t)) )
└─────────────────────────────────────────────────────────────────┘
```

$$\text{Cancel-Meeting} \triangleq \text{Cancel-Meeting}_1 \vee \text{Cancel-Meeting-Fail}$$

Informally, if the required pre-condition for the meeting cancellation is not satisfied, the system is unchanged. In practice, we would require an appropriate error message to be output.

For the sake of brevity, we shall present the remainder of the operations without going through this process.

The next two operations add visitors to, and delete visitors from, a meeting.

```
Add-Visitor-to-Meeting ≜
        M-OP ∧ Add-Visitor-to-Meeting_0 ∧ ≡CR-M ∧ ≡DR-M

Remove-Visitor-from-Meeting ≜
        M-OP ∧ Remove-Visitor-from-Meeting_0 ∧ ≡CR-M ∧ ≡DR-M
```

The pre-conditions for these operations are straightforward to determine in the usual way, and we shall omit them and those for the remaining operations also.

The next two operations deal with conference rooms.

```
Book-Conf-Room   ≜  M-OP ∧ ≡M-V ∧ Book-Conf-Room_0   ∧ ≡DR-M

Cancel-Conf-Room ≜  M-OP ∧ ≡M-V ∧ Cancel-Conf-Room_0 ∧ ≡DR-M
```

We now have the two operations concerning dining rooms.

$$\text{Book-Dining-Room} \quad \triangleq \text{M-OP} \wedge \equiv\text{M-V} \wedge \equiv\text{CR-M} \wedge \text{Book-Dining-Room}_0$$

$$\text{Cancel-Dining-Room} \quad \triangleq \text{M-OP} \wedge \equiv\text{M-V} \wedge \equiv\text{CR-M} \wedge \text{Cancel-Dining-Room}_0$$

There is one final operation to be defined in this section: namely the cancellation of both dining room and conference room(s) associated with a particular meeting. This is **not** the conjunct of the two cancellation operations already given because each of these leaves the components it is not acting on **fixed**. Hence we need a different operation defined by

$$\text{Cancel-Meeting-Arrangements} \quad \triangleq$$
$$\text{M-OP} \wedge \equiv\text{M-V} \wedge \text{Cancel-Conf-Room}_0 \wedge \text{Cancel-Dining-Room}_0$$

9.2.2 Operations which involve visitors only

This section contains operations which involve V-SYS only and leave M-SYS unchanged. We denote this group by

$$\text{V-OP} \quad \triangleq \quad \Delta\text{CAVIAR} \wedge \equiv\text{M-SYS}$$

The first pair of operations introduce visitors to and remove visitors from the visitor system.

$$\text{Create-Visitor} \quad \triangleq \quad \text{V-OP} \wedge \text{Create-Visitor}_0 \wedge \equiv\text{HR-V} \wedge \equiv\text{TR-V}$$

$$\text{Destroy-Visitor} \triangleq \quad \text{V-OP} \wedge \text{Destroy-Visitor}_0 \wedge \equiv\text{HR-V} \wedge \equiv\text{TR-V}$$

The Caviar invariant induces the following pre-condition for the Destroy operation.

$$\forall t : t?_V \bullet x?_V \notin \text{users}_{HR-V}(t)$$
$$\cup \cup \{ t : \text{date-of-time}^{-1}(\!(t?_V)\!) \bullet \text{users}_{TR-V}(t) \}$$
$$\cup \cup \{ s : \text{date-of-session}^{-1}(\!(t?_V)\!) \bullet \text{users}_{M-V}(s) \}$$

The two operations concerned with hotel rooms are as follows:

$$\text{Book-Hotel-Room} \quad \triangleq \text{V-OP} \wedge \equiv\text{V-P} \wedge \text{Book-Hotel-Room}_0 \quad \wedge \equiv\text{TR-V}$$

$$\text{Cancel-Hotel-Room} \triangleq \text{V-OP} \wedge \equiv\text{V-P} \wedge \text{Cancel-Hotel-Room}_0 \wedge \equiv\text{TR-V}$$

The two operations concerned with transport reservations are

Book-Transport $\triangleq$ V-OP $\wedge$ $\equiv$V-P $\wedge$ $\equiv$HR-V $\wedge$ Book-Transport$_0$

Cancel-Transport $\triangleq$ V-OP $\wedge$ $\equiv$V-P $\wedge$ $\equiv$HR-V $\wedge$ Cancel-Transport$_0$

9.2.3 A general visitor removal operation

Finally we define an operation which removes a visitor entirely from the system for a particular set of dates.

```
┌─ Delete-Visitor ─────────────────────────────────────────────┐
│ ΔCAVIAR                                                        │
│ ≡CR-M                                                          │
│ ≡DR-M                                                          │
│ Cancel-Hotel-Room₀                                            │
│ Cancel-Transport₀                                            │
│ Remove-Visitor-from-Meeting₀                                 │
│ Destroy-Visitor₀                                             │
├───────────────────────────────────────────────────────────────┤
│ x?ᵥ = u?_HR-V = u?_TR-V = u?_M-V ∧                           │
│ t?ᵥ = t?_HR-V ∧                                              │
│ t?_TR-V = { d : t?ᵥ; t : Time | date-of-time(t) = d          │
│                          ∧ u?_TR-V ∈ users_TR-V(t) • t } ∧   │
│ t?_M-V = { d : t?ᵥ; s : Session | date-of-session(s) = d     │
│                          ∧ u?_M-V ∈ users_M-V(s) • s }       │
└───────────────────────────────────────────────────────────────┘
```

10. Conclusion

This specification has created a conceptual model for the CAVIAR system which provides a precise description of the system state and its external interface, together with an exact functional specification of every operation. The subtle inter-relationships between constituent subsystems are described in the predicates which constrain the combination of these subsystems, and these have been taken into account in the specification of the operations. The system designer can now concentrate on the important parts of the design task: namely selecting appropriate data structures and algorithms, without having to be simultaneously concerned with the complexity of subsystem interactions. This reflects the classical principle of *separation of concerns*.

It may be argued that a specification such as we have given above is far from being an actual product. Experience shows, however, that such specifications reduce substantially the effort required to develop executable software. And in the case of CAVIAR, a Pascal implementation was constructed directly and quickly, working from the specification.

11. Acknowledgements

A formal specification of CAVIAR was given in 1981 by J.-R. Abrial. This work was carried out at the Programming Research Group at Oxford University in collaboration with B. Sufrin, T. Clement and one of the co-authors. T. Clement implemented a prototype version of the specification on an ITT-2020 computer in UCSD Pascal. J.-R. Abrial's original specification document listed most of the properties of the system that appear in this document, though the style of the presentation, the notation, and the conventions used in this paper have since been developed by members of the Programming Research Group.

We would like to thank J.-R. Abrial for his original contribution, I. Hayes for editing this paper and all those involved in helping with the project, particularly the personnel in the Visitor Services Department of STL, who willingly provided the team with information about the current manual system in operation at that time.

We would also like to thank Bernie Cohen, Tim Denvir and Tom Cox for their initial effort in setting up this collaborative effort between STL and the Programming Research Group and their continuing interest.

12. References and Related Work

1. Abrial, J.-R. The specification language Z: Basic library. *Oxford University Programming Research Group internal report*, (April 1980).

2. Morgan, C. C.   Schemas in Z: A preliminary reference manual. *Oxford University Programming Research Group Distributed Computing Project report*, (March 1984).

3. Sufrin, B. A., Sørensen, I. H., Morgan, C. C., and Hayes, I. J. Notes for a Z Handbook. *Oxford University Programming Research Group internal report*, (July 1985).

4. Morgan, C. C., and Sufrin, B. A. Specification of the UNIX file system. *IEEE Transactions on Software Engineering*, Vol. *10*, *No. 2*, (March 1984), pp. 128-142 (and in part B of this monograph).

13. Index of schemas and components

Following is an index of schema and component names. The first column gives the name of the schema or component; the second column, when present, gives the schema within which the name occurs; and the third column gives the page number of the occurrence.

Towards a Formal Specification
of the
ICL Data Dictionary

Bernard Sufrin

Abstract

We present a formal specification of the ICL Data Dictionary
system, paying particular attention to the facilities it provides
for controlling the retrieval and updating of dictionary
elements. We conclude by suggesting some modifications to the
design which would render the system simpler to understand
and to implement whilst retaining its full power. The
specification notation Z, which is based on set theory,
[Sufrin83&84], *[Morgan84]* is used, and familiarity with the
mathematical notions of predicate, set, relation and function is
assumed throughout.

Background

The potential benefits of applying formal, or at least mathematically rigorous, methods to the design and production of software are currently a topic of much discussion and have been eloquently expounded elsewhere, for example in [Hoare82] and in [Jones80]. In common with many others, we believe that the time is ripe, perhaps even overripe, for the application of these methods in an industrial context. This report arose out of a challenge from ICL to work with a group of their practising programmers to investigate the applicability of the methods to a real commercial product, the ICL Data Dictionary system (henceforward DDS). The company sponsored a ten-day pilot project, during which we used mathematical techniques to investigate two areas of DDS which its designers believe to be difficult to understand and explain, namely the means provided for controlling access to dictionary elements, and the support provided for multiple versions. Here we report on our investigation of access control.

1. Introduction

It is by now a matter of common knowledge that a substantial proportion of the total costs of "bugs" discovered during the lifetime of a computer-based system can be attributed to mistakes made during the earliest stages of its development. It is for this reason that we believe that the most appropriate time to construct — and to use — a formal specification for a large system is before the system is built. Why, then, attempt a mathematical specification of parts of a software product which is already several years old? Firstly, the standard DDS documentation of access control is rather difficult to understand, partly because the answers to many questions can only be discovered by reading the complete product documentation in its entirety. A concise formal description of the dictionary system from which the answers to questions about access can easily be deduced will be useful in its own right, and perhaps provide a basis for better product documentation. Secondly, a by-product of the specification activity will be the construction of a conceptual framework within which the consequences of simplifying the design of the system can be investigated. Thirdly, even though we hardly expect the majority of DDS users to be able to read a mathematical specification, in order to produce it at all we are forced to ask questions of the implementers of the system which the product documentation presently fails to answer adequately. These questions and their answers will certainly be of use to the authors of subsequent editions of the product documentation. Finally, if used in the spirit that it was made, the specification should also help to ensure compatibility of successive versions and new implementations of the Dictionary.

2. Overview of the Data Dictionary System

The potential application areas of the Data Dictionary system are outlined in detail in the first chapter of its reference manual [ICL]. In essence it is a database system specially adapted to the needs of supporting the construction, documentation and maintenance of collections of programs which must be kept mutually consistent. Such collections are to be found at computer installations everywhere, and without computer-based support they can quickly become very difficult to manage.

For the purposes of this report it is enough for us to note that the system provides a means of naming, storing, manipulating, and enquiring about any number of *elements* each of which may have several named *properties* which possess *values*. Some properties are possessed only by certain types of element, for example the *TITLE-PAGE property of REPORT-PROGRAM elements. Other properties may be possessed by any or all elements but are never acted upon by DDS, for example the *DESCRIPTION and *NOTE properties, whose values are uninterpreted text. Finally there is a class of properties which are administrative in nature and may be possessed by any or all elements and which are interpreted (acted upon) by the DDS, for example the *PRIVACY and *AUTHORITY properties which are possessed by almost all elements. It is by setting administrative properties such as these that an administrator may control aspects of the behaviour of a Data Dictionary at a particular installation, and users may control how the elements they define can be manipulated by others.

In order to begin constructing a mathematical model we must first introduce some nomenclature. Let P denote the set of all possible names for *properties* possessed by elements in the database, and let V denote the set of all possible *values* which these properties may take. For the moment we need not investigate the internal structure of the sets P and V, although we will do so later.

In the manual, the term "element" means an object consisting of a collection of named properties which have values. Such an object may be modelled as a finite mapping from property names to values. Let E denote the set of all possible elements storable in a DDS database; we define it formally by:

$$E \triangleq P \nrightarrow V$$

Notice that this definition merely explains the essence of "elementhood", but gives us no clues about how to represent elements using the data structures which are available in a conventional programming language.

If we take some liberties with the way in which we write values, and suppose that *authority, description, note,* and *privacy* are among the possible property names, then we can give a couple of (possibly untypical) examples of elements:

{ *authority* ↦ Bernard; *description* ↦ "Formal Documentation" }

{ *authority* ↦ Bernard; *privacy* ↦ 99; *note* ↦ "What's a note?" }

The term "element identifier" means the *name* by which an element is known to the DDS. If we let EI denote the set of *all possible* element identifiers, then the current state of a DDS may be modelled as an object from the set

EI ⇸ E   which can be expanded to EI ⇸ (P ⇸ V)

That is to say, a mapping from element identifiers to elements, which are themselves mappings from property names to storable values. Notice that in order to describe the state of a DDS at this level of abstraction it is not necessary for us to give details of the internal structure of element identifiers, although we will be forced to reveal this structure later.

3. Access Control

In the first part of this section we present a sequence of successively more accurate descriptions of the abstract information structures of a DDS which support access control. We do so without making explicit the fact that the dictionaries are self-describing — in the sense that these information structures are completely described by elements present in the dictionaries themselves. In the second part we consider the state of a running DDS, and show how some simple commands issued by users affect that state. In the third part we demonstrate in detail the relationship between our abstract description and the stored elements with which the dictionary implements the structures introduced in the first. Finally we describe several more complex commands, whose effects depend on the details just demonstrated.

3.1 Abstract Information Structures of DDS

Our first approximation is rather simple; we simply observe the set of element names known to the system and the correspondence between these names and their stored

values.   More formally, we define a schema DD which characterises the possible
states of a DDS.

```
 ___ DD _____
| elements:  F EI                               |
| store:     EI -+> E                           |
|_____                        |
| elements = dom store                          |
|_____|
```

The predicate below the bar records the invariant relationship we expect to hold
between the two observations: the element names which are known to the system are
exactly those which correspond to elements in the store.

A formalisation at this level of abstraction could serve as the basis of a model for the
data stored in *any* entity-attribute database! Since it fails to take into account the
specific characteristics of DDS that we are trying to explain, we shall discard it.

In our second approximation we record the fact that some elements have owners.
These are called *authority elements* in the product documentation, and form the
basis for one of the methods by which access to elements is controlled. When an
ordinary user runs one of the DDS programs, he may do so under the aegis of an
authority. His access to elements in the dictionary depends amongst other things upon
this authority.

We begin to formalise this situation by introducing additional observations, namely
the finite set of authority element identifiers which have been introduced by the
dictionary administrator into the system, and a mapping from the identifiers of stored
elements to those of their owners.

```
 ┌─ DD ──────────────────────────────────┐
 │   store:     EI ⇻ E                    │
 │   elements: F EI                       │
 │   auth:      F EI                      │
 │   owner:     EI ⇻ EI                   │
 ├────────────────────────────           │
 │   elements  = dom store               │
 │   ran owner ⊆ auth ⊆ elements         │
 │   dom owner ⊆ elements - auth         │
 └────────────────────────────────────────┘
```

The new predicates below the bar record the additional invariant relationships between our observations: all owners of elements must be authority elements, all authority elements must be present in the store, but no authority element has an owner.

Notice that the last predicate is such that not all elements need an owner; indeed it is consistent with a state in which *no* elements have owners. It turns out that it is easier to explain the system if we invent a special "mythical" authority — the nil authority, and insist that every non-authority element has an owner (which might be the nil authority). We formalise this in two steps: first we introduce a constant element identifier, nil, to stand for the identifier of the mythical nil authority.

```
│ nil: EI
```

Next we give a new description of a DDS state, which incorporates the second approximation but strengthens the invariant with two additional predicates: the first states that nil is an authority element, and the second that *all* non-authority elements must now have owners.

```
 ┌─ DD ──────────────────────────────────┐
 │   DD                                  │
 ├────────────────────────────           │
 │   nil ∈ auth                          │
 │   dom owner = elements - auth         │
 └────────────────────────────────────────┘
```

Technical Note: In our formalism, this description is not self-referential, but is an extension of DD – i.e. a redefinition which incorporates the prevailing definition. Of course for such an extension to be useful, the predicates which are added should be consistent with those already present.

We now engage in a little speculation (with the best of pedagogical motives): if the DDS designers had had an authoritarian or individualistic cast of mind, they might have stopped their design activity at this point and insisted that only the owner of an element can retrieve or update it. Under these circumstances we would have been able to end our modelling activity by making just one more observation of the state of a dictionary: the relation canaccess, which can be completely determined by the values of the remaining observations of DD, holds between an authority and an element exactly when that authority would allow access to the element.

```
┌─ AuthoritarianDD ──────────────────────────────┐
│ DD                                               
│ canaccess:    EI ↔ EI
│ ────────────────────────
│ ∀ user:auth; elt:elements •
│    user canaccess elt ⟺ owner elt = user
└─────────────────────────────────────────────────┘
```

Technical Note: In this extension we have added a new observation as well as an additional invariant to the definition of DD.

A marginally more libertarian group of designers might have interpreted ownership by the nil authority somewhat differently and allowed anybody to retrieve or update such elements:

```
┌─ NotQuiteSoAuthoritarianDD ─────────────────────┐
│ DD                                               
│ canaccess:    EI ↔ EI
│ ────────────────────────
│ ∀ user:auth; elt:elements •
│    user canaccess elt ⟺ owner elt ∈ {user, nil}
└─────────────────────────────────────────────────┘
```

As might be expected the ICL designers wanted to make their system a little more flexible than either of these descriptions indicate and we find both that they have included a number of ways in which elements may be shared between authorities and that they distinguish between retrieval and updating.

An authority may delegate rights to retrieve an element to one or more other authorities. We formalise this by introducing the relation delegates, which holds between an authority a and an authority a' if and only if a has taken steps to permit a' to retrieve all the elements which a owns.

```
┌ DD ─────────────────────────────────────────┐
│ DD                                           │
│ delegates: EI ↔ EI                           │
├──────────────────────────────┤              │
│ delegates ∈ (auth ↔ auth)                    │
└──────────────────────────────────────────────┘
```

Rights to a *single* element may be given by its owner to another authority, so we introduce another relation, mayretrieve, which holds between an authority a and an element e only if e's owner has explicitly taken steps to allow a to retrieve it.

```
┌ DD ─────────────────────────────────────────┐
│ DD                                           │
│ mayretrieve: EI ↔ EI                         │
├──────────────────────────────┤              │
│ dom mayretrieve ⊆ auth                       │
│ ran mayretrieve ⊆ elements - auth            │
└──────────────────────────────────────────────┘
```

As we shall see in the next section, part of the stored description of an authority element is a description of the types of element which it may not update. Since our description is not yet at a level of detail which includes types, we can discuss the right of an authority to *update* an element in the database only in rather general terms. In order to begin the discussion we add a relation maynotupdate to our observations. This relation holds between a declared authority and the names of elements which it has explicitly been forbidden to update; these can include elements which are not yet in the store.

```
┌─ DD ────────────────────────────────────┐
│  DD                                      │
│  maynotupdate: EI ↔ EI                   │
│  ─────────────────────────               │
│                                          │
│  dom maynotupdate ⊆ auth                 │
└──────────────────────────────┘
```

Note: Readers familiar with DDS will recognise that delegates
is closely related to the *RETRIEVE *property of authority
elements, that* mayretrieve *is related to the* *RETRIEVE
property of non-authority elements, and that maynotupdate *is
related to the* *INHIBIT *properties of authority elements.*

If the designers had stopped here, we would characterise an authority's rights to
retrieve and update elements by beginning to define the relation canretrieve which
holds between an authority and the elements it is permitted to retrieve, and the
relation canupdate which holds between an authority and the elements which the
system will allow it to update. At this stage the only thing we can say about the
updating is negative: namely that if an authority has explicitly been forbidden to
update an element then the system will prevent it from doing so.

```
┌─ DD ──────────────────────────────────────────────┐
│  DD                                                │
│  canretrieve: EI ↔ EI                              │
│  canupdate:   EI ↔ EI                              │
│  ──────────────────────                            │
│                                                    │
│  ∀ user:auth; elt: elements •                      │
│      ( owner elt ∈ {user, nil}    ∨                │
│        (owner elt) delegates user ∨                │
│        user mayretrieve elt       ) ⇒ user canretrieve elt │
│                                                    │
│  ∀ user:auth; elt: elements •                      │
│        (user maynotupdate elt)  ⇒ ¬ (user canupdate elt) │
└────────────────────────────────────────────┘
```

Although the system we have described above might have satisfied many designers, it
turns out that orthogonal to the system of ownership the DDS has a notion of *levels
of privacy*. Stored elements have a privacy level, which is a number between 0 and
99.

Level ≙ 0..99

Irrespective of the possibilities for retrieval afforded by the ownership system, a user running under the aegis of an authority may retrieve any element whose privacy level is less than or equal to that of the authority. (Incidentally, the product documentation indicates that the privacy level of an element may be higher than that of its owner, a fact which we find puzzling).

The nil authority is given a privacy level of 0, which reflects its role as the "owner" of elements intended to be universally retrievable. More formally

```
┌ DD ────────────────────────────────────────────────────────┐
│ DD                                                          │
│ privacy:    EI ⇸ Level                                      │
│ ───────────────────────────────────────────────            │
│ dom privacy = elements                                      │
│ privacy nil = 0                                             │
│                                                             │
│ ∀ user: auth; elt: elements •                               │
│    privacy elt ⩽ privacy user ⇒ user canretrieve elt        │
└─────────────────────────────────────────────────────────────┘
```

A dictionary administrator may decide for operational reasons to nominate one authority as the master authority. This authority (if one has been nominated) may retrieve and update any element in the dictionary, irrespective of ownership. A master authority should not be confused with the dictionary administrator: although the two roles might be played by the same person in many organisations, their functions are entirely different.

The only element which does not have a privacy level in the range 0..99 is the master authority (if there is one). For our purposes it will simplify matters if we attribute privacy level 99 to a master element if one exists: whilst this is not strictly in accordance with the choice of representation made by the ICL designers, its consequences are precisely the same. Note that the master authority (if there is one) may not be forbidden to udpate elements. Note also that, by virtue of its privacy level, the master authority has the right to retrieve any element at all.

```
┌─ DD ──────────────────────────────────────────┐
│  DD                                            │
│  master:    F¹ EI                              │
│  ──────────────────────────────────            │
│  master ⊆ auth                                 │
│  privacy (master) ⊆ {99}                       │
│  master ∩ (dom maynotupdate) = {}              │
└────────────────────────────────────────────────┘
```

Technical Note: F^1 EI *means a finite set of* EI *with at most one element.*

This almost concludes the first part of our description of the information structures which characterise a DDS and the invariant relations which hold between them. In Figure 1 we summarise these information structures, formally simplifying some of the predicates and recording two more things. The first of these is that the conditions hitherto outlined are the *only* conditions under which retrieval can take place: this is signified by strengthening the implications ($\Longrightarrow$) of DD to equivalences ($\Longleftrightarrow$). The second characterises updating more positively: an element may be updated by its owner or by the master authority. Notice that it is possible for a non-master authority which owns an element to be prevented from updating it.

Since we have not yet given any details of the structure of values, we have no way yet of recording the fact that the owner of a stored element is stored as its *authority* property. Nor can we record the fact that the set of authorities to whom an authority has delegated all his access rights is stored as the *retrieval* property of that authority element, and that the set of authorities which have been given the right of access to an element by its owner is stored as that element's *retrieval* property. We will only be able to go into these details after revealing more of the internal structure of stored values, element identifiers, and property names in section 3.3.

```
┌─ DD ──────────────────────────────────────────────────────────┐
│                                                                 │
│  store:                                     EI ⇸ E             │
│  elements, auth:                            F EI              │
│  owner:                                     EI ⇸ EI           │
│  delegates, mayretrieve, maynotupdate:      EI ↔ EI          │
│  privacy:                                   EI ⇸ Level        │
│  master:                                    F¹ EI            │
│  canretrieve, canupdate:                    EI ↔ EI          │
│ ─────────────────────────                                      │
│                                                                 │
│  elements  = dom store                                          │
│  ran owner ⊆ auth ⊆ elements                                   │
│  dom owner ⊆ elements - auth                                    │
│                                                                 │
│  nil ∈ auth                                                     │
│  dom owner = elements - auth                                    │
│                                                                 │
│  delegates ∈ (auth ↔ auth)                                     │
│  dom mayretrieve ⊆ auth                                         │
│  ran mayretrieve ⊆ elements - auth                              │
│  dom maynotupdate ⊆ auth                                        │
│                                                                 │
│  dom privacy = elements                                         │
│  privacy nil = 0                                                │
│  master ⊆ auth                                                  │
│  privacy (master) ⊆ {99}                                      │
│  master ∩ (dom maynotupdate) = {}                              │
│                                                                 │
│  (∀ user:auth; elt:elements • user canretrieve elt ⇔          │
│        user = owner elt                    ∨                   │
│        (owner elt) delegates user          ∨                   │
│        user mayretrieve elt                ∨                   │
│        privacy elt ≤ privacy user)                             │
│                                                                 │
│  (∀ user:auth; elt:EI • user canupdate elt ⇔                  │
│        user ∈ {owner elt} ∪ master ∧                          │
│        ¬(user maynotupdate elt))                               │
│                                                                 │
└─────────────────────────────────────────────────────────────┘
```

Figure 1: Summary of the Information Structures of a DDS

3.2 DDS Dynamics: Part 1

In this section and its companion we describe the way in which certain commands affect DDS information structures. In fact there are two distinct kinds of DDS run: administrative runs during which administrative commands may be issued, and ordinary runs during which they may not. For the purposes of our investigation the main difference is that certain kinds of element (in particular *AUTHORITY elements) may be inserted only during administrative runs, but otherwise may not.

Although one might expect the administrator to be the same as the master authority, this turns out not to be so. For simplicity, therefore, we have avoided consideration of administrative commands and concentrated on the most important non administrative commands. Later we suggest a small simplification of the design which would avoid the distinction between administrative and ordinary runs.

3.2.1 The State of a Running DDS

In characterising the state of a running DDS we must account for the fact that users "log in" under the aegis of an authority, which is deemed in our model to be the nil authority for those users who run under "no authority". In fact a password-based scheme is used to check that an individual has the right to log in as a particular authority, but the details of logging in are beyond the scope of this report.

Once the running authority is established, elements are processed by establishing the "element context", i.e. the identifier of the element to which subsequent commands will refer. One thing which the product documentation doesn't make quite clear is whether or not the element context identified by the user must always refer to an already-defined element. This seems plausible, however, since there is a special element whose identifier is null; the null element context prevails at the beginning of a run, after certain classes of errors, and after the stop command has been issued. We therefore introduce a constant

| null: EI

and characterise the state of a running DDS by:

```
 ┌─ DDS ──────────────────────────────────┐
 │  DD
 │  user:              EI
 │  elementcontext:    EI
 ├─────────────────────────────
 │  user ∈ auth
 │  null ∈ elements
 │  ∀ a: auth • a mayaccess null
 │  user canretrieve elementcontext
 └─────────────────────────────────────────┘
```

It is worth noting that the final constraint is a requirement *imposed* on the user, namely that he should be *able* to retrieve the element to which commands will subsequently refer.

In order to capture the effect of a command on a DDS, we relate the observations made before the command is performed (denoted by the undashed names) to those which can be made afterwards (denoted by dashed names). As is customary we factorise our description of the commands into those properties which all the commands have in common and those which are peculiar to particular commands.

The schema ΔDDS summarise the common characteristics of the effects of non-administrative commands on a DDS: the set of declared authorities may not change, nor may the master authority, nor may the authority of the running user.

```
 ┌─ ΔDDS ─────────────────────────────────┐
 │  DDS
 │  DDS'
 ├─────────────────────────────
 │  auth'   = auth
 │  master' = master
 │  user'   = user
 └─────────────────────────────────────────┘
```

Some commands change the element context, or just display parts of the stored dictionary, but don't change the information structures concerned with access control; their additional common properties are summarised in the schema ⎕DDS

```
 ⌈─ ⟦DDS ──────────────────────────────────────┐
 │  ΔDDS                                        ┘
 │  ────────────────────
 │
 │  owner'       = owner
 │  delegates'   = delegates
 │  privacy'     = privacy
 │  mayretrieve'    = mayretrieve
 │  maynotupdate'   = maynotupdate
 └──────────────────────────────────────────┘
```

3.2.2 The Display Command

The simplest command to describe is the DISPLAY command, which displays parts of the current element in a readable form. Below, we simply indicate that the user must supply some property names, and that on completion of the command he is presented (readable') with the values of the required properties as stored for the element currently in context. We do not concern ourselves with the precise form in which the display is presented.

```
 ⌈─ Display ───────────────────────────────────┐
 │  properties: F P                            ┘
 │  ⟦DDS
 │  readable':  P↛V
 │  ────────────────────
 │
 │  #properties=1 ∨ properties=P
 │  readable' = properties ◁ (store elementcontext)
 │  store' = store
 │  elementcontext' = elementcontext
 └──────────────────────────────────────────┘
```

(Those familiar with DDS should note that the ALLPROPERTIES variant of the DISPLAY command corresponds to properties=P whilst the *property-keyword variant corresponds to #properties=1. In order to simplify our description we have not formalised either the PROMPTLIST or the EXPLOSION variants of this command. To do either would require a more detailed model than we have so far presented, though the detail is not complex.)

3.2.3 Setting the Element Context

One command which plays at least three roles in the system is the FOR command: all three variants of which the author is aware set "context" in one way or another. They are:

FOR VERSION   `<version element identifier>`

FOR AUTHORITY `<authority element identifier>`

FOR `<element identifier>`

Since we do not treat version control here, we shall not consider the first of these. The second corresponds to the beginning of a DDS run: it just sets the user authority after checking a password and we shall not consider it here either. The third command is used to set the current element context: it sets the null context if presented with an element name which the current authority is not allowed to retrieve, or one which has not yet been defined.

```
┌─FOR ──────────────────────────────────────────────────┐
│   eid: EI                                              │
│   ⍙DDS                                                 │
├────────────────────────────                            │
│                                                        │
│   store' = store                                       │
│                                                        │
│   user canretrieve eid      ∧                          │
│   eid ∈ elements            ∧                          │
│   elementcontext' = eid                                │
│ ∨                                                      │
│   eid ∉ elements            ∧                          │
│   elementcontext' = null                               │
│ ∨                                                      │
│   ¬(user canretrieve eid)   ∧                          │
│   elementcontext' = null                               │
└────────────────────────────────────────────────────────┘
```

This concludes our account of the commands which have no effect on the stored information. Before we can describe the remaining commands it will be necessary for us to take a small detour and explain the relationship between the stored elements and the access-control information.

3.3 The Representation of Access-Control Information

In this section we formalise the fact that data dictionaries are self-describing. To put this another way, the abstract information structures which we introduced in order to explain the control of access to elements are actually represented by means of elements and properties stored in the dictionary.

In a DDS the properties named *AUTHORITY, *PRIVACY, and *RETRIEVAL are defined for most elements, so we introduce distinct constants into our specification which will henceforth stand for these property names:

> $authority,\ privacy,\ retrieval\colon\ \mathsf{P}$
> ___
> $authority \neq privacy \neq retrieval \neq authority$

Technical Note: "a≠b≠c≠d" *abbreviates* "a≠b ∧ b≠c ∧ c≠d".

Properties may take values from a variety of types, but in the first part of this section the only types we shall be concerned with are the numbers, N, single element identifiers, EI, and finite sets of element identifiers, $\mathsf{F}\ EI$. We can formalise the idea that elements of these types can all be represented as values by introducing the three injective functions:

> $\text{Number:} \quad \mathsf{N} \rightarrowtail \mathsf{V}$
> $\text{Element:} \quad EI \rightarrowtail \mathsf{V}$
> $\text{Elements:}\ (\mathsf{F}\ EI) \rightarrowtail \mathsf{V}$
> ___
> $\text{disjoint [ran Number, ran Element, ran Elements]}$

Technical Note: The definition above signifies that V *contains exactly one value for each number* $n\colon\mathsf{N}$, *one value for each single element identifier* $ei\colon EI$, *and one value for each set of element identifiers* $eis\colon\mathsf{F}\ EI$. *These values are distinct and denoted respectively by the terms* $\text{Number } n$, $\text{Element } ei$, *and* $\text{Elements } eis$.

All that now needs doing is to strengthen the invariant of the existing DDS description. In Figure 2 we summarise the qualities inherent in our use of the term "self-describing."

```
┌─ DD ──────────────────────────────────────────────────────────┐
│ DD                                                             │
│ has: EI ↔ P                                                    │
│ ─────────────────────────────                                 │
│                                                               │
│ ∀ ei: EI; p: P •                                              │
│   ei has p ⟺ ei ∈ elements ∧ p ∈ dom(store ei)               │
│                                                               │
│ ∀ ei: elements •                                              │
│   ei has privacy ∧ Number(privacy ei) = store ei privacy  ∨   │
│   ¬(ei has privacy) ∧ privacy ei = 0                          │
│                                                               │
│ ∀ a: auth •                                                   │
│   a has retrieval ∧ Elements(delegates⟦ a ⟧) = store a retrieval ∨ │
│   ¬(a has retrieval) ∧ delegates⟦ a ⟧ = {}                    │
│                                                               │
│ ∀ ei: (elements - auth) •                                     │
│   (ei has retrieval ∧                                         │
│    Elements(mayretrieve⁻¹⟦ ei ⟧) = store ei retrieval         │
│   )                                                           │
│   ∨                                                           │
│   ¬(ei has retrieval) ∧ mayretrieve⁻¹⟦ ei ⟧ = {}             │
│                                                               │
│ ∀ ei: (elements - auth) •                                     │
│   ei has authority ∧ Element(owner ei) = store ei authority ∨ │
│   ¬(ei has authority) ∧ owner ei = nil                        │
│                                                               │
└────────────────────────────────────────────────────────────────┘
```

Figure 2: Data Dictionaries are Self-Describing

In order to simplify our account of the default values provided by the system, we have introduced an additional observation: the relation has which holds between an element identifier ei and a property name p exactly when ei has been stored with a property named p. The first additional predicate records the fact that the privacy level of each stored element is represented by the numeric value of its privacy property. The second predicate records that the retrieval property of each authority element represents the set of authorities who stand in the relation <u>delegates</u> to it. The third predicate records that the value of the retrieval property of each non-authority element represents the set of authorities which may retrieve it, and the fourth predicate that its authority property represents its owner. Notice the different intepretations given to the *retrieval* property of an authority element and the same property of a non-authority element.

Hitherto we have given a rather abstract characterisation of the information structure which prevents certain authorities updating certain types of element, but we are now in a position to give a fuller account. In order to do so we need to examine the structure of the space of element identifiers (EI) in a little more detail. In fact this space is two dimensional; an element is identified by an element-type-identifier (known in the product documentation as an element keyword) and a within-type identifier. If we let K denote the set of element type identifiers, and I denote the set of within-type identifiers, then we can define

$$EI \cong K \times I$$

An authority is prevented from updating certain types of element if the element which describes it has a property called *INHIBIT. The value of this property is the set of element type identifiers to which the authority is denied update rights — despite any retrieval rights it may have. First we introduce another constant:

inhibit: P

inhibit $\notin$ {*authority, retrieval, privacy*}

and indicate that sets of element type identifiers may also be stored:

Types: **F** K $\rightarrowtail$ V

disjoint [ran Types, ran Number, ran Element, ran Elements]

We then strengthen the DD invariant a little further, to indicate that the type keyword of the element identifier is one of the set of keywords stored as the *INHIBIT property of the authority a:

```
┌─ DD ─────────────────────────────────────────────────────────────┐
│  DD                                                               │
│  ──────────────────────────                                       │
│                                                                   │
│  ∀ a: auth; et:K; i:I •                                           │
│    a maynotupdate (et, i)  ⇔                                      │
│       a has inhibit  ∧  et ∈ Types⁻¹(store a inhibit)             │
│                                                                   │
└───────────────────────────────────────────────────────────────────┘
```

Our account of self-description is now as detailed as it needs to be for the purposes of this report. Interested readers may care to take the account further and formalise the fact that details of the properties possessed by elements of each type are recorded in the database, as are details of the representation of each property. As a hint, we will show how the authority elements in the dictionary are identified. First we introduce the constant

$$AUERITY\colon K$$

to denote the **AUTHORITY** element keyword.

> *Note: In fact all elements with the same type have property names drawn from the same set of names; these are stored as the* *SYSTEM-PROPERTIES and *USER-PROPERTIES properties of the element which describes the type. A complete formalisation of this is possible within the framework we have already established, but goes beyond the scope of this report.*

All that remains is to strengthen the DD invariant yet again.

```
┌─ DD ─────────────────────────────────────────────────────────────┐
│  DD                                                               │
│  ──────────────────────────                                       │
│                                                                   │
│  auth = { (k, i):elements | k = AUTHORITY }                       │
│                                                                   │
└───────────────────────────────────────────────────────────────────┘
```

In other words, the authority elements are exactly those whose keyword is **AUTHORITY.**

3.4 DDS Dynamics: Part 2

In this section we complete our description of the DDS commands with a formalisation of the behaviour of the INSERT and DELETE commands. The REPLACE command is simply a combination of DELETE followed by INSERT, so we leave its formalisation as an exercise for interested readers. Our formalisation is partial, in the sense that we account only for the behaviour of successful commands. Whilst behaviour in the case of erroneous commands can easily be described within the present framework, doing so would not be particularly useful, especially in view of the simplifications we have made (see Appendix to this paper).

3.4.1 Inserting Elements

From its description in the product documentation, the INSERT command appears to have two variants. The first takes a new element identifier and a set of property-name, property-value pairs — in other words, an element — and stores the element as the value of the identifier. If no *authority* property is given, then the owner of the new element will be the current user; if no *privacy* property is given, then the element will be given the privacy level of the current user.

The command sets the current element context.

```
┌─ InsertNewElement ──────────────────────────────────────────┐
│ eid:          EI                                             │
│ newelement:  P ⇻ V                                           │
│ ΔDDS                                                         │
│ ┌───────────────────────────                                │
│                                                             │
│  eid ∉ dom store                                            │
│  store' = store ⊕ { eid ↦ newelement' }                     │
│  elementcontext' = eid                                      │
│  where                                                      │
│  newelement' =                                              │
│      { authority ↦ user; privacy ↦ privacy user } ⊕ newelement │
└─────────────────────────────────────────────────────────────┘
```

This description is such that if the *privacy* and *authority* properties are specified in such a way that `elementcontext'` is no longer accessible, then the insert operation will fail (the last invariant of DDS will not be satisfied). It seems to indicate that a user running under one authority can add an element to the database but give ownership rights to another authority. Whilst we found this rather difficult to rationalise, we could not discover anything in the documentation which forbids it. On asking the designers what really happens — an option which might not be open to the average DDS user — we discovered that only the master authority can give ownership rights to another authority when creating a new element. When the current user is not the master and *authority* and *privacy* properties are supplied, then they must be the ones which the system would provide by default anyway. Formalised concisely we have:

```
┌─ InsertNewElement ──────────────────────────────────────┐
│ InsertNewElement                                         │
│ ─────────────────────                                    │
│                                                          │
│ user ∉ master  ⟹                                         │
│     newelement⟦ authority ⟧ ⊆ {user} ∧                   │
│     newelement⟦ privacy   ⟧ ⊆ {privacy user}             │
└──────────────────────────────────────────────────────────┘
```

The second variant of the insert command takes a set of property-name, property-value pairs and incorporates them into the current element, providing that it has no existing property with any of the names supplied.

```
┌─ InsertNewProperties ───────────────────────────────────┐
│ newprops: P ↠ V                                          │
│ ΔDDS                                                     │
│ ──────────────────                                       │
│                                                          │
│ user canupdate elementcontext                            │
│ ¬∃ p:(dom newprops) • elementcontext has p               │
│ store' =                                                 │
│     store ⊕                                              │
│     { elementcontext ↦ ((store elementcontext) ∪ newprops) } │
│ elementcontext' = elementcontext                         │
└──────────────────────────────────────────────────────────┘
```

The documentation does not make it clear whether or not administrative properties may be added to an element by authorities other than its owner once it has been inserted. On asking the designers, we discovered that the only administrative property for which the description given above fails to account is the *authority* property: the master authority can give ownership of an unowned element to any authority, but non-master authorities can only take the ownership of such elements for themselves. More formally:

```
┌─ InsertNewProperties ──────────────────────┐
│  InsertNewProperties                        │
│  ────────────────────────                   │
│                                             │
│  authority ∈ dom newprops  ⟹               │
│      user ∈ master ∨                        │
│      newprops authority = user              │
└─────────────────────────────────────────────┘
```

3.4.2 Deleting Elements

DELETE appears in two variants: in the first, the user explicitly mentions an element for the command to delete:

```
┌─ DeleteElement ──────────────────────┐
│  eid:    EI                           │
│  ΔDDS                                 │
│  ─────────────────────                │
│                                       │
│  user canupdate eid                   │
│  store'            = {eid} ◁ store    │
│  elementcontext'  = null              │
└───────────────────────────────────────┘
```

In its second form, the user mentions some properties to be removed from the current element. Unfortunately, the documentation does not make it clear whether or not users may delete administrative properties from elements to which they have update rights, nor is it quite clear what happens if the last remaining property of an element is deleted. At first we assumed, albeit uneasily, that administrative properties can be deleted, and that elements with no properties can remain in the store, so to that extent our formalisation was inaccurate. Discussions with the implementation team proved our unease to be well founded; we learned that if administrative properties are deleted from an element by the user, then they revert to the default values which the system would have provided if the element had just been inserted.

```
┌─ DeleteProperties ──────────────────────────────────────┐
│  props: F P                                              │
│  ΔDDS                                                    │
│ ┌────────────────────────────────┘                      │
│  user canupdate elementcontext                           │
│  store' = store ⊕ { elementcontext ↦ element' }          │
│  elementcontext' = elementcontext                        │
│  where                                                   │
│  element' = { authority ↦ user; privacy ↦ privacy user } ⊕│
│             props ◁ (store elementcontext)               │
└──────────────────────────────────────────────────────────┘
```

4. Prospects

Whilst we would have liked to go on to describe the control of multiple versions in DDS, the present design proved too hard for us to formalise simply. The specification, therefore, has its limitations and it would be an unwise user who relied upon formal deductions from it to discover the consequences of actions he might take whilst running the system itself. It nevertheless remains useful as a pedagogical tool because it provides a discursive introduction to the concepts which underlie access control.

In our view the principal benefit of constructing the formal specification is the fact that we have developed a framework within which designs of future dictionaries can easily be investigated. Whilst it has been an interesting challenge to build a mathematical model of a software system such as the Data Dictionary System, the enterprise would remain simply an academic exercise if we were to stop at this point, so we have tried to indicate how to use the framework by using it to make a tentative proposal for simplifying the system. This is presented in the Appendix.

Appendix – Potential Simplifications

Those familiar with DDS will have noticed that we have made an important simplification already, by ignoring the "facility" to refer to as-yet-undefined authorities when adding or modifying properties. Although we have no definite knowledge about the operational consequences of this facility, we hazard a guess that it causes more aggravation than it saves: readers who have been victims of implicit declarations in Fortran may care to comment on this.

The most obvious additional simplification would be to drop the independent notion of privacy level, which seems to be orthogonal to authorities and ownership. We are tempted to wonder if there are any DDS installations where both privacy and authority are employed within the same dictionary.

A further simplification would be to remove the distinction between the system administrator and other authorities. This might well pay dividends in terms of enhancing the functionality of the system and reducing the complexity of its documentation and implementation. Our design goal is based on a new interpretation of the meaning of an authority element, which we prefer to think of as a role, or locus of responsibility, rather than a particular person. Indeed it is often the case that one individual plays several distinct roles in an organisation.

In the design outlined below we make every authority subordinate to ("owned by") some other authority; the root of this tree of authorities is the system administration authority (which owns itself). Power to alter properties of elements reposes ultimately in the administrator, which is able to delegate them to subordinate authorities, which in turn can delegate them further if need be. Any element which several authorities need to retrieve or to update should be owned by an authority which is higher in the tree than all of them, and which delegates its retrieval or update rights to them all.

In order to formalise this design, we first need to introduce the idea of a "loop-free" function, sometimes called a "tree" or "forest". Consider a homogeneous function

$$f: X \twoheadrightarrow X$$

We say that an element $x':X$ is *reachable via* f from an element $x:X$ if there is at least one nonzero number, $n:N^+$ for which $x' = f^n x$. When this is the case, we write

$$x \underline{f}^+ x'$$

More formally, we can define:

$$\underline{}^+ : (X \twoheadrightarrow X) \rightarrow (X \twoheadrightarrow X)$$

$$\forall f:X \twoheadrightarrow X; \ x, x':X \ \bullet$$
$$x \ \underline{f}^+ \ x' \iff \exists n:N_1 \ \bullet \ x' = f^n \ x$$

A function $f: X \nrightarrow X$ is said to be *loop-free*, or a *tree*, if there is no $x: X$ which is reachable from itself via f. More formally:

$$[X]$$
$$\text{Tree} \triangleq \{\ f: X \nrightarrow X \mid \neg(\exists\ x: X \bullet x\ \underline{f}^+\ x)\ \}$$

Our first approximation to a description of the design outlined above recalls our description of the standard data dictionary: the main difference is that all elements (including authority elements) are owned, and that if we confine our attention to authorities other than the administrator, the ownership function is a tree.

The administrator is reachable from every element via the ownership function, *i.e.* the administrator is ultimately responsible for everything in the dictionary.

```
┌─ DD ─────────────────────────────────────────┐
│  store:      EI ⇸ E                           │
│  elements:   F EI                             │
│  auth:       F EI                             │
│  owner:      EI ⇸ EI                          │
│  admin:      EI                               │
├───────────────────────────────────────────────┤
│  elements  = dom store                        │
│  dom owner = elements                         │
│  ran owner ⊆ auth ⊆ elements                  │
│  admin ∈ auth                                 │
│  {admin} ◁ owner  ∈ Tree[EI]                  │
│   ∀ ei:elements • ei owner⁺ admin             │
└───────────────────────────────────────────────┘
```

The information structures from which the relations `canretrieve` and `canupdate` can be derived are similar to those in the original design, except that there is no longer a role for privacy levels, the `nil` authority no longer exists, and update permission is characterised positively rather than negatively.

```
┌─ DD ──────────────────────────────────┐
│ DD                                     │
│ delegates:   EI ↔ EI                   │
│ mayretrieve: EI ↔ EI                   │
│ mayupdate:   EI ↔ EI                   │
│ ├─────────────────────────────         │
│ delegates ∈ auth ↔ auth                │
│ dom mayretrieve ⊆ auth                 │
│ dom mayupdate ⊆ auth                   │
│ delegates ⊆ owner⁻¹                    │
└────────────────────────────────────────┘
```

The last predicate states that an authority may only delegate its rights to authorities for which it is responsible.

An authority can retrieve an element if it or any of its subordinates own the element, or if it has been given explicit permission to retrieve it, or if it has been delegated rights to retrieve the element. An authority can update an element if it or any of its subordinates owns the element, or if it has been given permission to update the element.

```
 ┌─ DD ────────────────────────────────────────────┐
 │  DD                                              │
 │  canretrieve: EI ↔ EI                            │
 │  canupdate:   EI ↔ EI                            │
 │ ─────────────────────                            │
 │                                                  │
 │  dom canretrieve ⊆ auth                          │
 │  dom canupdate ⊆ auth                            │
 │                                                  │
 │  ∀ user:auth; elt:elements •                     │
 │    user canretrieve elt ↔                        │
 │          elt owner⁺ user              ∨          │
 │          owner elt delegates user ∨              │
 │          user mayretrieve elt                    │
 │                                                  │
 │  ∀ user:auth; elt:elements •                     │
 │    user canupdate elt ↔                          │
 │          user canretrieve elt      ∧             │
 │          elt owner⁺ user           ∨             │
 │          user mayupdate elt                      │
 └──────────────────────────────────────────────────┘
```

It might be nice if no authority possessed any capabilities that its owner does not also possess. In other words, if within a dictionary:

```
  canretrieve ⊆ owner ⍮ canretrieve
  canupdate ⊆ owner ⍮ canupdate
```

Interested readers may care to check whether or not this is the case, and if not, to modify our formalisation so that it is.

Finally we propose a small project for the interested reader. Devise representations (along the lines suggested by Figure 2) for mayretrieve, mayupdate, and delegates. These should make the relations canretrieve and canupdate simple to compute, and also make the system invariant simple to check.

Acknowledgements

ICL sponsored the ten-day pilot experiment in technology transfer which led (*inter alia*) to the production of this report. It is a pleasure to acknowledge the help of Roger Stokes of ICL, who despite the multiplicity of demands imposed on his time and talents, always remained interested enough in the experiment to convince me that it was worthwhile. Jean-Raymond Abrial first showed me how to apply mathematics to software specification and remains a continuing source of inspiration.

References

[ICL]

Reference Manual for the ICL Data Dictionary System (DDS.600)
ICL Document RP0120, May 1982.

[Hoare,82]

C.A.R. Hoare
"Programming is an Engineering Profession"
Technical Monograph #27
Oxford University Programming Research Group, 1982.

[Jones,80]

C.B. Jones
"Software Development: A Rigorous Approach"
Prentice-Hall International, 1980.

[Morgan,84]

Carroll Morgan & Bernard Sufrin
"Specification of the Unix Filing System"
IEEE Trans. Soft. Eng. Volume SE-10 Number 2. March 1984

[Sufrin,83]

Bernard Sufrin
"Mathematics for System Specification"
Computation MSc Course Notes
Oxford University Programming Research Group, 1983.

[Sufrin,84]

Bernard Sufrin, Carroll Morgan, Ib Sørensen, Ian Hayes
"Notes for a Z Handbook. Part 1: the Mathematical Language"
Oxford University Programming Research Group, 1984.

Flexitime Specification

Ian Hayes

Abstract

This paper gives a simplified specification of an actual flexitime system. It is interesting for a number of reasons. It is brief and not too complicated, and gives some good examples of the power of set theory in specification. A state is used which is far richer than that necessary for an implementation, and this approach has as its reward an overall simplification of the specification. It is simplified also by using an absolute time frame rather than one using times only within the current pay period.

Flexitime is a compromise between the rigidity of fixed working hours (*e.g.*, "9am to 5pm") and the relative freedom having only to work a certain *number* of hours (*e.g.*, 35 hours per week). A flexitime system requires a certain number of hours to be worked in each pay period, and in addition requires that all of those hours should be within certain limits (*e.g.*, between 6am and 8pm).

Keeping track of the time worked for each employee can be computerised, by having employees "clock in" whenever they start work and "clock out" whenever they stop.

State

We will only record working time to the nearest minute.

$$\text{Time} \triangleq \mathbb{N} \qquad \text{-- in minutes}$$

A period of time can be represented by a set of (not necessarily contiguous) minutes.

$$\text{Period} \triangleq \mathbb{P}\ \text{Time}$$

We can represent the standard working times for a pay period by a set containing all the minutes between 9am and 5pm, excluding the lunch break from 12noon to 1pm, for all the days in the pay period. In a similar way we can represent the range of permissible flexitime working hours by a set of times.

The function Standard_Hours takes a time as argument, and gives the set of standard working times for the pay period encompassing the time given as its argument. For example, if pay periods were weekly, Standard_Hours (12:00 14 February 1986) might return the set of all minutes between 9am and 1pm, 2pm and 5pm on each day of the week from 10th to 14th February 1986.

Similarly, the function Flexitime_Hours gives the set of minutes that *could* be worked (and credited) in the period encompassing the time given as an argument.

Our model of the system will record the times worked for all the employees, plus the time at which people currently working clocked in. Each employee is assigned a unique identifier from the set Id.

```
┌─Flexi──────────────────────────────────────
│ Standard_Hours,
│ Flexitime_Hours : Time → Period
│ worked : Id ⇸ Period
│ in     : Id ⇸ Time
├──────────────────
│ dom(in) ⊆ dom(worked)
└────────────────────────────────────────────
```

Operations

Each operation transforms a state before (Flexi) to a state after (Flexi′).

ΔFlexi ≙ Flexi ∧ Flexi′

Some operations do not change the state.

≡Flexi ≙ [ΔFlexi | Flexi′ = Flexi]

Clocking in and out operations performed by employees involve them inserting their unique (card) key into a special terminal which transmits the employee's identifier and the current time to the system. The system responds with an indicator of the operation performed. The common part of the clocking operations is given by

```
┌─ΔClocking───────────────────────────────┐
│ ΔFlexi                                    │
│ id?  : Id                                 │
│ t?   : Time                               │
│ ind! : Response                           │
│ ─────────────────────────────────         │
│ id? ∈ dom(worked) ∧                       │
│ Standard_Hours′ = Standard_Hours ∧        │
│ Flexitime_Hours′ = Flexitime_Hours        │
└───────────────────────────────────────────┘
```

where Response ≙ { "ClockIn", "ClockOut", "ReadOut", "Unknown" }. The identity of the employee must be known. Clocking operations do not affect Standard_Hours or Flexitime_Hours.

The operation of clocking in is given by

```
┌─ClockIn₀ ──────────────────────────────────────────┐
│  ΔClocking                                          │
│  ─────────────────────                              │
│  id? ∉ dom(in) ∧                                    │
│  t?  ∈ Flexitime_Hours(t?) ∧                        │
│  in' = in ∪ { id? ↦ t? } ∧                          │
│  worked' = worked ∧                                 │
│  ind! = "ClockIn"                                   │
└─────────────────────────────────────────────────────┘
```

The employee must not have clocked in already and the current time must be in the bounds of the flexitime working hours for the current pay period. The employee is clocked in at the given time.

The operation of clocking out is given by

```
┌─ClockOut₀ ─────────────────────────────────────────┐
│  ΔClocking                                          │
│  ─────────────────────                              │
│  id? ∈ dom(in) ∧                                    │
│  worked' = worked ⊕                                 │
│            { id? ↦ (worked(id?) ∪ in(id?)..(t?-1)) } ∧ │
│  in' = { id? } ◁ in ∧                               │
│  ind! = "ClockOut"                                  │
└─────────────────────────────────────────────────────┘
```

The employee must have clocked in. The minutes worked since clocking in are credited to the employee's time worked. Only the period that lies within flexitime hours really counts towards flexitime, but we have chosen to record the total working time in this specification in order to simplify it and allow extensions to keep track of overtime worked etc. The minutes worked are all those minutes from the time the employee clocked in (although he may not have worked the whole of that minute) upto but not including the minute in which he clocks out (even though he has worked part of that minute). On average, partial minutes not worked at clock in should cancel out partial minutes worked at clock out.

On each transaction the system responds with the current credit or debit of time worked by the employee within the current pay period, relative to the standard times.

```
┌─Worked──────────────────────────────────────────┐
│ ΔClocking                                        │
│ cr!  : RelMinutes                                │
│ ────────────────────────────────────────────    │
│ cr! = #(worked'(id?) ∩ Flexitime_Hours(t?))      │
│        - #{ t : Standard_Hours(t?) | t < t? }    │
└──────────────────────────────────────────────────┘
```

where $RelMinutes \triangleq Z$. The credit ($cr!$) is of type $RelMinutes$ (relative minutes) which, when positive, indicates a credit and, when negative, indicates a debit. Only the period of time worked within the flexitime hours for the current pay period counts.

The clocking operations in full are

$$ClockIn \triangleq ClockIn_0 \wedge Worked$$

$$ClockOut \triangleq ClockOut_0 \wedge Worked$$

If an employee not currently working inserts a card outside flexitime hours he will not be clocked in. However, he will receive an indication of the current time credit.

```
┌─ReadOut────────────────────────────────────┐
│ Worked                                      │
│ ─────────────────────────────────────────   │
│ id? ∉ dom(in) ∧                             │
│ t? ∉ Flexitime_Hours(t?) ∧                  │
│ ind! = "ReadOut" ∧                          │
│ Flexi' = Flexi                              │
└─────────────────────────────────────────────┘
```

If an unknown key is inserted an error response is given

```
┌─Unknown!──────────────────────────────┐
│  ≡Flexi                               │
│  id?  : Id                            │
│  ind! : Response                      │
│ ─────────────────────────────────     │
│  id ∉ dom(worked) ∧                   │
│  ind! = "Unknown"                     │
└───────────────────────────────────────┘
```

An administrative operation is required to add a new employee. The identity of the new employee is chosen from those not already in use.

```
┌─Add_Employee──────────────────────────┐
│  ΔFlexi                               │
│  id! : Id                             │
│ ─────────────────────────────────     │
│  id! ∉ dom(worked) ∧                  │
│  worked' = worked ∪ { id! ↦ {} } ∧    │
│  in' = in ∧                           │
│  Standard_Hours' = Standard_Hours ∧   │
│  Flexitime_Hours' = Flexitime_Hours   │
└───────────────────────────────────────┘
```

Acknowledgement

This paper treats a simplified version of a problem first specified by Jolanta Imbert of the GEC Research Laboratories, Marconi Research Centre.

Formal Specification
and
Design
of a
Simple Assembler

Ib Holm Sørensen

Bernard Sufrin

Abstract

We present the formal specification of a simple assembler, outline the
design of a simple implementation, and demonstrate its correctness. Both
specification and design are presented at a rather abstract level, and are
therefore unrealistic to some extent. However, it is this very high level of
abstraction which allows the specification and the design to be simply
explained and easily understood, and permits a proof that the design meets
the specification.

Introduction

An assembler is a program which translates a sequence of assembly language instructions into a sequence of machine language instructions ready to place in the store of a computer for execution. In this paper we assume that the computer for which we are going to specify our assembler is a "one address machine" — in other words each machine instruction has an opcode field and an operand field, and resides at a certain address in the store of the machine. Depending on the value of the opcode field, the operand field may be treated as an address or a number when the instruction is executed by the machine.

Each assembly language instruction determines the value of the opcode and address fields of a corresponding computer instruction, so an assembly language instruction has a symbolic opcode field and a symbolic or numeric operand field. When a symbol appears in the operand field of an assembly language instruction, the assembler should place the address with which the symbol is associated in the operand field of the corresponding machine instruction. A symbol is associated with an address by including a symbolic label field in the assembly language instruction which determines the content of that address.

Some assembly language instructions, known as *directives*, do not correspond to machine instructions, but are used to signify things such as the end of the input, or a change of the radix in which numbers are expressed. In order to simplify our discussion we will not consider this kind of directive at all.

A typical translation performed by the assembler might be

Assembly Language			Machine Store		
				Machine Language	
Label	Opcode	Operand	Location	Opcode	Operand
v1:	.const	100	1		100
v2:	.const	4095	2		4095
loop:	load	v2	3	01	2
	subn	8	4	03	8
	store	v2	5	02	2
	compare	v1	6	50	1
	jumple	exit	7	61	9
	jump	loop	8	71	3
exit:	return		9	77	

We can specify the task an assembler must perform by explaining the relationship of its input (a sequence of assembly language instructions) to its output (a sequence of machine language instructions). We will find it easier to investigate the essence of this relationship if we avoid considering things like error listings. This is not to say that such things would not be important in a more complete specification of requirements for the assembler, but at present we are interested in capturing the essence of its task which is the translation of assembler instructions into machine instructions.

The Structure of Instructions

The first abstraction step we take is to decide that we need not understand how assembler instructions are represented as character sequences nor how machine instructions are represented as bit sequences. In particular, all we need to know about assembler instructions is that they have a label field or an opcode field or both, and that they *may* have an operand field which is *either* a symbolic reference or a number, but cannot be both. Similarly, all we need to know about machine instructions is that they must have an opcode field or an operand field and may have both.

Let A denote the set of all possible assembly language instructions and M the set of all possible machine language instructions. The next step in our construction of the predicate is to investigate the structure of the two kinds of instruction, A and M. In order to do so we shall need to discuss label symbols and operation code symbols. So, let the set of all possible label symbols be denoted by SYM and the set of all possible opcode symbols by OPSYM.

We can now formalise our idea of the essential structure of an assembly language instruction.

$$
\begin{array}{lll}
\text{lab:} & \text{A} \twoheadrightarrow \text{SYM} & \qquad \ldots A1 \\
\text{op:} & \text{A} \twoheadrightarrow \text{OPSYM} & \qquad \ldots A2 \\
\text{ref:} & \text{A} \twoheadrightarrow \text{SYM} & \qquad \ldots A3 \\
\text{num:} & \text{A} \twoheadrightarrow \text{N} & \qquad \ldots A3 \\
\hline
\multicolumn{2}{l}{\text{dom ref} \cap \text{dom num} = \{\}} & \qquad \ldots A3 \\
\multicolumn{2}{l}{\text{dom op} \cup \text{dom num} \cup \text{dom ref} = \text{A}} & \qquad \ldots A4
\end{array}
$$

A1 formalises the requirement that assembly instructions *may* have a label, *A2* that they may have an opcode, *A3* that the optional operand may be numeric or symbolic but not both, and *A4* the requirement that they must all have an opcode or an operand.

The essential structure of machine instructions may be formalised similarly.

$$
\begin{array}{lll}
\text{opcode:} & \text{M} \twoheadrightarrow \text{N} & \qquad \ldots M1 \\
\text{operand:} & \text{M} \twoheadrightarrow \text{N} & \qquad \ldots M2 \\
\hline
\multicolumn{2}{l}{\text{dom opcode} \cup \text{dom operand} = \text{M}} & \qquad \ldots M3
\end{array}
$$

Finally, we assume that we have been given a way of translating symbolic opcodes to the numbers which they represent; that is, a function:

$$
\text{mnem:} \quad \text{OPSYM} \twoheadrightarrow \text{N}
$$

The domain of this function is the set of valid mnemonic opcode symbols.

Part 1: Requirements

We require that the assembler translate symbolic operands, where they appear, to numbers representing the corresponding address, translate numeric operand fields without changing them, and that it translate symbolic opcodes to their corresponding number. Our specification will effectively be the conjunction of predicates which formalise these requirements.

Symbol Definitions

Suppose that the input sequence of assembly instructions is

    in: seq A

A sequence is a special kind of function from the natural numbers, so the composition:

    in ⍮ lab

is a function of type

    N ⤀ SYM

which maps the position of each assembler instruction in which a symbolic label is defined to the label which is defined there. For the example in the introduction we have:

    in ⍮ lab = { 1↦V1,   2↦V2,   3↦loop,   9↦exit }

The inverse of this function is in general a relation which maps each symbol to the places in the input where it is defined as a label. For this reason we will find it convenient to define:

    symtab ≙ (in ⍮ lab)⁻¹   ... S1

In order to formalise the idea that there should be *no multiply defined symbols*, we require that symtab be a *function*.

    symtab ∈ SYM ⤀ N   ... S2

In general the inverse of a function may be a one-to-many relation: requiring that symtab be a function is the same as requiring that it map each symbol in its domain to a *unique* address. Later we will be able to give additional justification for this intuitively obvious requirement.

Symbolic Operands

The composition

in ⁏ ref

is a function of type

N ⟶ SYM

which maps the position of an assembler instruction in the input to the symbol which is referenced there. For the example in the introduction:

in ⁏ ref = { 3↦v2, 5↦v2, 6↦v1, 7↦exit, 8↦loop }

In addition,

rng(in ⁏ ref)

is the set of symbols which are referenced in the input. So, to express the requirement that all symbols which are referenced by the input are defined there, we write:

rng(in ⁏ ref) ⊆ dom symtab   ... *S3*

Numeric Operands

The function

in ⁏ num

of type

N ⟶ N

maps the position of an assembler instruction in the input to the number which appears there. For our example:

in ⁏ num = { 1↦100, 2↦4095, 4↦8 }

Because of the axioms for ref and num, the two functions (in ⁏ ref) and (in ⁏ num) have disjoint domains.

Symbolic Opcodes

The function

        in ⍮ op

of type

        ℕ ⇸ OPSYM

maps the position of an assembler instruction in the input to the opcode symbol which is referenced by it. To formalise the requirement that all referenced opcode symbols be valid mnemonics, we write:

        rng(in ⍮ op) ⊆ dom mnem   ... S4

Operands of Machine Instructions

Suppose that the output sequence of machine instructions is

        out: seq M

then the function

        out ⍮ operand

of type

        ℕ ⇸ ℕ

maps each machine address to the value of the operand field of the instruction stored there. If the assembler instruction at position n has a symbolic operand, then the operand field of the instruction at location n should take the value of the symbol

        (in ⍮ ref) n   i.e. ref(in(n))

Provided that symtab is a function and that the symbol is indeed defined, then its value is uniquely determined by

        (in ⍮ ref ⍮ symtab) n   i.e. symtab(ref(in(n)))

If the assembler instruction at position n has a numeric operand then the operand of the corresponding machine instruction should take the value

(in ¦ num) n

We can express both of these requirements as a single equality, namely:

(out ¦ operand) = (in ¦ ref ¦ symtab) ∪ (in ¦ num)   ... S5

In order to check that our formalisation is sensible, we should ensure that the right hand side of this equality is a *function* (since we have already established that the left hand side must be so).

Since in¦ref and in¦num must by virtue of the structure of the assembly language be functions with disjoint domains, the only thing left to ensure is that symtab itself is a function; this condition corresponds to the *no multiply defined symbols* condition which we discussed earlier.

Opcode Fields

All that remains is for us to state the relationship we require between the opcode fields of the input and the instruction fields of the output. This is simply:

out ¦ opcode = in ¦ op ¦ mnem   ... S6

Ensuring that every assembler instruction with an opcode field gives rise to a machine instruction with a corresponding field is just a question of ensuring that the domain of the right hand side is equal to the domain of in¦op. This is so provided that the range of in¦op is a subset of the domain of mnem, which corresponds to the condition *all referenced opcodes must be valid mnemonics* discussed earlier.

Specification Summary

In this section we summarise the specification by defining the schema ASSEMBLY which characterises the relationship we wish to hold between the inputs and outputs of an assembler. We have labelled the clauses of the specification so as to illuminate the proof steps we take later.

Context:

[A, M, SYM, OPSYM]

lab: A $\twoheadrightarrow$ SYM	... *A1*
op: A $\twoheadrightarrow$ OPSYM	... *A2*
ref: A $\twoheadrightarrow$ SYM	... *A3*
num: A $\twoheadrightarrow$ N	... *A3*

dom ref ∩ dom num = {}	... *A3*
dom op ∪ dom num ∪ dom ref = A	... *A4*

opcode: M $\twoheadrightarrow$ N	... *M1*
operand: M $\twoheadrightarrow$ N	... *M2*

dom opcode ∪ dom operand = M	... *M3*

mnem: OPSYM $\twoheadrightarrow$ N

Specification:

```
 ___ASSEMBLY _____
|    in :  seq A
|    out:  seq M
|   _____
|
|    symtab ∈ SYM ⇸ N                                          ... S2
|    rng( in ; ref ) ⊆ dom symtab                             ... S3
|    rng( in ; op  ) ⊆ dom mnem                               ... S4
|    (out ; operand) = (in ; ref ; symtab) ∪ (in ; num)      ... S5
|    (out ; opcode)  = (in ; op ; mnem)                        ... S6
|   where
|    symtab ≙ (in ; lab)⁻¹                                     ... S1
|_____
```

Consequences of the Specification

It is easy to show that when an assembly is successful, the length of the output sequence is the same as that of the input sequence. More formally,

$$\text{ASSEMBLY} \vdash \#out = \#in$$

Proof:

1.	dom out = dom(out ;operand) ∪ dom (out ;opcode)		... *M3*
2.	= dom(in ;ref ;symtab) ∪		
	dom(in ;num)	∪	
	dom(in ;op ;mnem)		... *S5, S6*
3.	= dom(in ;ref)	∪	
	dom(in ;num)	∪	
	dom(in ;op)		... *2,S3,S4*
4.	= dom in		... *3,A4*
5.	#(dom out) = #(dom in)		... *4*
6.	#out = #in		... *5* □

The precondition for a successful assembly is the existence of an output which satisfies the predicate of ASSEMBLY. This is formally denoted by hiding the output.

$$\text{PreASSEMBLY} \triangleq \text{ASSEMBLY} \setminus out$$

Technical note: Recall that the hiding operator __ of the schema calculus is defined as follows: the variables which are to be hidden are removed from the signature of the schema in which it is to be hidden; and the predicate of the schema is existentially quantified by the hidden variables. The definition above is therefore equivalent to

```
┌─ PreASSEMBLY ──────────────────────────┐
│  in: seq A                             │
│  ─────────────────                     │
│                                        │
│  ∃ out: seq M • the predicate of ASSEMBLY │
└────────────────────────────────────────┘
```

Nontechnical note: we could, of course, have written out the predicate of ASSEMBLY in full again, but here the benefits of concision clearly outweigh the virtues of precision.

Provided that we now insist that each machine instruction is *uniquely* characterised by its opcode and operand fields, *i.e.*

$$\forall\ m, n : M\ |\ (\text{opcode } m) = (\text{opcode } n) \wedge (\text{operand } m) = (\text{operand } n)\ \bullet\ m = n$$

the schema PreASSEMBLY simplifies to:

```
┌─ PreASSEMBLY ──────────────────────────┐
│  in: seq A                             │
│  ─────────────────                     │
│                                        │
│  symtab ∈ SYM ⤀ N                      │  ... S2
│  rng( in ⨾ ref ) ⊆ dom symtab          │  ... S3
│  rng( in ⨾ op  ) ⊆ dom mnem            │  ... S4
│  where                                 │
│  symtab ≙ (in ⨾ lab)⁻¹                 │  ... S1
└────────────────────────────────────────┘
```

Thus the specification states, amongst other things, that a program which is to be assembled correctly must have no multiply-defined labels, no undefined symbolic references, and no invalid opcode mnemonics.

Discussion

We have established the basis for a small theory of simple assemblers. Such a theory, however simple and abstract, gives us an intellectual handle by which we may grasp much more complicated machine and assembly languages, such as those outlined in exercises 4 and 5 below.

By formalising the essence of the relationship required between inputs and outputs of the simple assembler we have illustrated the two principal techniques used in system specification, namely representational abstraction and procedural abstraction. By representational abstraction we mean the statement of all essential characteristics of the information structures involved in describing a situation, without defining the storage structures used in their representation. By procedural abstraction we mean the statement of the input-output relationships involved in an activity without defining the computational structures used to achieve them.

Any program which can be proved to behave in the manner indicated by the ASSEMBLY schema, is, as far as we are concerned, an assembler. Of course we haven't yet given any clues about how to go about constructing such a program, but that enterprise is the subject of the next section of our paper.

Exercises

1. What should the output sequence of instructions look like for erroneous input? Is it important?

2. Specify the appearance of a listing on which errors, such as multiply-defined and undefined symbolic references, are noted.

3. How could the specification be extended to cover radix directives in the input language?

4. How could the specification be extended so as to describe an assembler for a machine with registers?

5. Specify an assembler for a Vax-like machine, whose machine instructions don't all occupy the same number of addressable units.

Part 2: High Level Design of an Assembler

In this section we outline the design of a simple two-phase implementation of the assembler. During the first phase the assembler completely builds the machine instructions of the output which have operands specified numerically (or not at all) in the input. It only partly builds the instructions which have operands which are symbolically specified in the input, leaving the values of the operand fields of such instructions indeterminate. It also constructs a reference-table, which records the positions where symbols were referenced in the input, and a symbol table, which records their values. It uses these tables in the second phase to complete the building of the machine instructions by giving values to symbolically specified operands.

We shall describe the first phase by defining a schema Phase1, which specifies the value of the intermediate state in terms of the input. The second phase will be described by defining a schema Phase2, which uses the intermediate state to derive a value for the output. Once we have made and explained these definitions we will show how to put them together to describe the complete implementation.

The definition and reference information of the intermediate state is characterised as abstractly as possible below — as the relation st (symbol table) and the function rt (reference table). The sequence core consists of machine instructions, some of which may only be partly determined after the first phase.

```
┌─ IS ──────────────────┐
│  st:    SYM ↔ N        │
│  rt:    N ↠ SYM        │
│  core:  seq M          │
└───────────────────────┘
```

Design of the first phase

After the first phase, the symbol and reference tables should have been built, and all the opcode and numeric operand fields should take the values in core that they will have in the final output.

```
 ┌─ Phase1 ──────────────────────────────────────────────┐
 │   in: seq A                                            
 │   IS                                                   
 ├─────────────────────────┐                              
 │                                                        
 │   st = (in ⦂ lab)⁻¹                              ... P1.1
 │   rt = (in ⦂ ref)                                ... P1.2
 │   (dom rt) ◁ (core ⦂ operand) = (in ⦂ num)      ... P1.3
 │   (core ⦂ opcode) = (in ⦂ op ⦂ mnem)            ... P1.4
 │   rng(in ⦂ op) ⊆ dom mnem                       ... P1.5
 └───────────────────────────────────────────────────────┘
```

More precisely, the first condition $(P1.1)$ specifies that the symbol table records all definitions of each label. $P1.2$ specifies that the reference table records the symbol referenced at each location whose assembly instruction had a symbolic operand. $P1.3$ specifies the in-core values of operand fields derived from numeric operands in the input. The fourth condition $(P1.4)$ specifies the in-core values of the opcode fields. Finally, a precondition of the first phase is that all opcode symbols are valid mnemonics $(P1.5)$.

The reader may have noticed that the operand fields of instructions with *symbolic* operands are left unspecified. Our reason for leaving them so is that at least one well-known implementation technique uses the unfilled operand fields to store most of the information present in the reference-table, and we do not wish to exclude such an implementation technique at this early stage of design.

Design of the second phase

The second phase may assume that the output values of all opcode and numeric operand fields are already present in core. It must determine the values of operand fields which were specified symbolically. Since the input is no longer accessible, the only way to tell the difference between symbolic and numeric operand fields is by inspecting the domain of the reference table.

Formally, we have:

```
┌─ Phase2 ──────────────────────────────────────────────────┐
│  IS
│  out: seq M
│ ──────────────────────────
│  st ∈ SYM ⇸ N                                          ... P2.1
│  rng rt ⊆ dom st                                       ... P2.2
│  (out ⨾ opcode) = (core ⨾ opcode)                      ... P2.3
│  (dom rt) ◁ (out ⨾ operand) =
│                  (dom rt) ◁ (core ⨾ operand)           ... P2.4
│  (dom rt) ◁ (out ⨾ operand) = (rt ⨾ st)                ... P2.5
└───────────────────────────────────────────────────────────┘
```

The first two conjuncts constitute a precondition for this phase (since out does not occur in them): there must be no multiply-defined symbols $(P2.1)$ and all referenced symbols must be defined $(P2.2)$. $P2.3$ specifies that the opcode fields of the output be exactly the same as they were in core, and condition $P2.4$ specifies that the operand fields of the output instructions with numeric operands must also be the same as they were in core. The last condition $(P2.5)$ specifies that the operand fields of the output instructions with symbolic operands are given the values of the appropriate symbols.

Putting the phases together

It is tempting to describe the two phase implementation by defining a schema

        Implementation ≙ Phase1 ∧ Phase2

However, when an assembly is complete we do not particularly care what the value of the intermediate state was, so we shall *hide* it in our definition:

        Implementation ≙ (Phase1 ∧ Phase2) \ (st, rt, core)

Correctness of the Design

In order to prove that our design is correct it would be sufficient to prove that it is at least as applicable as the specification, and that the result prescribed by the design is consistent with the specification whenever the specification is applicable. In fact we shall be able to show here that the implementation is *equivalent to* the specification. We do this by expanding and simplifying the definition of the implementation using the rules of the schema calculus and the laws of mathematics.

Taking the formal schema conjunction of the two phases and hiding the intermediate state gives

```
 ┌─ Implementation ──────────────────────────────────────────┐
 │  in:    seq A                                              │
 │  out:   seq M                                              │
 ├────────────────────────                                    │
 │  ∃ st: SYM ↔ N; rt: N ↠ SYM; core: seq M •                 │
 │     st = (in ⦂ lab)⁻¹                               ... P1.1│
 │     rt = (in ⦂ ref)                                 ... P1.2│
 │     (dom rt) ◁ (core ⦂ operand) = (in ⦂ num)       ... P1.3│
 │     (core ⦂ opcode) = (in ⦂ op ⦂ mnem)             ... P1.4│
 │     rng(in ⦂ op) ⊆ dom mnem                         ... P1.5│
 │     st ∈ SYM ↠ N                                    ... P2.1│
 │     rng rt ⊆ dom st                                 ... P2.2│
 │     (out ⦂ opcode) = (core ⦂ opcode)               ... P2.3│
 │     (dom rt) ◁ (out ⦂ operand) =                           │
 │                       (dom rt) ◁ (core ⦂ operand)   ... P2.4│
 │     (dom rt) ◁ (out ⦂ operand)  = (rt ⦂ st)        ... P2.5│
 └────────────────────────────────────────────────────────────┘
```

If we exploit the equalities *P1.1, P1.2, P2.3,* and *P2.4* this can be simplified to

```
┌─ Implementation ──────────────────────────────────────┐
│ in:    seq A                                           │
│ out:   seq M                                           │
│ ─────────────────────                                  │
│ ∃ st: SYM ↔ N •                                        │
│   st = (in ⅷ lab)⁻¹                                    │
│   (dom (in ⅷ ref)) ◁ (out ⅷ operand) = (in ⅷ num)      ... IX
│   (out ⅷ opcode) = (in ⅷ op ⅷ mnem)                    │
│   rng(in ⅷ op) ⊆ dom mnem                              │
│   st ∈ SYM ⇸ N                                         │
│   rng(in ⅷ ref) ⊆ dom st                              │
│   (dom (in ⅷ ref)) ◁ (out ⅷ operand) = (in ⅷ ref ⅷ st)  ... IY
└────────────────────────────────────────────────────────┘
```

thus eliminating core and rt from the quantified predicate.

We now combine *IX* and *IY* to yield *I5* (using the *restriction elimination law* given in the appendix) and reorder the conjuncts of the quantified predicate, thus obtaining our final simplified description of the implementation

```
┌─ Implementation ──────────────────────────────────────┐
│ in:    seq A                                           │
│ out:   seq M                                           │
│ ─────────────────────                                  │
│ ∃ st: SYM ↔ N •                                        │
│   st = (in ⅷ lab)⁻¹                              ... I1 │
│   st ∈ SYM ⇸ N                                   ... I2 │
│   rng(in ⅷ ref) ⊆ dom st                        ... I3 │
│   rng(in ⅷ op) ⊆ dom mnem                       ... I4 │
│   (out ⅷ operand) = (in ⅷ num) ∪ (in ⅷ ref ⅷ st) ... I5 │
│   (out ⅷ opcode) = (in ⅷ op ⅷ mnem)             ... I6 │
└────────────────────────────────────────────────────────┘
```

Eliminating the where clause of the specification (using the *where elimination law* given in the appendix), we see that the specification is equivalent to

```
 ┌─ ASSEMBLY ──────────────────────────────────────────────────────┐
 │   in : seq A                                                      │
 │   out: seq M                                                      │
 ├──────────────────────────────                                     │
 │  ∃ symbtab: SYM ↔ N •                                             │
 │     symtab = (in ⦂ lab)⁻¹                             ... S1       │
 │     symtab ∈ SYM ⇸ N                                 ... S2       │
 │     rng( in ⦂ ref ) ⊆ dom symtab                     ... S3       │
 │     rng( in ⦂ op  ) ⊆ dom mnem                       ... S4       │
 │     (out ⦂ operand) = (in ⦂ ref ⦂ symtab) ∪ (in ⦂ num)  ... S5    │
 │     (out ⦂ opcode)  = (in ⦂ op ⦂ mnem)               ... S6       │
 └──────────────────────────────────────────────────────────────────┘
```

Since we may rename the bound variables of a quantified predicate without changing the meaning of the predicate, the two schemas ASSEMBLY and Implementation are clearly equivalent, and we have therefore demonstrated the correctness of our design.

The two phases may now be used almost independently as subjects for further refinement. To be precise, independent refinements of the phases will refine the entire specification provided *either* that the refinement of Phase1 is deterministic, *or* that all intermediate states produced by the refinement of Phase1 satisfy the precondition of the refinement of Phase2.

Discussion

We have constructed specifications for the two phases of an in-store assembler. In each case we have captured the essence of the information processed by the phases, but in neither case have we specified the order in which the information is processed, nor have we specified the form in which this information will be stored in the computer. This leaves several possibilities open to those who will define a more computer-oriented realisation of the intermediate data structures and algorithmically more explicit realisations of the two phases. In particular, our earlier suggestion that the symbol-reference table be stored in the unfilled operand fields of core is consistent with the specification of both phases, and might usefully be explored further by those interested in completing a formally-justified derivation of a real assembly program based on this design.

Acknowledgements

This paper is a much altered version of [Sorensen82]. We have benefited from discussion over the years with colleagues and students at the Programming Research Group. Jean-Raymond Abrial first showed us how to put set theory to productive use as a Software Engineering tool, and remains a continuing source of inspiration.

Bibliography

[Sorensen82]

      Specification of a Simple Assembler
      CICS Project Working Paper
      Ib Holm Sørensen
      Oxford University Programming Research Group, 1982

[Sufrin84]

      Notes for a Z Handbook: Part 1 -- Mathematical Language
      Bernard Sufrin, Carroll Morgan, Ib Holm Sørensen, Ian Hayes
      Oxford University Programming Research Group, 1984

Appendix: laws used in the proof

Restriction Elimination

The law of *restriction elimination* follows directly from the definition of the domain exclusion ($\triangleleft$) and domain restriction ($\triangleleft$) operators.

$$R:X \leftrightarrow Y; \; S:\mathbb{P} X \vdash R = (S \triangleleft R) \; \cup \; (S \triangleleft R)$$

Where Elimination

The two laws of *where-clause elimination* follows directly from the semantics of predicates which are qualified by where-clause definitions. A predicate qualified by a where clause is syntactically equivalent to an existentially-quantified predicate.

$$(P_1 \; \underline{where} \; v:T \; | \; P_2) \quad \hat{=} \quad (\exists \; v:T \bullet P_2 \wedge P_1)$$

$$(P \; \underline{where} \; v \; \hat{=} \; E) \quad \hat{=} \quad (\exists \; v:T \bullet v=E \wedge P)$$

(where T is the type of the term E).

For example, using the second law the predicate

$$x=y^2 \; \underline{where} \; y\hat{=}4$$

is equivalent to the predicate

$$\exists \; y:N \bullet y=4 \wedge x=y^2$$

which may be simplified further to $x=16$

PART C — DISTRIBUTED COMPUTING

Roger Gimson

Carroll Morgan

Work on the Distributed Computing Software Project began at Oxford University Programming Research Group in 1982. The goal of the project is to construct and publish the specification of a loosely-coupled distributed operating system, based on the model of autonomous clients having access to a number of shared services.

A fundamental objective of the project is to make use of mathematical techniques of program specification to assist the design, development and presentation of distributed system services.

In this section we present some of the results of the first stage of the project.

The section begins with an overview of the use of mathematics in system design, and its application to the specification of an example file service. It illustrates how abstraction from details of implementation can allow the exploration of novel system designs.

The rest of the section contains the user documentation for some of the services which have been implemented to date. Surprisingly, it was possible to place the original specifications wholly within the corresponding user manuals; and so they illustrate how we have been able to blend our abstract mathematical descriptions with the detail even of the concrete syntax of a programming language interface.

The project is funded by a grant from the Science and Engineering Research Council.

Contents

1. The Role of Mathematical Specifications

This chapter appeared in the book "Distributed Computing Systems Programme" (ed. D.A.Duce), published by Peter Peregrinus Ltd. 1984, under the title "Ease of use through proper specification".

1.1 Introduction

The aim of the Distributed Computing Software Project is to explore the new possibilities of distributed operating system design which have been made possible by the low cost of distributed processing hardware. The mathematical techniques of program specification and development play a crucial part in this aim because:

we can use *mathematical specifications* to explore designs motivated purely by ease-of-use rather than by ease-of-implementation (since specification allows abstraction from implementation constraints);

we will have a precise notation in which such designs can be reliably communicated to others, and which will assist the discovery and discussion of the designs' implications;

it will be possible to present the specifications directly in the user manuals of the distributed operating system, thus increasing their precision while decreasing their size; and

we will be able to use the mathematical techniques of *refinement* to produce implementations which are highly likely to satisfy their specifications (and hence will also be accurately described by their user manuals).

It is especially important that those benefits should be realised in the construction of a *distributed* operating system - because distributed operating systems offer the rare opportunity for the user to control the system, rather than vice versa. The high bandwidth of current local area networks allows an efficient modularity; for example, a structure consisting of largely autonomous services and clients is entirely feasible. In such a system, the choice between (rival) services, and the manner in which they are used, would be entirely up to the clients. This is the basis of the *open systems* approach: provided services are well-specified, clients are free to make use of them in whatever manner is consistent with their specification.

1.2 A first example

One of the most visible parts of any operating system is its file system. Even today, the design of these range in quality from excellent to horrific. But others of course may think instead that they range from horrific to excellent: the features one user cannot do without, another may abhor. It is through such *features* that an operating system controls (even the thoughts of) its clients, and this is exactly what we hope to avoid.

A file *service* in a distributed operating system is there to be shared by as many clients as possible. To achieve this, it must be unopinionated: it must have so *few* features that there is nothing anyone could object to. It is only in the context of specification that we can propose such a radical design; any less abstract context introduces efficiency constraints. Some of these, of course, will have to be met eventually, but perhaps not all of the ones that might conventionally be presumed. We must not introduce such constraints simply because we could not express ourselves without them: first we state what we would like - then we can compromise.

As an example, let us consider the simplest file system design one could imagine. We describe it as a partial function "files" from the set "NAME" of file names to the set "FILE" of all possible files; and we say nothing about the structure of the sets NAME and FILE themselves:

files: NAME $\rightarrow$ FILE

The mathematical notation above introduces the variable files, and gives its type as NAME $\rightarrow$ FILE. The English text states that this variable is to describe the file system. Our style of mathematical specification is an example of the Z specification technique, and we will continue to use it below. It is not possible for us to explain Z itself in any detail in this document, but we hope its flavour will be evident; and in any case the bulk of the meaning will be conveyed by the English. Sufrin [8] and Morgan [3,4] together give an introduction to Z.

We propose two operations only on the file system: StoreFile stores a (whole) file, and RetrieveFile (destructively) retrieves it.

StoreFile

Let files be the state of the file system before the operation, and let files' be the state afterwards. Let file? be the file to be stored, and let name! be some filename, chosen by the filesystem, which will refer to the newly stored file (we conventionally use words ending in ? for inputs, and in ! for outputs). That is, given

```
files, files': NAME ⇸ FILE
file?         : FILE
name!         : NAME
```

the effect of StoreFile is to choose a new name, which is not currently in use

$$name! \notin dom\ files$$

and to update the partial function by overriding its current value, so that after the operation it maps the new name to the newly-stored file

$$files' = files \oplus \{name! \mapsto file?\}$$

(We notice as an immediate advantage of our abstraction that we have given the implementor the freedom to store identical but differently named files using shared or separate storage, as he chooses.)

RetrieveFile

Let files be the state of the file system before the operation, and let files' be the state afterwards. Let name? be the name of the file to be retrieved, and let file! be the file itself. That is, given

```
files, files': NAME ⇸ FILE
name?         : NAME
file!         : FILE
```

the effect of RetrieveFile is to return the named file to the client

$$file! = files\ (name?)$$

provided it exists

    name? ∈ dom files

and to remove the name (and hence the file) from the partial function which represents the file system

    files' = {name?} ⊴ files

The description above is "of course" not feasible with today's technology - which is a pity. It would be too impractical to have to retrieve a whole large file if we wished, say, just to read one small piece of it. But how wonderful it would be if a file system could be so simple! At least we were able to describe it.

1.3 The first compromises

The best we can do with our simple file system is to use it as the basis for a development of a more practical design - and the description above provides a context into which the necessary compromises can be introduced. Here are some of them (in no particular order):

<u>Compromise</u>	<u>Reason</u>
It must be possible to read the file without deleting it.	The communication medium is not entirely reliable - a breakdown during retrieval could destroy the file without returning its contents.
Clients must be prevented from destroying the files of others (remember, a file can't be updated).	Mistakes are inevitable - even honest clients could accidentally destroy other clients' files.
Files must be given a limited lifetime, and clients must be charged for their storage.	Any implementation of the file system, however capacious, will still be finite.

We introduce these compromises in a revised design. First, we name three new sets:

CLIENT   - the set of client identifications,

TIME   - the set of instants (e.g. seconds from 1st January 1980 - but we need not be specific here),

COST   - the set of costs (e.g. pence).

The definition of a file is extended to include the identification of its owner, and its time of creation and (eventual) expiry. DATA is a fourth new set which contains all the possible values a client could store in a file (its contents). We will collect these attributes in a schema FILE, and state at the same time that in any file, the creation time must precede the expiry time:

```
FILE
        owner     : CLIENT
        created,
        expires  : TIME
        contents : DATA

        created ≤ expires
```

The schema FS below describes the state of the file storage system itself:

```
FS
        files: NAME ⇸ FILE
```

and the schema ΔFS describes the general aspects of any operation on it:

```
ΔFS
        files, files': NAME ⇸ FILE
        who            : CLIENT
        when           : TIME
```

who is the identity of the client performing the operation, and when is the time at which it is performed. We can abbreviate ΔFS (without changing its meaning) by building it from the schema FS instead of directly from the variable files:

```
ΔFS
    FS
    FS'
    who : CLIENT
    when: TIME
```

StoreFile

The (revised) StoreFile operation we will present as a schema including the variables files, files', who, and when (supplied by ΔFS), as well as the data to be stored (contents?), the expiry time (expires?), the new name chosen by the service (name!), and the charge made in advance (cost!):

```
StoreFile
    ΔFS
    contents?: DATA
    expires? : TIME
    name!    : NAME
    cost!    : COST

    (∃FILE' •
                owner'     = who
                created'   = when
                expires'   = expires?
                contents'  = contents?

                name!    ∉ dom files
                files'   = files ⊕ {name! ↦ FILE'}
                cost!    = Tariff (FILE'))
```

A new file FILE′ is constructed which is owned by the client storing it, which records its creation time as the time it was stored, which will expire at the time the client specified (then becoming inaccessible), and whose contents the client supplies.

A new name name!, not currently in use, is chosen and the file is stored under that name. The charge made is some function Tariff of the file (hence of its owner, creation and expiry times, and contents). Here is a possible definition of Tariff (which depends in turn on some function Size):

$$\text{Tariff} = (\lambda \text{FILE} \bullet (\text{expires} - \text{created}) * \text{Size(contents)})$$

ReadFile

The ReadFile operation returns the expiry time and the contents of the file stored under a given name. Its parameters are the name of the file to be returned (name?), when it will expire (expires!), and its contents (contents!):

```
ReadFile
      ΔFS
      name?     : NAME
      expires! : TIME
      contents!: DATA

      FS′ = FS

      (∃FILE •
            FILE        = files (name?)
            expires    > when
            expires!   = expires
            contents!  = contents)
```

ReadFile does not change the state of the service. The map files is applied to the name, to determine the file's value FILE, which must not have expired. Its expiry time and contents are returned.

DeleteFile

The DeleteFile operation removes a file from the service. A rebate is offered as an incentive to deletion before expiry. name? is the name of the file to be deleted, and cost! is the (possibly negative) charge made for doing so (we assume negation "–" is defined on COST):

```
DeleteFile
      ΔFS
      name?: NAME
      cost!: COST

      (∃FILE •
            FILE    = files (name?)
            expires > when
            owner   = who
            files'  = {name?} ◁ files
            cost!   = - Rebate (FILE, when))
```

The map files is applied to the name, to determine the file's value FILE, which must not have expired. It must be owned by the deleting client. The file's name name? (and hence the file itself) are removed from the partial function which represents the stored files, and the cost is determined by a function Rebate of the file and its deletion time. Here is a possible definition of Rebate:

$$
Rebate = (\lambda FILE;\ when:\ TIME\ \bullet\ (expires\ -\ when)\ *\ Size(contents))
$$

Naturally, there are other compromises which could be made, in addition to or instead of those above. In the next section, however, we discuss a compromise which we suggest should *not* be made.

1.4 A compromise avoided

One glaring inefficiency remains in our proposal: that we must transfer whole files at once. Many clients will not have time or the resources (e.g. local memory) to do this. But here we will not compromise by modifying our file storage service to cater for this inefficiency - rather we insist that the business of the file storage service will be file storage exclusively. Partial examination and updating will be the business of a file updating service.

To propose a service which treats the contents of files as having structure, we must propose a structure. The proposal we make is the very simple view that the contents of a file is a sequence of *pieces*. (Recall that sequences are functions from the natural numbers N to their base type, and begin at index 1.) We do not wish to say what a piece is, however, for this description.

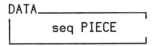

```
DATA
        seq PIECE
```

The file updating service in fact has no state; all its work is done in the calculation of its outputs from its inputs. Its two operations are ReadData and UpdateData.

ReadData

ReadData takes the contents of a file contents?, a starting position start?, and a number of pieces to be read number?, and returns the data pieces! at that position within contents?. (#pieces! is the length of the sequence pieces!, and 1..#pieces! is the set $\{i: N \mid 1 \leqslant i \leqslant \#\text{pieces}!\}$.)

ReadData _____

      contents?: DATA
      start?,
      number? : N
      pieces! : DATA

      #pieces! = min (number?, (#contents? - start?))

      $(\forall i: 1..\#\text{pieces}! \bullet \text{pieces}!(i) = \text{contents}?(i + \text{start}?))$

The length of the data returned is equal to the number of pieces requested, if possible; otherwise, it is as large as the length of contents? will allow. The ith piece of pieces! returned is equal to the $(i+\text{start}?)^{\text{th}}$ piece of contents?.

UpdateData

UpdateData takes the contents of a file contents?, a position start?, and some data pieces?, and returns an updated contents contents!.

UpdateData _____

      contents?,
      contents! : DATA
      start?   : N
      pieces? : DATA

      #contents! = max (#contents?, (start? + #pieces?))
      start? $\leqslant$ #contents?

      $(\forall i: 1..\#\text{contents}! \bullet$
         $(i - \text{start}?) \in 1..\#\text{pieces}?$
            $\Rightarrow \text{contents}!(i) = \text{pieces}?(i - \text{start}?)$

         $(i - \text{start}?) \notin 1..\#\text{pieces}?$
            $\Rightarrow \text{contents}!(i) = \text{contents}?(i))$

The length of the new contents is equal to its original length, unless an extension was necessary to accommodate the new data; however, the new data must begin within the original contents or immediately at its end. The ith piece of contents! is equal to the $(i-start?)^{th}$ piece of pieces?, if this is defined; otherwise, it is equal to the ith piece of contents?.

Our proposal is of course only one of the many possible (for a different proposal, see the definition of these operations in Morgan and Sufrin [5]). We could, of course, propose *several* updating services, each providing its own set of facilities. Moreover, the original operations which transferred whole files would still be available to those clients able to use them (see figure 1).

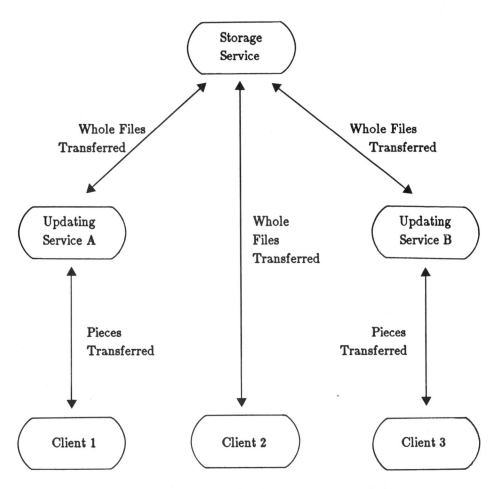

Figure 1: Separate updating and storage services

1.5 Modularity and composition of services

The structure we have presented above separates the issues of how files should be stored from how they should be manipulated. As a result, we have offered the user an unusual freedom of choice - he can read just one piece of a file, or he can treat a file as a single object (with the corresponding conceptual simplification; Stoy and Strachey [7] for example allow this in their operating system OS6).

Still, it is likely that a further compromise will be necessary: for large files, the time taken to transfer the file between the two services (storage and updating) may not be tolerable. We solve this not by changing our design, but by an engineering decision: for applications that require it, we will provide the two services together *in one box*, and the transfers will be internal to it (see figure 2). Its specification we construct by combining the material already available.

StoreFile, ReadFile, and DeleteFile will be available as before. However, we introduce two new operations, ReadStoredFile and UpdateStoredFile, whose specifications will be formed by composing the specifications given above. (The schema composition operator "⅋", used for this, is defined in the glossary.)

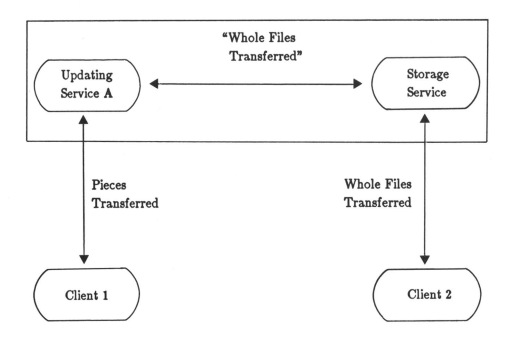

Figure 2:   Combined updating and storage service

ReadStoredFile

Reading a stored file is performed by first reading the whole file with ReadFile, and then reading the required portion of its contents using ReadData. In Z we write this

$$\text{ReadStoredFile} \; \hat{=} \; \text{ReadFile} \; \text{;} \; \text{ReadData}$$

If we were to expand this definition of ReadStoredFile, the result would be as below:

```
ReadStoredFile
    ΔFS
    name?    : NAME
    start?,
    number? : N
    expires!: TIME
    pieces! : DATA

    FS' = FS

    (∃FILE •
      FILE    = files (name?)
      expires > when
      expires! = expires

      #pieces! = min (number?, (#contents - start?))
      (∀i: 1..#pieces! •
          pieces!(i) = contents(i + start?)))
```

ReadStoredFile takes a file name name?, a starting position start?, and a number of pieces number?, and returns the expiry time of the file expires!, and the data pieces! found at the position specified. (expires! is returned by ReadStoredFile because ReadFile returns it; we could have dropped this extra output, but choose not to introduce the Z notation for doing so.)

UpdateStoredFile

The complementary operation UpdateStoredFile is a more difficult composition, since we must accumulate the costs of the component operations, and we must ensure that the updated file is (re-)stored under its original name. For the sake of honesty, we will give the definition, but we will not expand it:

UpdateStoredFile ≙

        ReadFile ⁏
        DeleteFile [dcost!/cost!] ⁏
        UpdateData ⁏
        StoreFile [name?/name!, scost!/cost!] ⁏
        (dcost?, scost?, cost!: COST | cost! = dcost? + scost?)

UpdateStoredFile first reads the whole file, then deletes it, then updates it, and then stores its new value under its original name. Finally, it presents as its overall cost the sum of the two charges made by DeleteFile (which may well be negative) and StoreFile.

What we have done is to compose two simple but infeasible operations to produce a more complicated but feasible one (rather like the use of complex numbers in electrical engineering, for example). Naturally, the implementor need not transfer whole files back and forth within his black box on every read and update operation - but nevertheless the updating and storage service provided by the box *must* behave as if he does: that is, it must behave as we have specified. Our decomposition was chosen for economy of concept; the implementor's must be chosen for economy of time and equipment, and the whole range of engineering techniques are available to him to do so (caches, update-in-place, *etc.*).

1.6 Experience so far

The Distributed Computing Project has followed the general principles above, but it has in fact adapted to constraints in different ways. Its storage service, which we have implemented in prototype, stores *blocks* of a fixed size (rather like the service described by Biekert and Janssen[1]). This distinguishes it as a "universal" storage service from, say, the one implemented at Cambridge (described by Needham and Herbert[6]). Organisation of blocks into files, the keeping of directories, etc. is done by software in the clients' own machines (for example, using a "File Package" as described by Gimson [2]). This allows clients freedom in the choice of what file structure they build, but of course makes the sharing of files more difficult. If one package should become popular, however, it could be placed in a machine of its own, and so become a service.

There are many aspects of the project that it has not been possible to cover. For example, the specification of the errors that may occur in use is an essential part of the full specification of a service. We include such details in the user manuals of the services we have implemented. The manuals follow the style of specification presented here, combining formal text and English narrative to give a precise yet easily understandable description of the user interface to a service.

So far, the pressure of simplicity in our mathematical descriptions has kept the designs correspondingly simple. At present, they are perhaps too much so; but by using mathematical specification techniques we have built basic services which genuinely are simple. And that is where one must begin.

1.7 Future plans

The styles of specification, and of presentation of user manuals, has to some extent been developed in parallel with the software to which they have been applied. These styles are now more stable, and further services will be specified, designed, and implemented in the same way.

The goal of the project is to produce a suite of designs from which implementations can be built on a variety of machines. Each design will be documented, in a mathematical style, both for the user and for the implementor. Thus the primary goal is to construct a distributed system on paper.

For a paper construction to have any value, the designs proposed in it must be widely applicable, and genuinely useful. Machine-independent techniques of description will take care of the first requirement. To ensure that the second is met, prototype implementations must be constructed of each of the designs, and experience must be gained of their use.

Acknowledgements

Our thanks go to Sue Waters, for her help with the two figures.

References

[1]   Biekert, R., and Janssen, B., 1983, "The implementation of a file system for the open distributed operating system Amoeba", *Informatica Rapport, Vrije Universitiet, Amsterdam.*

[2]   Gimson, R. B., 1983, "A File Package - User Manual", *Distributed Computing Project Working Paper, Programming Research Group, Oxford University.*

[3]   Morgan, C. C., 1984, "Schemas in Z - a preliminary reference manual", *Distributed Computing Project Working Paper, Programming Research Group, Oxford University.*

[4]   Morgan, C. C., 1984, "Schemas in Z - an example", *Distributed Computing Project Working Paper, Programming Research Group, Oxford University.*

[5]   Morgan, C. C., and Sufrin, B., 1984, "Specification of the Unix File System", *IEEE Trans. Soft. Eng.*, March 1984 (and in part B of this monograph).

[6]   Needham, R., and Herbert, A., 1982, "The Cambridge file service", in *The Cambridge Distributed Computing System*, Addison-Wesley, 41-63.

[7]   Stoy, J. E., and Strachey, C., 1972, "OS6 - An operating system for a small computer", *Comp. J. 15, 2*, 195-203.

[8]   Sufrin, B., 1983, "Mathematics for system specification", *Lecture Notes 1983-1984, Programming Research Group, Oxford University.*

2. Authentication of User Names

2.1 Nicknames and usernames

As a short-term measure, a very simple scheme has been chosen to make it difficult for one client to impersonate another.

Each registered client has a *nickname* and a *username*. Nicknames are allocated from a set Nickname, and the allocation is public - that is, it is common for clients to know each others' nicknames. It is expected that nicknames will change only rarely, if at all.

Usernames are allocated privately, from a set User; a client should not reveal his username to anyone else. Since usernames may become compromised (known by too many people) or forgotten (known by too few!), it might be necessary to change a client's username from time to time.

2.2 Authentication

Authentication is achieved by the existence of a (secret) partial function

$$\mathsf{GetNickname} \;:\;\; \mathsf{User} \;\nrightarrow\; \mathsf{Nickname}$$

which gives for any username the nickname of the client who should be its sole possessor. Since the set User of usernames has been made very large, and the set

$$\mathsf{dom}\ \mathsf{GetNickname}$$

of *authentic* usernames has been made a relatively small part of it, it will be hard for clients to guess the usernames of others. Services therefore may use the function GetNickname to authenticate their clients; they might reject requests for which

$$\mathsf{client?} \;\notin\; \mathsf{dom}\ \mathsf{GetNickname}$$

2.3 Guest user

There is a *guest* username GuestUser which some services might recognise as a special case. This username is public, and is expected to be used by clients temporarily without a private username of their own. It is guaranteed that the guest username is not the authentic username of any client

$$\mathsf{GuestUser} \;\in\; \mathsf{User}\ -\ \mathsf{dom}\ \mathsf{GetNickname}$$

3. Time Service - User Manual

3.1 Time service operation

The time service provides only one user operation, *GetTime*, which returns the current time

> *in seconds since 00:00:00 1 January 1980.*

The description of the operation has three sections, titled **Abstract**, **Definition** and **Reports**.

The Abstract section gives a procedure heading for the operation, with formal parameters, as it might appear in some programming language. The correspondence between this procedure heading and an implementation of it in some real programming language must be obvious and direct.

Each formal parameter is given a name ending with either ? or !. Those ending with ? are inputs, and those ending with ! are outputs.

The Definition section defines the meaning of the operation.

The Reports section lists the possible (success or failure reporting) values which the report! formal parameter can assume. Reports are discussed in more detail in section 3.2.

GETTIME

Abstract

```
GetTime (client?: User;
             now!   : Time;
             cost!  : Money;
             report!: Report)
```

Definition

The current time now! is returned, measured in seconds from 00:00:00 1st January 1980. The cost cost! is fixed. The client's username client? must be authentic (see Chapter 2).

```
client? ∈ dom GetNickname
```

Reports

```
Success
ServiceError
```

3.2 Error reports

The report parameter report! indicates whether the operation succeeded or failed. The value Success indicates that the operation succeeded.

The value ServiceError indicates that the operation failed; in this case, no reliance should be placed on any other values returned. Possible reasons for this report are:

The service isn't running
There was a communication error

3.3 UCSD Pascal interface

```
UNIT TI;

INTERFACE {UNIT TI   28-Nov-83}

{Time Service  -  UCSD-Pascal Interface}

  USES {$U SVTYPES.CODE} SV_Types;


TYPE
  TI_Report = (TI_Success, TI_ServiceError);


PROCEDURE TI_GetTime (    InClient   : SV_User;
                      VAR OutNow    : SV_Time;
                      VAR OutCost   : SV_Money;
                      VAR OutReport : TI_Report);

  {return current time}
```

3.4 Modula-2 interface

```
DEFINITION MODULE TI;  (* Roger Gimson  22-Feb-84 *)


(* Time Service  -  Modula-2 Interface *)


FROM SVTypes IMPORT User, Time, Money;

EXPORT QUALIFIED Report, GetTime;


TYPE
  Report = (Success,
            ServiceError);

PROCEDURE GetTime (    InClient  : User;
                   VAR OutNow    : Time;
                   VAR OutCost   : Money;
                   VAR OutReport : Report);
  (* return current time *)

END TI.
```

4. Reservation Service - User Manual

4.1 Introduction

The distributed operating system at the Programming Research Group is made up of various services which are largely independent. In particular, it is possible that one service can be turned on or turned off while other services and clients continue to run.

When a service is turned off (*shutdown*), there should not be any client who is at that moment involved in some *series* of interactions with it - because interruption of such a series could be quite inconvenient (for the client). If such series (or *transactions*) can be recognised by the service, it is possible to avoid this inconvenience as follows.

Shutdown procedure:

1. The operator *requests* shutdown of the service.

2. The service rejects any attempt to begin a new transaction, but allows current transactions to continue.

3. When all transactions have completed, the service notifies the operator that shutdown is complete.

However, there are some problems; for example, a client might *himself* fail to complete a transaction (presumably due to accidental failure of his own software). If this happened, the service would *never* shutdown. A more serious problem is that for some services (*e.g.* the block storage service) there is no recognisable transaction structure, and so the above scheme cannot be used at all. We solve both problems with an independent *Reservation Service*.

The reservation service does not interact at all with the service it reserves; it interacts only with its own clients, and with the operator. It allows clients to state when, and for how long, they would like to use the reserved service, and it allows the operator to state a *shutdown time* beyond which all reservations are to be rejected. It becomes the clients' responsibility to protect themselves from sudden shutdown of the service (by making reservations), and the operator's responsibility to turn off the service only after the shutdown time (which he may set). Thus a shutdown can be unexpected only by those clients who have made no reservation.

A typical use of the reservation service would be for clients to include a reservation request at the start of every program which uses the reserved service. The duration of the reservation should be long enough to allow the program to complete, but short enough to allow the operator to make a reasonably spontaneous decision to shutdown.

The state of the reservation service has two components:

expires   a map from clients' nicknames (their public identities - see Chapter 2) to the time at which their current reservation expires

shutdown   the shutdown time most recently set by the operator.

```
RS
  expires : Nickname ⇸ Time
  shutdown: Time
```

Each operation requested by clients includes the three values:

client?   the username of the client
cost!   the cost of the operation
report!   a report indicating whether the operation succeeded or failed.

```
ΔRS
  RS
  RS'

  client? : User
  nickname: Nickname

  cost!   : Money
  report! : Report

  client?  ∈ dom GetNickname
  nickname = GetNickname (client?)
```

The username `client?` is supplied by the user; it is his *private* username (as distinct from his public nickname). `client?` must be authentic; that is,

$$\text{client?} \in \text{dom GetNickname}$$

if the service is not to ignore the request.

The client's nickname is calculated by the service. `cost!` and `report!` are returned to the user by the service.

4.2 Reservation service operations

Three operations are described in this section: *Reserve*, which is requested by clients, *SetShutdown*, which is requested by the operator, and *Scavenge*, which is performed by the service itself (at its discretion). The latter two operations are included here only as an aid to the reader's intuition.

The description of each operation can have up to four sections, titled **Abstract**, **Definition, External Calls** and **Reports**.

The Abstract section gives a procedure heading for the operation, with formal parameters, as it might appear in some programming language. The correspondence between this procedure heading and an implementation of it in some real programming language must be obvious and direct.

Each formal parameter is given a name ending with either ? or !. Those ending with ? are inputs, and those ending with ! are outputs.

A short description may accompany the procedure heading.

The Definition section mathematically defines the operation, by giving a schema which includes as a component every formal parameter of the procedure heading. Within the schema appear also subschema(s) whose components include the service state before and after the operation (this can be more (RS, RS') or less (ΔRS) explicit). Any other components appearing in the schema are either local to the operation (that is, temporary) or represent values exchanged with other services (invisibly to the client).

Only the formal parameters of the procedure heading are exchanged directly between client and service.

A short description may accompany the schema.

The External Calls section lists the calls which this service may make on other services, in order to complete the requested operation. These appear as procedure calls which match the procedure headings given in the description of the operation called. (These are found in the user manual for the called service.) The correspondence between formal and actual parameters is positional, with missing (*i.e.* irrelevant) actual parameters indicated by commas.

The Reports section lists the possible (success or failure reporting) values which the formal parameter report! can assume. If such a value is followed by a component in parentheses and/or a predicate, it is to suggest that the reported value would occur *because* that component satisfied the predicate. The component and predicate are therefore a hint to the cause of the report.

Reports are discussed in more detail in section 4.3.

RESERVE

Abstract

```
Reserve (client?  : User;
              interval?: Interval;
              until!   : Time;
              cost!    : Money;
              report!  : Report)
```

A reservation is made for a period of interval? seconds. until! returns the expiry time of the new reservation.

A client can cancel his reservation by making a new reservation in which interval? is zero; see *Scavenge* below.

Definition

```
Reserve _____
  ΔRS
  interval?: Interval
  until!,
  now       : Time
 _____
  until! = now + interval?
  until! ≤ shutdown

  expires'  = expires ⊕ {nickname ↦ until!}
  shutdown' = shutdown

  cost! = ReservationCost
_____
```

The reservation must expire before the shutdown time. The current time now is obtained from the time service (see previous section).

External Calls

Time Service

```
GetTime (,now,,Success)
```

now is obtained by a successful call of *GetTime*. It is measured in seconds from 00:00:00 1st January 1980.

Reports

```
Success
ServiceError

NotAvailable              ⟹         shutdown < now + interval?
                                    shutdown = until!

TooManyUsers              ⟹         #expires = Capacity
```

SETSHUTDOWN

Abstract

SetShutdown (shutdown? : Time;
                    threatens!: Boolean)

The operator may set a new shutdown time. He is informed if the new time threatens existing reservations; if it does, it is his responsibility to negotiate with the clients affected.

Definition

```
SetShutdown ─────────────────────────────────────────────┐
  RS
  RS'
  shutdown? : Time
  threatens!: Boolean
 ─────────────────────
  shutdown'  =  shutdown?

  threatens! = true ⇔
   (∃ expiry: ran expires • expiry > shutdown')

  expires'  = expires
└──────────────────────────────────────────────────────────┘
```

The shutdown time is changed to the new value *regardless of existing reservations*. Reservations are unaffected.

SCAVENGE

Abstract

```
Scavenge()
```

The service can at any time remove reservations whose expiry time has passed. This is in fact the *only* way in which reservations are removed (by client, operator or service).

Definition

```
Scavenge ────────────────────────────────────────────┐
 │  RS
 │  RS'
 │  now: Time
 │──────────────────────────────
 │  shutdown' = shutdown
 │
 │  expires' ⊆ expires
 │
 │  (∀removed: dom expires •  removed ∉ dom expires'
 │                        ⟹ expires(removed) ⩽ now)
 └────────────────────────────────────────────────────┘
```

Scavenge does not change the shutdown time.

Scavenge can remove reservations, but it never makes new ones. A reservation is removed only if its expiry time has passed.

External Calls

Time Service

```
GetTime (,now,,Success)
```

now is obtained by a successful call of *GetTime*. It is measured in seconds from 00:00:00 1st January 1980.

4.3 Error reports

The report! parameter of each operation indicates either that the operation has succeeded or suggests why it failed; in most cases, failure leaves the service unchanged.

An operation can return only the report values listed in the Reports section of its description. If it returns the value Success, it must satisfy its defining schema. If it returns any other value, it must satisfy instead the appropriate schema below.

ServiceError

```
┌─ ServiceError ─────────────────┐
│   RS                           │
│   RS'                          │
│  ──────────────────────        │
│   report! = ServiceError       │
└────────────────────────────────┘
```

ServiceError indicates an unexpected failure, which might not be the client's fault. These are typical causes:

Service not running

Network (hardware or protocol) failure
Service hardware fault
Service software error

NotAvailable

```
NotAvailable _____
  ΔRS
  interval?: Interval
  until!,
  now       : Time
 ─────────────────────
  report! = NotAvailable

  shutdown < now + interval?
  until! = shutdown

  RS' = RS
```

If the reservation cannot be made due to early shutdown, the shutdown time itself is returned in until!.

now is obtained from the time service.

TooManyUsers

```
TooManyUsers _____
 ΔRS
 now: Time
 _____
 report! = TooManyUsers

 #expires = Capacity

 nickname ∉ dom expires

 RS' = RS
```

The service has finite capacity Capacity for recording reservations; this report
occurs when that capacity would be exceeded. The report *cannot* occur if the client
has a reservation (since it is overwritten by the new one).

now is obtained from the time service.

Clients who cannot themselves make reservations might be able to rely temporarily on
the reservations of others.

4.4 UCSD Pascal interface

```
UNIT RI;

INTERFACE {UNIT RI   28-Nov-83}

{Reservation Service  -  UCSD-Pascal Interface}

  USES  {$U SVTYPES.CODE} SV_Types;


TYPE
  RI_Report = (RI_Success, RI_ServiceError, RI_NotAvailable,
               RI_TooManyUsers);


PROCEDURE RI_Reserve (    InClient    : SV_User;
                          InInterval  : SV_Interval;
                      VAR OutUntil    : SV_Time;
                      VAR OutCost     : SV_Money;
                      VAR OutReport   : RI_Report);

  {reserve use of the service for InInterval, terminating at
   OutUntil, otherwise return the time at which the service
   becomes unavailable in OutUntil}
```

4.5 Modula-2 interface

```
DEFINITION MODULE RI;  (* Roger Gimson   22-Feb-84 *)


(* Reservation Service  -  Modula-2 Interface *)


FROM SVTypes IMPORT User, Time, Interval, Money;

EXPORT QUALIFIED Report, Reserve;


TYPE
  Report = (Success,
            ServiceError,
            NotAvailable,
            TooManyUsers);

PROCEDURE Reserve (     InClient   : User;
                        InInterval : Interval;
                    VAR OutLimit   : Time;
                    VAR OutCost    : Money;
                    VAR OutReport   : Report);
  (* reserve use of the service for InInterval, terminating at
     OutLimit, otherwise return the time at which the service
     becomes unavailable in OutLimit *)

END RI.
```

PART D — TRANSACTION PROCESSING

Ian Hayes

The papers presented in this section were produced as part of a joint project between IBM (UK) Laboratories at Hursley, England and the Programming Research Group of Oxford University into the application of formal software specification techniques to transaction processing.

The work documented consists of specifications of parts of the IBM Customer Information Control System (CICS). The first paper contains a description of the work carried out; this paper has been published in the IEEE Transactions on Software Engineering (February 1985). A number of modules of the CICS command level application programmer's interface were specified; these include the CICS Exception Handling which is documented within the first paper and CICS Temporary Storage which is described in the second paper. The paper on the CICS Message System was later work not directly related to the other papers.

The work documented here was supported by research contract between IBM and Oxford University and is published by kind permission of the Company. Carroll Morgan gave much needed and appreciated critiques of the specifications. The project was lucky to have had Rod Burstall, Tony Hoare and Cliff Jones as consultants. Peter Collins and John Nicholls have been responsible for the project from the IBM end and Ib Sørensen was responsible for setting up the project from the Oxford end; the work reported here owes much to his guidance throughout the project.

Contents

Applying Formal Specification to
Software Development in Industry*

Ian Hayes

Abstract

This paper reports experience gained in applying formal specification techniques to an existing transaction processing system. The system is the IBM Customer Information Control System (CICS) and the work has concentrated on specifying a number of modules of the CICS application programmer's interface.

The uses of formal specification techniques are outlined, with particular reference to their application to an existing piece of software. The specification process itself is described and a sample specification presented. The specifications are written in the specification notation Z, which is based on the notation of set theory from mathematics.

One of the main benefits of applying specification techniques to existing software is that questions are raised about the system design and documentation during the specification process. Some problems that were identified by these questions are discussed.

Problems with the specification techniques themselves, which arose in applying the techniques to a commercial transaction processing system, are outlined.

Introduction

Oxford University and IBM United Kingdom Laboratories Limited are engaged in a joint project to evaluate the applicability of formal specification techniques to industrial scale software. The project is attempting to scale up formal mathematical methods, used so far within a research environment, to large-scale software in an industrial environment. This paper reports the experience gained so far in applying these techniques to describe the application programmer's interface of the IBM Customer Information Control System (CICS).

CICS is widely used to support online transaction processing applications such as airline reservations, stock control, and banking. It can support applications involving large numbers of terminals (thousands) and very large data bases (requiring gigabytes). The CICS General Information manual [3] gives the following description:

> CICS/VS provides (1) most of the standard functions required by application programs for communication with remote and local terminals and subsystems; (2) control for concurrently running user application programs serving many online users; and (3) data base capabilities . . .

CICS is general purpose in the sense that it provides the primitives of transaction processing. An individual application is implemented by writing a program invoking these primitives. The primitives are similar to operating system calls, but are at a higher level: they also provide such facilities as security checking, logging, and error recovery.

CICS has been in use since 1968, and has undergone continuous development during its lifetime. In the original implementation, the application programmer's interface was at the level of control blocks and assembly language macro calls. This is referred to as the *macro*-level application programmer's interface. In 1976 a new interface, the *command*-level application programmer's interface, was introduced. It provides a cleaner interface which does not require the application programmer to have knowledge of the control blocks used in the implementation of the system. The command-level interface is the subject of our work on specification.

CICS is supported on a number of IBM operating systems: DOS/VSE, MVS, and MVS/XA, in such a way that application programs written using the application programmer's interface may be transferred from one environment to another without recoding. In addition, the command-level interface supports a number of programming languages: PL/I, Cobol, Assembly language, and RPG II. This is achieved by the use of a preprocessor that translates programs containing CICS commands into the appropriate statements in the language being used (usually a call on a CICS module). Hence the application programmer's interface provides a level of abstraction that hides a number of significantly different implementations.

The command level interface is split up into a number of relatively independent modules responsible for controlling various resources of the system. The formal specification work has so far concentrated on specifying individual modules in relative isolation. Of the sixteen modules comprising the command level interface, three — temporary storage, exceptional condition handling, and interval control — have been specified. Temporary storage provides facilities for setting up named temporary storage *queues* that may be used to communicate information between transactions or as temporary storage by a single transaction. Exceptional condition handling provides facilities to handle exceptions raised by calls on CICS commands in a manner similar to PL/I condition handling. Interval control provides facilities to set up time-outs and delays, as well as to start a new transaction at a given time and to pass data to it.

With the large number of CICS systems around the world, the usage of the CICS command level application programmer's interface is on a par with many programming languages. As with programming languages, it is important that the interface be clearly specified in a manner independent of a particular implementation.

Uses of Formal Specification

The work reported in this paper deals with the specification of parts of an existing system. Before considering the benefits of specification when applied to existing software we will briefly review the benefits of specification in general. (For a more detailed discussion see [8].)

In software development a formal specification can be used by:

- o designers — to formulate and experiment with the design of the system;

- o implementors — as a precise description of the system being built, particularly if there is more than one implementation;

- documentors — as an unambiguous starting point for user manuals; and

- quality control — for the development of suitable testing strategies.

Using a specification, the designer of a system can reason about properties of the system before development starts; and during development, formal verification that an implementation meets its specification can be carried out.

When an existing system is being specified there are both short and long term benefits. In the short term performing the specification

1. uncovers those parts of the existing manuals that are either incomplete or inconsistent; and

2. gives insights into anomalies in the existing system and can suggest ways in which the system could be improved.

In the longer term the specification can be used

1. for re-implementation of all or part of the system;

2. as a basis for discussing and developing specifications for changes or additions to the system; and

3. to provide a model of the functional behaviour of the system suitable for educating new staff.

Re-implementation may involve a new machine architecture, programming language, or operating system, or a restructuring to take advantage of multi-processor or distributed systems. As the specification is implementation independent, it provides a suitable starting point for each of the above alternatives.

When changes or additions to the system are to be made, new specifications can be developed with reference to the previous specification. These developments will give insights into the effect of the changes and their interaction with existing parts of the system.

As the specification is a formal document it provides a more precise description for communication between the designers than natural language descriptions. This should help to reduce misunderstandings among the people involved.

Experimentation with specification provides a much quicker and cheaper method of investigating a number of alternative changes to the system than implementing the changes. On the other hand, because the specification is implementation independent, it cannot provide direct answers to questions of how difficult the changes will be to implement, or their impact on the performance of the system. However, as it is at a high level of abstraction it can give a better insight into the interaction of changes with other components of the system; it is just these high level interactions which get lost in the detail of implementation.

While working predominantly at a more abstract level the specifier must be experienced in implementation and should be aware of the implementation consequences of his decisions. Those parts of the specification for which the implementation consequences are unclear should be further investigated before detailed implementation is begun.

The Specification Process

The starting point for our specification work was the CICS command level application programmer's reference manual [2]. The style of this manual is a combination of formal notation describing the syntax of commands and informal English explanations of the operation of the commands. We developed our initial specification of a module of the system by reference to the corresponding section of the manual. The main goal was to come up with a mathematical model of the module that is consistent with its description in the manual. This involves forming a crude initial model of the module and extending it to cover operations (or facets of operations) not initially dealt with, or refining or redesigning the specification as inconsistencies are discovered between it and the manual.

In attempting the initial specification, questions arose that were not satisfactorily answered by the manual. At this stage, a list of questions was prepared, and an expert on that module of the system (along with the source code) was consulted.

Questions can arise because:

1. the manual is incomplete or vague;

2. the manual is not explicit as to whether *possible* special cases are treated normally or not;

3. the manual is itself inconsistent; or

4. the chosen mathematical model is inconsistent with the manual in some small way: either the model or the manual is incorrect.

As the system has been in use for some time the answers to the more straightforward questions about its operation have already found their way into the manual. Hence most questions that arose in the specification process were rather subtle and required for their answers reference to the source code of the module. Some of the questions led to inconsistencies being discovered between the manual and the implementation. These inconsistencies would either be errors in the manual or bugs in the implementation. Which way they should be classified depends on the original intent of the designer.

The specification was also given to people experienced in formal specification who gave comments on its internal consistency and style, and who suggested ways in which the specification could be simplified or improved. They were also given a copy of the relevant section of the manual to read *after* they had understood the specification, and were asked to point out any inconsistencies they discovered between it and the specification.

The answers to questions and the review of the specification led to a revision of the specification, which led to further questions and further review, and so on.

Notation

The style of the specification document is a mixture of formal Z and informal explanatory English. The formal parts of the specification, given in Z, are surrounded in the text by boxes so that they stand apart from the explanatory surrounds and may be more easily found for reference purposes. To make a specification readable, both formal and informal parts are necessary; the formal text can be too terse for easy reading and often its purpose needs to be explained, while the informal natural language explanation can more easily be vague or ambiguous and needs the precision of a formal language to make the intent clear. The informal text provides the link between formality and reality without which the formal text would just be a piece of mathematics. To create a good specification the structuring of the specification and the composition and style of the informal prose are as important as the formal text.

The aim is to provide a specification at a high level of abstraction and thus avoid implementation details. The specification should reveal the operation of the system a small portion at a time. These portions can be progressively combined to give a specification of the whole. This style of presentation is preferred to giving a monolithic specification and trying to explain it; the latter can be rather overwhelming and incomprehensible since there are too many different facets to understand at once. It is hoped that by giving the specification in small portions each piece can be understood, and when the pieces are put together the understanding of the parts that has already been gained can lead more easily to an understanding of the whole.

For more complex specifications that are developed via numerous small steps, understanding the whole can be quite difficult, since one needs to remember the function of all the parts and understand the way in which they are combined. In such cases it can be useful to provide both a portion by portion development of the specification and an expanded monolithic specification as well. The latter is more assailable after one has been through a piece by piece development and has an understanding of its various components.

A Sample Specification

As a sample of the type of specification produced we will look in detail at the specification of exceptional condition handling within CICS. The exception check mechanisms of CICS are similar to those provided by PL/I [4]. This module was chosen for exposition because it is one of the smaller modules in the system. The manual entry on which the specification was initially based is given in the appendix. The specification given here is a final product of a specification process described in the previous section.

The *syntax* of the CICS commands depends of course on the environment in which they are written. Our notation below is intended to be uncommitted, but explicit enough to indicate exactly which command is meant.

Exceptional Conditions Specification

Exceptional conditions may arise during the execution of a CICS command. A transaction may either set up an action to be taken on a condition by using a Handle Condition command, or it may specify that the condition is to be ignored by using an Ignore Condition command. If a condition has been neither handled nor ignored, then the default action for that condition is used.

For example, to handle condition x with action y we can use

```
Handle Condition(c=x, a=y)
```

where the keyword parameter "c=" gives the condition and "a=" gives the action. To ignore condition z we use

```
Ignore Condition(c=z)
```

We introduce the set CONDITION, which contains all the exceptional conditions that may occur, and also contains two special conditions: *success* — the condition that indicates that a command completed normally, and *error* — a catchall condition that might be used if the exceptional condition that occurred is not handled.

We also introduce the set ACTION which contains all actions that could be taken in response to some exceptional condition. The exact nature of ACTION will not be discussed in detail here. For each programming language supported by CICS it has a slightly different meaning, but for all of the languages an action is represented by a label which is given control. There are five special actions used in this specification: *nil* — indicating a normal return (i.e., no action), *abort* — the action that abnormally terminates a transaction, *wait* — indicating that the transaction is to wait until the operation can be completed normally (e.g., wait until space becomes available), and *system* — used to simplify the specification of the Handle Condition command.

The State

The state of the exception controlling system can be defined by

```
┌─ Exceptions ──────────────────────────────────┐
│    Handler : CONDITION ⇸ ACTION               │
│   ─────────────────────────                    │
│    Handler(success) = nil                      │
└────────────────────────────────────────────────┘
```

The mapping Handler gives the action to be taken for those conditions that have been set up by either an Ignore Condition or Handle Condition command. The handling action for condition *success* is always *nil* (i.e., return normally). The action for other conditions is determined by some fixed function

```
Default : CONDITION → ACTION
```

We state two properties of Default:

```
Default(error) = abort
rng(Default) = { nil, abort, wait }
```

The default action for the special condition *error* is to abort and the only default actions are *nil*, *abort*, and *wait*.

The initial state of the exception handling system for a transaction is given by

```
┌─ Initial ──────────────────────────────────┐
│    Exceptions                               │
│   ─────────────                             │
│    Handler = { success ↦ nil }              │
└─────────────────────────────────────────────┘
```

The initial state of the handler is to return normally if the operation completes successfully.

As an example, if starting in the initial state the commands

```
Handle Condition(c=x, a=y)
Ignore Condition(c=z)
```

are executed, then the final state will satisfy

$$\text{Handler} = \{\ x \mapsto y,\ z \mapsto nil,\ success \mapsto nil\ \}$$

The Handle Condition sets up a mapping from condition x to action y and the Ignore Condition maps condition z onto the *nil* action.

The Operations

The two operations, Handle Condition and Ignore Condition, work directly on the above state. We describe a state change using the following schema, which is called "ΔExceptions":

```
┌─ ΔExceptions ──────────────────────────────────┐
│    Exceptions                                  
│    Exceptions'                                 
└────────────────────────────────────────────────┘
```

Exceptions represents the state of the exception handling system before an operation and Exceptions' the state after.

The operation Handle Condition is used to set up the action, a, to be performed on a particular exceptional condition, c; it is defined as

```
┌─ Handle Condition ──────────────────────────────────────────────┐
│   ΔExceptions                                                    │
│   c : CONDITION                                                  │
│   a : ACTION                                                     │
│ ──────────────────────────                                       │
│   c ≠ success ∧ a ∉ { nil, abort, wait } ∧                       │
│   (a=system) → Handler' = Handler ⊕ { c ↦ Default(c) },          │
│                Handler' = Handler ⊕ { c ↦ a }                    │
└──────────────────────────────────────────────────────────────────┘
```

The first predicate gives the pre-condition for the operation: the special condition *success* cannot be handled, and the special actions *nil*, *abort*, and *wait* cannot be given as handling actions. The second predicate describes the effect of the operation: if the action to be set up is specified as *system*, then instead the default action for the given condition will be set up as the handler for that condition; otherwise the supplied action, a, will be set up. For example, if the following command is executed in the initial state

```
Handle Condition(c=x, a=system)
```

where Default(x) = *wait*, the resulting state will satisfy

```
Handler = { x ↦ wait, success ↦ nil }
```

The operation to specify that an exceptional condition is to be ignored is given by

```
┌─ Ignore Condition ──────────────────────────────────────┐
│   ΔExceptions                                            │
│   c : CONDITION                                          │
│ ──────────────────────────                               │
│   c ≠ success                                            │
│   Handler' = Handler ⊕ { c ↦ nil }                       │
└──────────────────────────────────────────────────────────┘
```

The special condition *success* cannot be specified in an Ignore Condition command. The action to be taken on an ignored condition is to return normally (i.e., *nil*).

Exception Checking

Exception handling can take place on any CICS command except Handle Condition and Ignore Condition themselves. We need to describe the exception checking that takes place on all other commands. The exception checking process determines the action, a, to be taken on completion of a command. The value of a is dependent on the condition, c, returned by the command, and the current state of the exception handling mechanism. In addition, any command may specify whether all exceptions are to be handled or not for just the execution of that command. In describing the checking process we will include the Boolean variable handle to indicate this. The following defines the (complex) exception checking mechanism which is included in the definition of each operation (other than Handle Condition and Ignore Condition).

```
┌─ Exception Check ─────────────────────────────────┐
│   Exceptions                                       │
│   handle : Boolean                                 │
│   c : CONDITION                                    │
│   a : ACTION                                       │
│ ──────────────────────────                         │
│   ¬handle             → a = nil,                   │
│   c ∈ dom Handler     → a = Handler(c),            │
│   Default(c) ≠ abort  → a = Default(c),            │
│   error ∈ dom Handler → a = Handler(error),        │
│                         a = abort                  │
└────────────────────────────────────────────────────┘
```

If exceptions are not being handled for the command (¬handle) the action is to return normally; otherwise the action is determined from the exception handler. If the condition, c, has been ignored or handled (including the case where the handle action was specified as *system*) then the corresponding handler action is used. Otherwise, if the default action for the condition is not *abort* the default is used, else if the special condition *error* is handled its handler action is used, otherwise the action will be *abort*.

Questions Raised During Specification

The raising of questions about the system during the specification process is an important benefit of the process. They indicate problems either in the documentation of the system or in its logical design, and provide those responsible for maintaining the system with immediate feedback on problem areas.

In writing a formal specification one is creating a mathematical model of what is being specified, and in creating such a model one is encouraged to be more precise than if one were writing in a natural language. Because of the required precision, questions are raised during the specification process that are not answered by referring to the less formal manual. In fact, the task of formal specification is demanding enough to raise most of the questions about the functional behaviour of the system that would be raised by an attempt to implement it. The effort required for a specification, however, is considerably less than that required for an implementation.

We will now discuss some of the questions that were raised during the specification work on CICS modules. It is interesting to note that most of the questions raised required the expert on the module to refer to the source code to give a conclusive answer. We will begin with the questions about exceptional conditions, then a question about interval control, and finally a question about the interaction between temporary storage and exceptional conditions.

Exceptional Conditions

We will first list some questions that were raised during the specification of exceptional condition handling and then examine one of the more interesting questions in detail. All of these questions were resolved in producing the specification given in the previous section.

1. What is the range of possible default actions?

2. Is the default action for a particular condition the same for all commands that can raise that condition?

3. Can the special condition *error* be ignored?

4. Is the action for condition *error* only used if the default system action on a condition is *abort?*

5. If executed from the initial state, does the sequence

```
Handle Condition(c=x,  a=y)
...
Handle Condition(c=x,  a=system)
```

return the handler to the initial state?

The reader is invited to try to answer these questions from the manual entry given in the appendix and then from the specification given in the previous section. We will now look in detail at question 5 above. It shows a subtle operation of the exceptional conditions mechanism that is counter-intuitive.

In an earlier model of the Handle Condition command the following incorrect line was used in the specification.

$$(a = system) \rightarrow Handler' = \{c\} \lhd Handler$$

That is, if the action is *system* then the entry for the condition c is removed from the handler (c $\notin$ dom Handler'). The final model contains the line

$$(a = system) \rightarrow Handler' = Handler \oplus \{ c \mapsto Default(c) \}$$

In this version, if the action is *system* the entry in the handler for condition c is set up to be Default(c) (therefore c $\in$ dom Handler').

To see the effect of the difference we need to look at the Exception Check mechanism given in the previous section. If we use the second line above then the action when that exception c occurs will be Default(c) (assuming handle is true). In the earlier model, however, the action also depends on whether a handler has been set up for the special condition *error*: the action will be Default(c) unless Default(c) is *abort* and *error* $\in$ dom Handler, in which case the action will be Handler(*error*). The difference between the two versions is subtle and the reader is encouraged to study the definitions of Handle Condition and Exception Check in order to understand the difference.

The exception check mechanism is quite complex. None of the people experienced with CICS who were questioned about exceptional condition handling was aware of the problem detailed above. It is interesting to conjecture why this is so. The most plausible explanation is that the operation of the exception check mechanism is counter-intuitive. For example, the sequence given in question 5:

```
Handle Condition(c=x, a=y)
...
Handle Condition(c=x, a=system)
```

does not leave the exceptional condition handler in its initial state if the default action for condition x is abort and a handler has been set up for the special condition *error*; before the above sequence the *error* handler will be used on an occurrence of condition x, but after, the action Default(x) (i.e., abort) will be used on an occurrence of x.

If the above sequence did restore the exception condition handler to its initial state, then it could be used to temporarily handle condition x for the duration of the statements between the Handle Condition commands. This form of operation is more what those using the exceptional conditions module expect.

The Exception Check mechanism is so complex that most readers of either the manual or the specification given in the previous section do not pick up the above subtle operation unless it is explicitly pointed out in some form of warning. This is probably a good argument in favour of revising exception handling so that it becomes more intuitive.

The discussion about question 5 above also raises the point that a specification can be incorrect. This case shows one advantage of getting a second opinion on the specification and how it compares with the manual, from a person experienced in formal specification. It is important that the reviewer should read the specification before reading the manual. The reviewer's mental model of the system is thus based on the mathematical model in the specification. When the reviewer reads the manual looking for inconsistencies with the specification, any questions that arise can be answered by consulting the precise model given in the specification. This contrasts with the person writing the specification who forms a model from the manual and often has to consult other sources to answer questions that arise. Getting a second opinion on the specification and how it compares to the manual is an important ingredient for increasing confidence in the accuracy and readability of the specification.

Interval Control

As another example we will consider one of the problems raised during the specification of the CICS interval control module. Interval control is responsible for operations that deal with the interval timer. The operations provided by interval control can be split logically into two groups: those concerned with starting new transactions at specified times, and those concerned with time-outs and delays.

In specifying a module of the system we define the state components of the module (in the case of exceptional conditions there was only one state component, Handler). The state components of interval control can be split into two groups that are concerned respectively with the two groups of interval control operations. For the most part, operations only refer to or change components of the corresponding state. One exception is the command Start (to start a new transaction) which in some circumstances changes the time-out state components. This can be considered to be a carefully documented anomaly of the current implementation. Both the implementation and documentation could be simplified if the Start command did not destroy the current time-out. More importantly, removal of this interaction would lead to a more useful time-out mechanism, since time-outs would not be affected by a transaction start.

This anomaly is interesting because it points out an unwanted interaction between different parts of a module. In attempting to write the specification this interaction stood out because it involved the Start operation using the time-out state. This form of interaction between parts of modules tends to be pinpointed in the formal specification process since the offending operations require access to state information other than that of the part to which they belong.

Two further facts reinforce the view that the current operation of the Start command is not the most desirable: if the new transaction is to be started on a different computer system to the one issuing the Start command, or if the start is protected (from the point of view of recovery on system failure) then the start does not destroy the current time-out. Ideally we do not want to have to specify distributed system and recovery effects individually with each operation. We would like to add extra levels of abstraction to describe these effects for the whole system.

Interaction Between Modules

As an example of an interaction between two CICS modules we will consider an interaction between exceptional conditions and temporary storage. When temporary storage is exhausted it can raise the exceptional condition *nospace*. This will be processed in the normal way if it has been explicitly handled; the default action, however, is to wait until space becomes available.

Thus the specification of the temporary storage operations that can lead to a *nospace* exception require access to the exceptional conditions state to determine whether or not the *nospace* exception is handled; if it is handled it can occur, but if it is not, it cannot. These operations would more simply be specified (and implemented) if they had an extra parameter indicating whether or not to wait. It is interesting to note that, in the implementation, such temporary storage commands are transformed into a call with an additional parameter after the exception handling state has been consulted. It is also interesting that these commands were not correctly implemented if the *nospace* exception was ignored.

Interactions between modules of the system are pinpointed during the formal specification process (just as they would be in an implementation) since an operation from one module will need access to the state components of another. Any such interactions discovered during the specification process should be examined closely as they indicate a breakdown in the modular structure of the system.

Problems With Specification

In this section the problems encountered in applying the formal specification techniques themselves will be examined. This is in contrast to the previous section, in which we concentrated on the system being specified.

The problems encountered in applying specification techniques can be split into communication problems between the people involved, the general problem of achieving the "right" level of abstraction in the specification, and more technical problems related to the particular specification technique.

Communication Problems

As a specification group from a university working with a commercial development laboratory we faced a communications problem. Each party has its own language: the specifiers use the language of mathematics based on set theory, while the developers use terminology and concepts specific to the system which they are developing. The communication problem is in both directions. This requires that each party learn the language of the other.

In performing a formal specification the specifier needs to understand what is being specified in order to be able to develop a mathematical model of it. To understand the system he needs to read manuals and consult experts, both of which use IBM and CICS terminology. Once a specification is written the specifier would like to get feedback on its suitability from these same experts. This requires that they need to be educated in mathematics to a level at which they can understand a specification. At the current stage of the project the educational benefit has been more to the advantage of the specifiers learning about the system. In performing a specification of part of a system the specifier, of necessity, becomes an expert on the functional behaviour of that part (but not on the implementation of the part).

The "right" level of abstraction

In this context "right" means that a piece of specification conveys the primary function of the part of the system it specifies and is not unduly cluttered with details. It is most important that a specification should not be biased towards a particular implementation. However, getting the right specification also involves choosing the most appropriate model and structuring the specification so that the minute details of the specified object do not obscure the primary function.

We can use hierarchical structuring to achieve this. Details of some facet of a component can be specified separately and then that specification can be referred to by the higher level specification. Different cases of an operation (e.g. the normal case and the erroneous case) can be specified independently and combined to give a specification of the whole.

The structure of a good specification may not correspond to the structure one may use to provide an efficient implementation. In specification one is trying to provide a clear logical separation of concerns, while in implementation one may take advantage of the relationships between logically separate parts to provide an efficient implementation of the combined entity. The intellectual ability required of a good specifier is roughly equivalent to that of a good programmer; however, the view taken of the system must be different.

Technical Problems

The technical specification problems discovered in applying formal specification techniques to CICS in particular were:

1. putting the module specifications together to provide a specific. tion of the system as a whole;

2. specifying parallelism;

3. specifying recovery on system failures; and

4. specifying distributed systems.

We shall briefly discuss each of these in turn.

Putting modules together: Currently, three modules out of the sixteen modules that form the application programmer's interface have been specified and we now feel we have enough insight into the system to consider the problem of putting the module specifications together. Each module has state components and a set of operations that work on those state components. Putting the modules together amounts to combining the states together to form the state of the system, and extending the operations of the modules to operations on the whole system.

The problems encountered in putting modules together were:

1. avoiding name clashes when the modules were combined;

2. specifying the effect on the whole system state of an operation defined within a module of the system; and

3. coping with situations in which an operation of one module refers to state components of another module.

Parallelism: In our current specifications the operations are assumed to be atomic operations acting on the state of the system. We have a sufficient underlying theory to allow one to reason formally about a single sequential transaction. An area for future research is to extend the theory to allow reasoning about the interactions between parallel processes. The current specifications will still be used but they will need to be augmented with additional specifications which constrain the way in which the parallel processes interact.

Recovery: An important part of a transaction processing system is the mechanism for recovery on failure of the system. The current specifications do not address the problem of recovery. Again we would like to augment the current specifications so that recovery can be incorporated without requiring the existing part of the specification to be rewritten.

Distributed Systems: A number of CICS systems may cooperate to provide services to users. The main facility provided within CICS to achieve this is the ability to execute certain operations or whole transactions on a remote system. While the individual operation specifications could be augmented to reflect remote system execution it was thought better to wait until we had a specification of the system and extend that to a distributed system. To reason effectively about a distributed system we need to be able to reason about parallelism.

Conclusions

Formal specification techniques have been successfully applied to modules of an existing system and as an immediate benefit have uncovered a number of problems in the current documentation as well as flaws in the current interface design. In the longer term the formal specifications should provide a good starting point for specifying proposed changes to the system, a more precise description for educating new personnel, and a basis for improved documentation.

In part the reason we have been successful in applying our specification techniques is that the modular structure of CICS is quite good, and we have been able to take advantage of this by concentrating on individual modules in relative isolation.

The main short term benefits that are obtained by applying formal specification techniques to existing software are the questions that are raised during the specification process. They highlight aspects of the system that are incompletely or ambiguously described in the manual, as well as focusing attention on problems with its structure, for example, undesirable interactions between modules.

In the longer term a formal specification provides a precise description which can be used to communicate between people involved with the system. The specification is less prone to misunderstanding than less formal means of communication, such as natural language or diagrams. It can be used as a basis for a new specification which incorporates modifications to the original design, and it provides an excellent starting point for people responsible for improving the documentation. (In another group at Oxford work on incorporating formal specifications into user manuals is being done by Roger Gimson and Carroll Morgan [5].)

The time required to specify a module of the system varied from about four weeks for Exceptional Conditions to 12 weeks for Interval Control. The time required was related to the size of the module (the number of operations, etc.) and also to the number and severity of problems raised about the behaviour of the module. The size of a module specification (in pages) turned out to be roughly comparable to the size of the manual entry for the module. The specification sizes ranged from 4 pages (handwritten) for Exceptional Conditions to 16 pages for Interval Control.

The difficulties encountered with the specification process itself were the language gap between university and industry, and the problem of achieving the right level of abstraction. There were also a number of more technical specification problems that arose when applying the techniques: the problem of putting together module specifications to provide a specification of the system as a whole, specifying parallelism, specifying recovery on system failure, and specifying distributed systems. These problems are areas for further research.

Acknowledgements

I would like to thank IBM for their permission to publish this paper and reproduce part of one of their manuals as an appendix. Several members of the IBM Development Laboratory at Hursley, England assisted the author to understand some parts of CICS; of special note are Peter Alderson, Peter Collins and Peter Lupton.

This work has benefited from consultations with Tony Hoare, Cliff Jones, and Rod Burstall. Tim Clement was responsible for the initial specification of temporary storage. Paul Fertig, Roger Gimson, John Nicholls and Bernard Sufrin gave useful comments on this paper. Finally, I would like to express my gratitude to Carroll Morgan and Ib Holm Sørensen for their help as reviewers of the specifications, and for their instruction in specification techniques.

References

[1] J.-R. Abrial, "The specification language Z: Basic library", Programming Research Group, Oxford University, Oxford, England, *Internal Report*, 1982.

[2] "CICS/OS/VS application programmer's reference manual (Command level)", IBM Corp., 1980.

[3] "CICS/VS general information", IBM Corp., 1980.

[4] "OS PL/I checkout and optimising compilers: Language reference manual", IBM Corp., 1976.

[5] C. C. Morgan, "Using mathematics in user manuals", Programming Research Group, Oxford University, Oxford, England, *Distributed Computing Project Technical Report*, 1983.

[6] C. C. Morgan and B. A. Sufrin, "Specification of the Unix filing system", *IEEE Trans. on Software Engineering*, vol. 10, no. 2, pp. 128-142, March 1984 (and in part B of this monograph).

[7] I. H. Sørensen, "A specification language", in *Program Specification* (Lecture Notes in Computer Science, Vol. 134), Springer-Verlag, pp. 381-401, 1982.

[8] J. Staunstrup, *Program Specification: Proceedings of a Workshop, Aarhus, Denmark, August 1981* (Lecture Notes in Computer Science, Vol. 134), Springer-Verlag, 1982.

Appendix

CICS/VS Version 1 Release 5
Application Programmer's Reference Manual (Command Level)
Exceptional Conditions

Exceptional conditions may occur during the execution of a CICS/VS command and, unless specified otherwise in the application program by an IGNORE CONDITION or HANDLE CONDITION command or by the NOHANDLE option, a default action for each condition will be taken by it. Usually, this default action is to terminate the task abnormally.

However, to prevent abnormal termination, an exceptional condition can be dealt with in the application program by a HANDLE CONDITION command. The command must include the name of the condition and, optionally, a label to which control is to be passed if the condition occurs. The HANDLE CONDITION command must be executed before the command which may give rise to the associated condition.

The HANDLE CONDITION command for a given condition applies only to the program in which it is specified, remaining active until the associated task is terminated, or until another HANDLE CONDITION command for the same condition is encountered, in which case the new command overrides the previous one.

When control returns to a program from a program at a lower level, the HANDLE CONDITION commands that were active in the higher-level program before control was transferred from it are reactivated, and those in the lower-level program are deactivated.

Some exceptional conditions can occur during the execution of any one of a number of unrelated commands. For example, IOERR can occur during file-control operations, interval-control operations, and others. If the same action is required for all occurrences, a single HANDLE CONDITION IOERR command will suffice.

If different actions are required, HANDLE CONDITION commands specifying different labels, at appropriate points in the program will suffice. The same label can be specified for all commands, and fields EIBFN and EIBRCODE (in the EIB) can be tested to find out which exceptional condition has occurred, and in which command.

The IGNORE CONDITION command specifies that no action is to be taken if an exceptional condition occurs. Execution of a command could result in several conditions being raised. CICS/VS checks these in a predetermined order and only the first one that is not ignored (by an IGNORE CONDITION command) will be passed to the application program.

The NOHANDLE option may be used with any command to specify that no action is to be taken for any condition resulting from the execution of that command. In this way the scope of the IGNORE CONDITION command covers specified conditions for all commands (until a HANDLE CONDITION for the condition is executed) and the scope of the NOHANDLE option covers all conditions for specified commands.

The ERROR Exceptional Condition

Apart from the exceptional conditions associated with individual commands, there is a general exceptional condition named ERROR whose default action also is to terminate the task abnormally. If no HANDLE CONDITION command is active for a condition, but one is active for ERROR, control will be passed to the label specified for ERROR. A HANDLE CONDITION command (with or without a label) for a condition overrides the HANDLE CONDITION ERROR command for that condition.

Commands should not be included in an error routine that may give rise to the same condition that caused the branch to the routine; special care should be taken not to cause a loop on the ERROR condition. A loop can be avoided by including a HANDLE CONDITION ERROR command as the first command in the error routine. The original error action should be reinstated at the end of the error routine by including a second HANDLE CONDITION ERROR command.

Handle Exceptional Conditions (HANDLE CONDITION)

```
HANDLE CONDITION condition [ (label) ]
                 [ condition [ (label) ] ]
                    . . .
```

This command is used to specify the label to which control is to be passed if an exceptional condition occurs. It remains in effect until a subsequent IGNORE

CONDITION command for the condition encountered. No more than 12 conditions are allowed in the same command; additional conditions must be specified in further HANDLE CONDITION commands. The ERROR condition can also be used to specify that other conditions are to cause control to be passed to the same label. If "label" is omitted, the default action for the condition will be taken.

The following example shows the handling of exceptional conditions, such as DUPREC, LENGERR, and so on, that can occur when a WRITE command is used to add a record to a data set. DUPREC is to be handled as a special case; system default action (that is, to terminate the task abnormally) is to be taken for LENGERR; and all other conditions are to be handled by the generalized error routine ERRHANDL.

```
EXEC CICS HANDLE CONDITION
          ERROR(ERRHANDL)
          DUPREC(DUPRIN)
          LENGERR
```

If the generalized error routine can handle all exceptions except IOERR, for which the default action (that is, to terminate the task abnormally) is required, IOERR (without a label) would be added to the above command.

In an assembler-language application program, a branch to a label caused by an exceptional condition will restore the registers in the application program to their values at the point where the EXEC interface program is invoked.

In a PL/I application program, a branch to a label in an inactive procedure or in an inactive begin block, caused by an exceptional condition, will produce unpredictable results.

Handle Condition Command Option

condition [(label)] "condition" specifies the name of the exceptional condition, and "label" specifies the location within the program to be branched to if the condition occurs. If this option is not specified, the default action for the condition is taken, unless the default action is to terminate the task abnormally, in which case the ERROR condition occurs. If the option is specified without a label, any HANDLE CONDITION command for the condition is deactivated, and the default action taken if the condition occurs.

Ignore Exceptional Conditions (IGNORE CONDITION)

```
IGNORE CONDITION   condition
                 [ condition ]
                   .  .  .
```

This command is used to specify that no action is to be taken if an exceptional condition occurs. It remains in effect until a subsequent HANDLE CONDITION command for the condition is encountered. No more than 12 conditions are allowed in the same command; additional conditions must be specified in further IGNORE CONDITION commands. The option "condition" specifies the name of the exceptional condition that is to be ignored.

CICS Temporary Storage

Ian Hayes

Abstract

Temporary storage provides facilities for storage of information in named "queues". The operations that can be performed on an individual queue are either the standard queue-like operations (append to the end and remove from the beginning), or array-like random access read and write operations.

A Single Queue

An element of a queue is a sequence of bytes.

$$TSElem \; \hat{=} \; seq \; Byte$$

A single queue may be defined by

$$
\begin{array}{|l}
\text{TSQ} \underline{\hspace{6cm}} \\
\quad ar \; : \; seq \; TSElem \\
\quad p \quad : \; \mathbb{N} \\
\hline
\quad p \; \leqslant \; \#ar \\
\end{array}
$$

The sequence ar contains the items in the queue. The size of the sequence is always equal to the number of append operations that have been performed on the queue since its creation — independent of the number of other (remove, read, or write) operations. The pointer p keeps track of the position of the item which was last removed or read from the queue.

The initial state of a queue is given by an empty sequence and a zero pointer.

$$TSQ\_Initial \; \hat{=} \; [\; TSQ \; | \; (ar = [\,]) \; \wedge \; (p = 0) \;]$$

Operations

We will define four operations on a single TSQ. The definitions of these operations will use the schema

$$\Delta TSQ \triangleq TSQ \wedge TSQ'$$

ΔTSQ (Δ for change) defines a before state TSQ, with components ar and p (satisfying $p \leqslant \#ar$), and an after state TSQ', with components ar' and p' (satisfying $p' \leqslant \#ar'$). The definitions of the operations follow.

```
┌─ Append₀ ──────────────────────────────────┐
│  ΔTSQ                                       │
│  from? : TSElem                             │
│  item! : ℤ                                  │
│  ─────────────────────────────────         │
│  ar' = ar ⌢ [from?] ∧                       │
│  item! = #ar' ∧                             │
│  p' = p                                     │
└─────────────────────────────────────────────┘
```

The new element from? (a "?" *at the end of a name indicates an input*) is appended to the end of ar to give the new value of the sequence. The position of the new item is returned in item! (a "!" *at the end of a name indicates an output*). The pointer position is unchanged.

```
┌─ Remove₀ ──────────────────────────────────┐
│  ΔTSQ                                       │
│  into! : TSElem                             │
│  ─────────────────────────────────         │
│  p < #ar ∧                                  │
│  p' = p + 1 ∧                               │
│  into! = ar(p') ∧                           │
│  ar' = ar                                   │
└─────────────────────────────────────────────┘
```

The pointer must not already have reached the end of the sequence. The pointer is incremented to indicate the next item in the queue and the value of that item is returned in into!. The contents of the sequence are unchanged.

```
┌─ Write₀ ─────────────────────────────────────────┐
│ ΔTSQ                                              │
│ item? : ℤ                                         │
│ from? : TSElem                                    │
├───────────────────────────────────────           │
│ item? ∈ 1..#ar ∧                                  │
│ ar′ = ar ⊕ { item? ↦ from? } ∧                    │
│ p′ = p                                            │
└──────────────────────────────────────────────────┘
```

The position item? must lie within the bounds of the current sequence. The item at that position in ar is overridden by the value of from? to give the new value of the sequence. The pointer position is unchanged.

```
┌─ Read₀ ──────────────────────────────────────────┐
│ ΔTSQ                                              │
│ item? : ℤ                                         │
│ into! : TSElem                                    │
├───────────────────────────────────────           │
│ item? ∈ 1..#ar ∧                                  │
│ into! = ar(item?) ∧                               │
│ p′ = item? ∧                                      │
│ ar′ = ar                                          │
└──────────────────────────────────────────────────┘
```

The value of the item at position item?, which must lie within the bounds of the sequence, is returned in into!. The pointer position is updated to assume the value item?. The sequence is unchanged.

In the above, all of the operations have been specified in terms of the sequence ar and pointer p. While this is reasonable for the Read and Write operations it does not show the queue-like nature of the Append and Remove operations. Let us now show that the queue-like operations are the familiar ones. We can define a standard queue by

$$Q \;\;\hat{=}\;\; \text{seq } TSElem$$

The standard "append to the end of a queue" operation is given by

```
┌─ Standard_Append──────────────────────┐
│  ΔQ                                     │
│  from? : TSElem                         │
│ ───────────────────────────            │
│  q' = q ⌢ [from?]                       │
└────────────────────────────────────────┘
```

where $\Delta Q \triangleq [\ q,\ q'\ :\ Q\ ]$.

The standard "remove from the front" of the queue operation is given by

```
┌─ Standard_Remove──────────────────────┐
│  ΔQ                                     │
│  into! : TSElem                         │
│ ───────────────────────────            │
│  q = [into!] ⌢ q'                       │
└────────────────────────────────────────┘
```

The predicate in the above specification may be unconventional to some readers. It states that the value of the queue before the operation is equal to the value returned in into! *catenated with the value of the queue after the operation. This form of specification more closely reflects the symmetry between* Standard_Append *and* Standard_Remove *than the more conventional*

```
into! = head(q)
q' = tail(q)
```

To see the relationship between standard queues and temporary storage queues we need to formulate the correspondence between the respective states.

```
┌─ QLike────────────────────────────────┐
│   q : Q                                 │
│   TSQ                                   │
│ ───────────────────────────            │
│   q = tailᵖ(ar)                         │
└────────────────────────────────────────┘
```

A standard q corresponds to the sequence ar with the first p elements removed. Given this relationship between states we will now show the relationship between Append$_0$ and Standard_Append. What we will show is that if we perform an Append$_0$ with initial state TSQ and final state TSQ', then the corresponding standard queue states Q and Q' (as determined by QLike and QLike' respectively) are related by Standard_Append. This can be formalised by the following theorem:

Theorem: Append$_0$ ∧ QLike ∧ QLike' ⊢ Standard_Append

Proof:

1. q, q':seq TSElem; from?:TSElem   from QLike, QLike' and Append$_0$
2. q' = tail$^{p'}$(ar')   from QLike'
3.   = tail^p(ar ⌢ [from?])   from Append$_0$
4.   = (tail^p(ar)) ⌢ [from?]   as p ≤ #ar from TSQ
5.   = q ⌢ [from?]   from QLike
6. Standard_Append   from (1), (5)   □

We can now do the same for Remove.

Theorem: Remove$_0$ ∧ QLike ∧ QLike' ⊢ Standard_Remove

Proof:

1. q, q':seq TSElem; into!:TSElem   from QLike, QLike' and Remove$_0$
2. p < #ar   from Remove$_0$
3. q = tail^p(ar)   from QLike
4.   = [ar(p+1)] ⌢ (tail^{p+1}(ar)) from (2) and property of tail
5.   = [into!] ⌢ (tail$^{p'}$(ar'))   from Remove$_0$
6.   = [into!] ⌢ q'   from QLike'
7. Standard_Remove   from (1), (6)   □

Errors

To cope with errors we can introduce a report to indicate success or failure of an operation. If an error occurs we would like the TSQ to remain unchanged. This can be encapsulated by

```
┌─ ERROR────────────────────────────────────┐
│  ΔTSQ                                      │
│  report! : CONDITION                       │
│ ──────────────────────                     │
│  TSQ′ = TSQ                                │
└────────────────────────────────────────────┘
```

where the set CONDITION contains all the error reports plus the report *Success*. In the operations described above there are three errors that can occur: trying to remove an item from a TSQ with no items left to remove, trying to read or write at a position outside the sequence, and running out of space to store an item.

```
┌─ NoneLeft!────────────────────────┐
│  ERROR                            │
│ ──────────────────                │
│  p = #ar ∧                        │
│  report! = ItemErr                │
└────────────────────────────────────┘
```

```
┌─ OutofBounds!────────────────────┐
│  ERROR                           │
│  item? : ℤ                       │
│ ──────────────────               │
│  item? ∉ 1..#ar ∧                │
│  report! = ItemErr               │
└────────────────────────────────────┘
```

```
┌─ NoSpace!─────────────────────────┐
│  ERROR                            │
│ ──────────────────                │
│  report! = NoSpace                │
└────────────────────────────────────┘
```

If the operations work correctly the report will indicate *Success*.

$$\text{Successful} \;\hat{=}\; [\; \text{report!} \;:\; \text{CONDITION} \;|\; \text{report!} \;=\; \textit{Success} \;]$$

The operations given previously can now be combined with the erroneous situations. We will redefine the operations in terms of their previous definitions.

$$\text{Append} \quad\hat{=}\quad (\text{Append}_0 \;\wedge\; \text{Successful}) \;\vee\; \text{NoSpace!}$$

$$\text{Remove} \quad\hat{=}\quad (\text{Remove}_0 \;\wedge\; \text{Successful}) \;\vee\; \text{NoneLeft!}$$

$$\text{Write} \quad\hat{=}\quad (\text{Write}_0 \;\wedge\; \text{Successful}) \;\vee\; \text{OutofBounds!} \;\vee\; \text{NoSpace!}$$

$$\text{Read} \quad\hat{=}\quad (\text{Read}_0 \;\wedge\; \text{Successful}) \;\vee\; \text{OutofBounds!}$$

Note that NoSpace! does not specify under what conditions it occurs. The specifications of Append and Write do not allow us to determine whether or not the operation will be successful from the initial state and inputs to an operation. This is an example of a non-deterministic specification. It is left to the implementor to determine when a NoSpace! report will be returned (we hope it will not be on every call).

Named Queues

We now want to specify a system with more than one queue. A particular TSQ can be specified by name and the above operations can be performed on it. We will use a mapping from queue names (TSQName) to queues. The state of our system of queues is given by

$$\text{TS} \quad\hat{=}\quad \text{TSQName} \;\nrightarrow\; \text{TSQ}$$

The initial state of the system of queues is given by an empty mapping:

$$\text{TS\_Initial} \quad\hat{=}\quad \{\}$$

Our operations require the updating of a particular named TSQ. We can introduce a schema, UpdateQ, to encapsulate the common part of updating for operations on queues that already exist.

```
┌─ UpdateQ ──────────────────────────────┐
│  ΔTS                                    │
│  queue? : TSQName                       │
│  ΔTSQ                                   │
│ ───────────────────────                 │
│  queue? ∈ dom(ts) ∧                     │
│  TSQ = ts(queue?) ∧                     │
│  ts' = ts ⊕ { queue? ↦ TSQ' }           │
└─────────────────────────────────────────┘
```

where $\Delta TS \triangleq [\ ts, ts'\ :\ TS\ ]$. Note that UpdateQ specifies that the named queue (alone) is updated but does not specify in what way it is updated. The latter is achieved by combining UpdateQ with the single queue operations to get the operation on named queues.

In adding named queues we have added the possibility of a new error: trying to perform operations on non-existent queues. This error is given by

```
┌─ NonExistent! ─────────────────────────┐
│  ΔTS                                    │
│  queue? : TSQName                       │
│  report! : CONDITION                    │
│ ───────────────────────                 │
│  queue? ∉ dom(ts) ∧                     │
│  ts' = ts ∧                             │
│  report! = QIdErr                       │
└─────────────────────────────────────────┘
```

Our operations, except AppendQ which is allowed on a non-existent queue, can now be redefined in terms of our previous definitions.

$$
\begin{aligned}
\text{RemoveQ} \ &\triangleq\ (\text{UpdateQ} \wedge \text{Remove}) \setminus \Delta TSQ \\
&\qquad \vee\ \ \text{NonExistent!} \\[1em]
\text{WriteQ} \ &\triangleq\ (\text{UpdateQ} \wedge \text{Write}) \setminus \Delta TSQ \\
&\qquad \vee\ \ \text{NonExistent!}
\end{aligned}
$$

ReadQ   ≙   (UpdateQ ∧ Read) \ ΔTSQ
            ∨   NonExistent!

The temporary variables in ΔTSQ (ar, p, ar′, p′) are hidden in the signatures of the final operations and the operations inherit the errors from the equivalent single queue operations.

A queue is created by performing an AppendQ operation on a queue that does not exist. The following schema describes the creation of a queue:

```
┌─ CreateQ ──────────────────────────┐
│ ΔTS                                 │
│ queue? : TSQName                    │
│ TSQ_Initial                         │
│ TSQ′                                │
│ ─────────────────────               │
│ queue? ∉ dom(ts) ∧                  │
│ ts′ = ts ∪ { queue? ↦ TSQ′ }        │
└─────────────────────────────────────┘
```

Again the relationship between TSQ_Initial (ar, p) and TSQ′ (ar′, p′) is not defined within this schema. This is supplied by Append in the following definition

AppendQ   ≙   ((UpdateQ ∨ CreateQ) ∧ Append) \ ΔTSQ

Note that for a non-existent queue, if an error occurs (i.e. a NoSpace condition), then an empty queue will be created.

In addition to these promoted operations on named queues we have an operation to delete a named queue:

```
┌─ DeleteQ₀ ──────────────────────────┐
│ ΔTS                                 │
│ queue? : TSQName                    │
│ report! : CONDITION                 │
│ ─────────────────────               │
│ queue? ∈ dom(ts) ∧                  │
│ ts′ = { queue? } ⩤ ts ∧             │
│ report! = Success                   │
└─────────────────────────────────────┘
```

An exception occurs if the queue to be deleted does not exist; DeleteQ becomes

$$\text{DeleteQ} \;\triangleq\; \text{DeleteQ}_0 \lor \text{NonExistent!}$$

A Network of Systems

Temporary storage queues may be located on more than one system. Let us call the set of all possible system identifiers SysId. We can represent temporary storage queues on a network of systems by

$$\text{NTS} \;\triangleq\; \text{SysId} \twoheadrightarrow \text{TS}$$

For a network

$$\text{nts} \;:\; \text{NTS}$$

dom(nts) is the set of systems that share temporary storage queues and for a system with identity sysid such that sysid $\in$ dom(nts), nts(sysid) is the temporary storage state of that system. The operations on temporary storage queues may be promoted to operate for a network of systems by the following schema:

```
┌─ Network ─────────────────────────────┐
│  ΔNTS                                  │
│  sysid? : SysId                        │
│  ΔTS                                   │
├───────────────────────────────────────┤
│  sysid? ∈ dom(nts) ∧                   │
│  ts = nts(sysid?) ∧                    │
│  nts' = nts ⊕ { sysid? ↦ ts' }         │
└───────────────────────────────────────┘
```

where $\Delta\text{NTS} \triangleq [\text{ nts}, \text{nts}' : \text{NTS }]$. As with the promotion of operations to work on named queues the above schema only specifies which system is updated but not how it is updated. The latter be supplied when Network is combined with the definitions of the operations on a single system.

Network operation also introduces the possibility of an error if the given system does not exist.

```
┌─ NoSystem!─────────────────────────────┐
│  ΔNTS
│  sysid? : SysId
│  report! : CONDITION
│ ───────────────────────────────────────
│  sysid? ∉ dom(nts) ∧
│  nts' = nts ∧
│  report! = SysIdErr
└─────────────────────────────────────────┘
```

The operations on a multiple system are given by

$$AppendQN_0 \triangleq (AppendQ \land Network) \setminus \Delta TS$$
$$\lor NoSystem!$$

$$RemoveQN_0 \triangleq (RemoveQ \land Network) \setminus \Delta TS$$
$$\lor NoSystem!$$

$$ReadQN_0 \triangleq (ReadQ \land Network) \setminus \Delta TS$$
$$\lor NoSystem!$$

$$WriteQN_0 \triangleq (WriteQ \land Network) \setminus \Delta TS$$
$$\lor NoSystem!$$

The sysid? and queue? name supplied as inputs are not necessarily those on which an operation takes place. A queue name on a given system may be marked as actually being located on another (remote) system, possibly with a different name on that system. We will model this by the following function which takes an input pair (sysid?, queue?) and gives the corresponding actual pair (sysid!, queue!) on which the operation will be performed:

$$remote : (SysId \times TSQName) \rightarrow (SysId \times TSQName)$$

In many cases the input sysid? and queue? name are the actual system and queue name; in these cases remote will behave as the identity function.

We will use the following schema to incorporate remote into the operations.

```
┌─ TSRemote ──────────────────────────────────────────┐
│   sysid?, sysid!  :  SysId                           │
│   queue?, queue!  :  TSQName                         │
├─────────────────────┐                                │
│   (sysid!, queue!) = remote(sysid?, queue?)          │
└──────────────────────────────────────────────────────┘
```

The outputs, sysid! and queue!, of TSRemote form the inputs to the operations. If a sysid? parameter is supplied then the operations on temporary storage queues are defined by

$$AppendQN_1 \ \hat{=} \ TSRemote \ >> \ AppendQN_0$$

$$RemoveQN_1 \ \hat{=} \ TSRemote \ >> \ RemoveQN_0$$

$$ReadQN_1 \ \ \hat{=} \ TSRemote \ >> \ ReadQN_0$$

$$WriteQN_1 \ \ \hat{=} \ TSRemote \ >> \ WriteQN_0$$

Recall that the schema operator ">>" (piping) identifies the outputs (variables ending in "!") of its left operand with the inputs (variables ending in "?") of its right operand; these variables are hidden in the result. All other components are combined together as for schema conjunction ($\wedge$).

If no sysid? parameter is given then the operations are given by

$$AppendQN_2 \ \hat{=} \ AppendQN_1[cursysid?/sysid?]$$

$$RemoveQN_2 \ \hat{=} \ RemoveQN_1[cursysid?/sysid?]$$

$$ReadQN_2 \ \ \hat{=} \ ReadQN_1[cursysid?/sysid?]$$

$$WriteQN_2 \ \hat{=} \ WriteQN_1[cursysid?/sysid?]$$

That is, the sysid? parameter is replaced by a parameter giving the identity of the current system (the system on which the operation was initiated).

A note on the current implementation

Each system keeps track of the names of queues that are located on other (remote) systems and, for each remote queue, the identity of the remote system and the name of the queue on that system. It is possible that the referred request could be for a queue name that is also remote to the referred system, in which case the request will be further referred to another system. To find the system on which the queue actually resides we need to follow through a chain of systems until we get to a system on which the queue name is considered local. We can model the implementation by the function

$$\text{rem} : \quad (\text{SysId} \times \text{TSQName}) \twoheadrightarrow (\text{SysId} \times \text{TSQName})$$

which for a sysid and queue name gives the sysid and queue name of the next link in the chain; if a sysid and queue name pair is not in the domain of rem then the chain is finished. The correspondence between rem and remote is given by

$$\text{remote} = \text{repeat rem}$$

where repeat applies the function rem repeatedly until the parameter to rem is no longer in the domain of rem

$$
\begin{aligned}
(\text{repeat } f) \ y &= y & \text{if } y \notin \text{dom}(f) \\
&= (\text{repeat } f) \ (f \ y) & \text{if } y \in \text{dom}(f)
\end{aligned}
$$

That is

$$
\begin{aligned}
\text{remote}(s, \ q) &= (s, \ q) & \text{if } (s, \ q) \notin \text{dom rem} \\
&= \text{remote } (\text{rem } (s, \ q)) & \text{if } (s, \ q) \in \text{dom rem}
\end{aligned}
$$

Since remote is a total function the equality of remote and (repeat rem) requires that no chain of rem's contains a loop (so that (repeat rem) is also total).

Given the function `rem` if we take the corresponding (curried) function with the following type

$$r \; : \; \mathsf{SysId} \; \rightarrow \; (\mathsf{TSQName} \; \twoheadrightarrow \; (\mathsf{SysId} \times \mathsf{TSQName}))$$

so that

```
r(s)(q)   = rem(s, q)
dom(r(s)) = { q : TSQName | (s, q) ∈ dom rem },
```

the mapping that needs to be stored on a system `s` is given by `r(s)`, and is of type

$$\mathsf{TSQName} \; \twoheadrightarrow \; (\mathsf{SysId} \times \mathsf{TSQName})$$

Acknowledgements

The work reported in this paper was supported by a grant from IBM. The starting point was an earlier specification created by Tim Clement. This specification has benefited greatly from the detailed comments of Carroll Morgan and Ib Holm Sørensen.

CICS Message System

Ian Hayes

Abstract

The following message system is based on the message handling in CICS. The specification itself is an interesting example: it combines states (of input and output devices), and gives a number of examples of the use of the ">>" operator on schemas.

Message Output

We can represent a set of output devices by a mapping from a device name to a sequence of messages that have been output to that device:

```
NOUT
    noq : Name ↦ seq Message
```

The operations on output that are discussed here neither create nor destroy devices:

$$\Delta NOUT \; \hat{=} \; [\; NOUT \wedge NOUT' \; | \; \text{dom } noq' = \text{dom } noq \;]$$

Sending a message to a device simply appends the message to the queue for that device:

```
NSend₀
    ΔNOUT
    n? : Name
    m? : Message
    ─────────────────
    noq' = noq ⊕ { n? ↦ noq(n?) ⌢ [m?] }
```

Multiple Destinations

A message may be sent to a set of destinations:

```
┌─ NSendM₀ ────────────────────────────────────┐
│  ΔNOUT                                         │
│  ns?  :  ℙ Name                                │
│  m?   :  Message                               │
├────────────────────────────────────────────── │
│  ns? ⊆ dom noq ∧                               │
│  noq′ = noq ⊕ { n : ns? • n ↦ noq(n) ⌢ [m?] }  │
└────────────────────────────────────────────────┘
```

All of the names in ns? must correspond to valid output devices. The message is sent to each device in n?.

Theorem:

Given

$$\mathsf{ToSet} \ \hat{=} \ [\ \mathsf{n?} \ : \ \mathsf{Name}; \ \mathsf{ns!} \ : \ \mathbb{P} \ \mathsf{Name} \ | \ \mathsf{ns!} = \{\ \mathsf{n?} \ \} \ ]$$

then

$$\mathsf{NSend_0} = \mathsf{ToSet} \gg \mathsf{NSendM_0}$$

Recall that the schema operator ">>" identifies the outputs (variables ending in "!") of its left operand with the inputs (variables ending in "?") of its right operand; these variables are hidden in the result. All other components are combined together as for schema conjunction (∧).

Message Input

We can represent a set of input devices by a mapping from a device name to a sequence of messages yet to be input from that device:

```
NIN
    niq : Name ↦ seq Message
```

The operations on input described here will neither create nor destroy devices:

$$\Delta NIN \;\;\hat{=}\;\; [\; NIN \wedge NIN' \;\;|\;\; \mathrm{dom}\; niq' = \mathrm{dom}\; niq \;]$$

Receiving a message from a device simply removes it from the head of the input queue for that device:

```
NReceive₀
    ΔNIN
    n? : Name
    m! : Message
    ─────────────────────
    m! = head(niq(n?)) ∧
    niq' = niq ⊕ { n? ↦ tail(niq(n?)) }
```

Send and Receive

We can define an operation that both sends a message to a device and receives a message from that device:

$$NSendReceive_0 \;\;\hat{=}\;\; NSend_0 \wedge NReceive_0$$

Combining Input and Output

We will introduce NDEV to describe the combined input and output state for all of the devices. If a device can be used for input then it must be able to be used for output:

```
NDEV_____
|   NIN
|   NOUT
|_____
|
|   dom niq ⊆ dom noq
|_____
```

Input and output operations will preserve the output and input states respectively.

$$\equiv NOUT \quad \hat{=} \quad [\ \Delta NDEV \ | \ NOUT' = NOUT \ ]$$

$$\equiv NIN \quad \hat{=} \quad [\ \Delta NDEV \ | \ NIN' \ = NIN \ ]$$

where $\Delta NDEV \quad \hat{=} \quad NDEV \wedge NDEV'$.

The operations on the combined state are

$$NSend \qquad \hat{=} \quad NSend_0 \qquad \wedge \quad \equiv NIN$$

$$NSendM \qquad \hat{=} \quad NSendM_0 \qquad \wedge \quad \equiv NIN$$

$$NReceive \qquad \hat{=} \quad NReceive_0 \qquad \wedge \quad \equiv NOUT$$

$$NSendReceive \quad \hat{=} \quad NSendReceive_0 \wedge \quad \Delta NDEV$$

Logical Names

Rather than work with actual (physical) device names, as we have up to this point, we would like to work with logical names that are mapped into physical device names. We use the following mapping from logical names to physical names.

```
LtoP
    ltop : LName ↦ Name
```

None of the operations discussed here modify the mapping from logical names to physical names. Hence we will use

$$≡LtoP \quad ≙ \quad [\ LtoP ∧ LtoP' \ | \ LtoP' = LtoP\ ]$$

If a logical name actually corresponds to a device we perform the operation on that device, otherwise we use the device with physical name console.

```
MapName
    ≡LtoP
    dev : Name ↦ seq Message
    ln? : LName
    n!  : Name

    ln? ∈ dom(ltop⨾dev)   ⟹   n! = ltop(ln?)  ∧
    ln? ∉ dom(ltop⨾dev)   ⟹   n! = console
```

The operations on a single device become

$$LSend \qquad ≙ \quad MapName[noq/dev]\ >>\ NSend$$

$$LReceive \qquad ≙ \quad MapName[niq/dev]\ >>\ NReceive$$

$$LSendReceive ≙ \quad MapName[niq/dev]\ >>\ NSendReceive$$

Multiple Logical Destinations

To send a message to a set of logical names we need to map the set of logical names into physical names. If none of the logical names correspond to a device we send the message to the device with physical name console.

```
┌─ MapSet ────────────────────────────────────────────────────────┐
│  ≡LtoP                                                           │
│  lns?  :  ℙ LName                                                │
│  ns!   :  ℙ Name                                                 │
│  NOUT                                                            │
├──────────────────────────                                       │
│                                                                  │
│  let  names = ltop⟦lns?⟧ ∩ dom noq  in                          │
│    names = {} ⟹ ns! = { console }  ∧                            │
│    names ≠ {} ⟹ ns! = names                                     │
└──────────────────────────────────────────────────────────────────┘
```

The operation to send a message to a set of logical devices is

$$\text{LSendM} \; \triangleq \; \text{MapSet} \gg \text{NSendM}$$

Theorem:

Given

$$\text{ToSetL} \; \triangleq \; [\; \text{ln? : LName; lns! : ℙ LName} \; | \; \text{lns! = \{ ln? \}} \;]$$

then

$$\text{LSend} \; = \; \text{ToSetL} \gg \text{LSendM}$$

Domains of the Operations

In practice we would like all the operations to be total (defined for all inputs). Unfortunately, this is not the case. If a name (or a set of names) does not correspond to an actual device, then the name will be translated to the special device console; if the console does not exist, the operation is not defined. For the output operations, ensuring that the console exists is a sufficient pre-condition for the operation to be defined (we will also need this pre-condition for input).

$$Pre \;\; \hat{=} \;\; [\; NDEV; \; LtoP; \; m? : Message \; | \; console \in dom \; niq \;]$$

Remember that dom niq ⊆ dom noq, so console ∈ dom noq.

Theorems:

$$Pre \quad \Rightarrow \quad pre \; LSend$$

$$Pre \quad \Rightarrow \quad pre \; LSendM$$

For the input operations we need the additional requirement that the queue of messages yet to be input on the device is not empty.

$$PreIn \;\; \hat{=} \;\; [\; Pre; \; n? : Name \; | \; niq(n?) \neq [] \;]$$

Theorems:

$$MapName[niq/dev] \gg PreIn \quad \Rightarrow \quad pre \; LReceive$$

$$MapName[niq/dev] \gg PreIn \quad \Rightarrow \quad pre \; LSendReceive$$

Acknowledgement

This specification is based on a message system specified by David Renshaw of IBM (U. K.) Laboratories, Hursley, England.